Death Work

A Study of the Modern Execution Process

Contemporary Issues in Crime and Justice Series
Roy Roberg, San Jose State University: Series Editor

Crime and Justice: Issues and Ideas (1984)
Philip Jenkins, Pennsylvania State University

Hard Time: Understanding and Reforming the Prison (1987)
Robert Johnson, The American University

The Myth of a Racist Criminal Justice System (1987)
William Wilbanks, Florida International University

Gambling Without Guilt: The Legitimation of an American Pastime (1988)
John Rosecrance, University of Nevada at Reno

Ethics in Crime and Justice: Dilemmas and Decisions (1989)
Joycelyn M. Pollock-Byrne, University of Huston

Sense and Nonsense about Crime: A Policy Guide, Second Edition (1989)
Samuel Walker, University of Nebraska at Omaha

Crime Victims: An Introduction to Victimology, Second Edition (1990)
Andrew Karmen, John Jay College of Criminal Justice

Death Work: A Study of the Modern Execution Process (1990)
Robert Johnson, The American University

Lawlessness and Reform: The FBI in Transition (1990)
Tony G. Poveda, State University of New York at Plattsburg

Women, Prison, and Crime (1990)
Joycelyn M. Pollock-Byrne, University of Houston

Death Work

A Study of the Modern Execution Process

Robert Johnson

The American University

 Brooks/Cole Publishing Company
Pacific Grove, California

Consulting Editor: *Roy R. Roberg*

Brooks/Cole Publishing Company A Division of Wadsworth, Inc.
© 1990 by Wadsworth, Inc., Belmont, California 94002.
All rights reserved. No part of this book may be reproduced,
stored in a retrieval system, or transcribed, in any form or
by any means—electronic, mechanical, photocopying, recording,
or otherwise—without the prior written permission of the
publisher, Brooks/Cole Publishing Company, Pacific Grove,
California 93950, a division of Wadsworth, Inc.

Printed in the United States of America
10 9 8 7 6 5 4 3 2 1

Library of Congress Cataloging-in-Publication Data

Johnson, Robert
    Death work : a study of the modern execution process / Robert
Johnson.
        p.   cm.
    Includes bibliographical references.
    ISBN 0-534-12828-9
    1. Executions and executioners—United States.   2. Death row-
-United States.   I. Title.
HV8699.U5J643   1989
364.6'6'0973—dc20   89-23899
                                                              CIP

Sponsoring Editor: *Cynthia C. Stormer*
Editorial Assistant: *Cathleen Sue Collins*
Production Editor: *Penelope Sky*
Production Assistant: *Meredy Amyx*
Manuscript Editor: *Lynne Y. Fletcher*
Permissions Editor: *Mary Kay Hancharick*
Interior and Cover Design: *Lisa Thompson*
Cover Illustration: *Ronald G. Grauer*
Typesetting: *Kachina Typesetting, Inc., Tempe, Arizona*
Printing and Binding: *Malloy Lithographing, Inc., Ann Arbor, Michigan*

Excerpts on pages 25–27 and page 50 from "Trial by Ordeal" by C. Chessman. In S. Levine (Ed.), *Death Row: An Affirmation of Life*. Copyright © 1972
by Volcano Press, Inc. (formerly Glide Publications). Reprinted by permission.

Excerpts throughout Chapters 3 and 4 first appeared in Johnson, R., *Condemned to Die: Life Under Sentence of Death* (Prospect Heights, Ill.: Waveland
Press, 1989).

For Deirdra, Brian, and Patrick,
who keep me ever in touch with how good life can be
and, by implication, with how tragically awry things can go
for the victims of violent crimes and violent punishments.

Through the Contemporary Issues in Crime and Justice Series, students are introduced to important topics that until now have been neglected or inadequately covered and that are relevant to criminal justice, criminology, law, political science, psychology, and sociology. The authors address philosophical and theoretical issues, and analyze the most recent research findings and their implications for practice. Consequently, each volume stimulates further thinking and debate on the topics it covers, in addition to providing direction for the development and implementation of policy.

Capital punishment continues to be a hotly debated subject, as the taking of a human life (especially by the state) is a serious and necessarily grievous act. The issue is complicated by changing public opinion: the death sentence was banned two decades ago, but it has made a strong comeback recently. If we attend to the insight Robert Johnson offers in this book, we can make informed decisions about capital punishment from an enlightened perspective.

None of the many volumes on the subject reflect a point of view like Johnson's. We become deeply entrenched in the lives and feelings of everyone involved in the execution process: the death watch team, the warden, the condemned prisoner and, finally, the official witnesses to the final event. Johnson's account derives power and veracity from the fact that he voluntarily served as a witness to an execution.

The execution process itself is also put under the magnifying glass. The death watch period begins with the team removing the condemned man's belongings, continues through shaving and showering, moves into the death cell to await the final minutes, and proceeds to the death chamber. There the prisoner is strapped into the chair and the death mask is placed over his face. In the end, after electrocution, he is removed to the "cooling room." This forceful and moving account of how we execute our least respected citizens makes it very clear that major societal decisions should not be made in a vacuum.

Robert Johnson does not attempt to shock us into changing our opinions about the death penalty. He does, however, force us to come to grips, both intellectually and emotionally, with the killing process we have institutionalized. *Death Work* is an eloquent and scholarly treatise on our current approach to capital punishment. Ultimately, Johnson's vigorous and persuasive argument for an alternative to capital punishment leaves us free to draw our own conclusions.

Roy R. Roberg

About the Author

Robert Johnson is Professor of Justice, Law and Society in the School of Public Affairs at The American University in Washington, D.C. He holds a bachelor's degree in psychology from Fairfield University, and master's and doctoral degrees in criminal justice from the University of Albany, State University of New York. Dr. Johnson's books include *Culture and Crisis in Confinement, Condemned to Die,* and *Hard Time*; he co-edited and contributed to *The Pains of Imprisonment;* he has published numerous articles in professional journals and anthologies. Professor Johnson received The American University Award for Outstanding Scholarship, and is a Distinguished Alumnus of the School of Criminal Justice, Nelson A. Rockefeller College of Public Affairs and Policy, University of Albany, State University of New York.

PREFACE

Death Work is about executions. I've studied this grim topic for about a decade now. My first concern was with the character of life on death row, where condemned prisoners await the outcome of their legal appeals. In this book I build on my earlier research, studying the executions that for more and more prisoners end the long, lonely wait on death row. It is in the death chamber that the condemned and their executioners make capital punishment a social reality. My aim is to place that fatal connection in historical perspective, and to probe its psychological and moral significance.

In a perverse sort of way, this is a timely topic. For roughly a decade, from the late sixties to the late seventies, there was a moratorium on executions, backed by the authority of the Supreme Court. This was the culmination of a gradual but persistent decline in the use of the death penalty in the Western world during the twentieth century. It appeared that executions would forever pass from the American scene. Nothing could have been further from the truth.

In 1977, the moratorium on carrying out the death sentence ended with the well publicized execution of Gary Gilmore. Since then, more than a hundred people have been put to death, most of them in the past few years. Some twenty-three hundred prisoners are presently confined on death rows across the nation. Most have lived under sentence of death for years, in some cases a decade or more. Many of them are coming to the end of the legal appeals process. It is fair to say that executions will be with us for the foreseeable future.

For better or worse, the modern death penalty is a man's affair. Of the prisoners executed recently, only one, less than 1 percent, was a woman; fewer than 1 percent of the prisoners waiting to die are women. More women were executed in the past, especially during the infamous witch hunts, but so far as I can determine, in every historical period women have been executed for crimes at substantially lower rates than men. I am aware of no instance, at any time in history, of a woman serving as an executioner. Certainly none of today's executioners are women. To be sure, women staff members may take on supporting roles, particularly when the condemned prisoner is a women, but their involvement stops at that point. Accordingly, my narration maintains a generic male perspective except where it is obviously inappropriate to do so.

The execution process today is distinctively mechanical, impersonal, and ultimately dehumanizing. This procedure may be routine, but it can never be mundane. Killing and dying under color of law always reflects a remarkable, elemental exercise of power. One cannot be complacent about the plight of those who wait to die on our nation's death rows. Nor can one be indifferent to the experiences of the prison staff who do our death work—who guard the condemned or carry out executions. When we examine the implications of the death penalty in detail, we recognize that it is a tragic social institution that matches the tragedy of violent crime with a punishment that is itself tragic and violent. We minimize or ignore the death penalty at our peril. To do so is to acquiesce, thoughtlessly, in a profound and irrevocable sanction that is imposed in our names. If nothing else, after reading this book you can give or withdraw your consent to executions with a better understanding of the human issues that lie at the root of this, our ultimate penal sanction.

Acknowledgments

I owe a debt of thanks to the many people who helped me with this book. Thomas Stevenson, a former graduate assistant, and Michele M. Provost, our administrative assistant, were kind enough to transcribe the research interviews that inform much of the text. I also wish to thank those who made my work possible by participating in the research. This cooperative group includes the prison warden and the execution team, the inmates of death row, and a host of prison reformers, all of whom spoke with me about the personal and sometimes painful ways in which death work has impinged on their lives.

The text of this book benefited from thoughtful reviews. Paul S. Leighton, my graduate assistant, and Jeffrey H. Reiman, my colleague and erstwhile officemate, reviewed not one but two separate drafts, each time making detailed, constructive comments. The book is noticeably better for their efforts. I am also indebted to the reviewers selected by Brooks/Cole whose comments enriched the book: James R. Acker, State University of New York, Albany; Michel Angela Coconis; Philip W. Harris, Temple University; Norval Morris, University of Chicago; and Hans Toch, State University of New York, Albany. The metamorphosis of the text from manuscript to bound book is the handiwork of the personnel at Brooks/Cole. I wish to thank Cindy Stormer, Penelope Sky, and Lynne Fletcher for their sensitive editorial suggestions; Mary Kay Hancharick for her help securing permissions; and Lisa Thompson for the appealing interior and cover design.

I reserve my deepest thanks for my wife, Deirdra, and our two sons, Brian and Patrick. This book is lovingly dedicated to them.

Robert Johnson

CONTENTS

PART II

Waiting to Die
A Study of Modern Death Rows

3 Death Row
Conditions of Confinement

4 Living and Working on Death Row

PART III

In Cold Blood
A Study of Modern Executions

5 Death Work
A Modern Execution Team

6 Deathwatch
The Final Hours   83

7 An Execution and Its Aftermath   102

PART IV

Moral Considerations   119

Death Work

A Study of the Modern Execution Process

PART I

Executions Past and Present

The scaffold, indeed, when it is prepared and set up, has the effect of a hallucination. . . . The scaffold is vision. The scaffold is not a mere frame, the scaffold is not a machine, the scaffold is not an inert piece of mechanism made of wood, of iron, and of ropes. It seems a sort of being which had some sombre origin of which we can have no idea; one would say that this frame sees, that this machine understands, that this mechanism comprehends; that this wood, this iron, and these ropes have a will. In the fearful reverie into which its presence casts the soul, the awful apparition of the scaffold confounds itself with its horrid work. The scaffold becomes the accomplice of the executioner; it devours, it eats flesh, and it drinks blood. The scaffold is a sort of monster created by the judge and the workman, a spectre which seems to live with a kind of unspeakable life, drawn from all the death which it has wrought.

Victor Hugo

The electric chair is a fearsome object. It's the end, no questions asked. It's a machine of total destruction. It's the biggest chair you'll ever see.

Prison warden

CHAPTER 1

Executions Past
From Antiquity to the Twentieth Century

There is an old joke, one I've told before, about a shipwrecked sailor. Adrift for days, he is washed ashore on an uncharted island. He looks about apprehensively. Presently his gaze falls on a gallows, whereupon he is visibly relieved. "At last," he sighs, "I've reached civilization!" The point of the joke is that only a comparatively settled, and hence civilized, society has the need for a permanent gallows and possesses the means, including skilled labor, to construct one. There is truth in that observation, though the earliest form of the death penalty involved stoning, which did not require a gallows or any other man-made instrument of execution.

The joke is funny, however, because the linking of civilization and the death penalty is, at least in the modern world, only half true. Civilized societies may execute some of their criminals, but executions are normally considered regrettable lapses from civilization. Executions today are necessary evils, surely, rather than hallmarks of a civilized way of life. No one, not even the staunchest supporter of the death penalty, would use the electric chair to symbolize the civilized quality of life in twentieth-century America. More to the point, civilized societies are less likely to execute criminals than are uncivilized ones. And when civilized societies execute criminals, they are likely to use less harsh means than are uncivilized societies. Perhaps the joke is on the sailor, after all.

Yet the death penalty is alive and well in contemporary America. Since we consider ours a highly civilized society, that would seem to belie my thesis (and perhaps comfort our sailor). My response, in brief, is that the death penalty is an anachronism that survives today because we hide it from our awareness and deny its violence. When we recognize the real nature of the death penalty, which in part means placing it in historical perspective, we will, I believe, do the right thing and abolish this sanction altogether.

For much of recorded history, executions were public spectacles (discussed in Part I). Often, gross bodily torture was inflicted upon the condemned. Offenders would be executed soon after their crimes with much of the community directly or indirectly involved. By contemporary standards, some of the crimes that were punished by death were decidedly trivial. The executions of petty thieves, for example—some of them children—strike us as primitive, bloodthirsty affairs.

Things are different today. Executions are preceded by years of confinement on death row; prisoners are no longer subjected to the indignity and pain of physical torture. The condemned are merely held captive until they have depleted their legal appeals, then they are killed with much dispatch and (we hope) little pain. Executions today are removed from the public view; they are somber, restrained, professional undertakings reserved almost exclusively for adult murderers. (Teenagers sixteen years of age or older can be sentenced to death for murder, but few are.) All of this produces an illusion of justice and humanity.

The reality is profoundly unjust and inhumane. The modern death penalty involves nothing less than a slow death by psychological torture, which no offender deserves. Today's condemned prisoner is literally and often completely dehumanized. He is reduced to the status of an object—a body and not a person—then put to death following an impersonal bureaucratic routine. His executioners are dehumanized as well, though only partially and symbolically, in the specific context of carrying out executions. This dehumanization allows prison officials to function as bureaucrats of violence while remaining largely unaffected in their personal lives.

The modern execution process, broadly conceived, is assessed in the central sections of this book. The nature of life and work on death row are examined in Part II; the killing and dying that constitute executions are considered in Part III. The main argument of the book, formally explicated in Part IV (Chapter 8), is that the modern execution process, which strips prisoner and executioner alike of their humanity, is an actual, and not merely a metaphorical, instance of torture. Since torture can never be just, the death penalty is rejected as an unjust punishment. The book closes with an examination of alternatives to the death penalty, including true or natural-life sentences.

Executions in Historical Perspective: An Overview

Sensibilities about violence—especially about the killing and dying that are at the heart of the death penalty—have evolved considerably over the ages. In general, these sensibilities impart a different form and significance to the death penalty at different stages of history. There was, first, the raw, passionate, largely unfettered rage that underlay stonings in antiquity (3000 B.C.–A.D. 500). Then, the violence was face-to-face, and the entire community was involved as spectators or executioners. Later, the rage of communal stoning, softened but not tamed, came to be expressed in the primitive marketplace hangings of the early medieval village (A.D. 500–1000). These hangings were rough-and-ready affairs, featuring the aggrieved party as the executioner. During the late Middle Ages (1000–1500), executions still took place in the marketplace or in the village square, but by then they had become more formal, dignified, even ceremonial undertakings. Procedures were more elaborate; rage was blunted by formalities. For the grievous offenders of this time—a category including heretics—executions were elaborate, highly planned exhibitions orchestrated by high officials. Rage was absent altogether in these pageants, but other strong emotions reigned. Most notably, there was excitement and awe, especially before the might and majesty of the Inquisition.

Executions marked by a restrained ceremony were the norm during the early modern period (1500–1800). Crowds of spectators could lapse into unseemly behavior (especially in England), but such behavior was sharply at odds with the formal execution script. These executions featured ritual and etiquette, as in the late Middle Ages, but little pomp or circumstance. Milder feelings, such as those of devotion, were given an outlet in ceremony; excitement or awe was deemed inappropriately expressive. Officials and spectators were instead expected to show a quiet reverence, tinged by sadness. In the modern period (from 1800 on), ceremony gradually gave way to bureaucratic procedure played out behind prison walls, in isolation from the community. Feelings are absent, or at least suppressed, in bureaucratically administered executions. With bureaucratic procedure, there is a functional routine dominated by hierarchy and task. Officials perform mechanistically before a small, silent gathering of authorized witnesses. Executions have come to be seen as "dirty work"; hence, there is no communal involvement of any sort. The proceedings are antiseptically arranged; few of us get our hands soiled.

The general trend in the conduct of executions is to remove ourselves from the violence. First, physically—we no longer throw stones. Then, existentially—we are no longer engaged in any meaningful way, individually or as a society. This trend reflects our growing awareness of the humanity of others, which makes it harder for us to kill criminals even when we believe they deserve to die. Gradually but inexorably, executions have become more formal undertakings that are detached from community life. Ultimately, what was once a public communal act has become the private preserve of prison officials, who approach the task of execution with the consummate impersonality of the modern bureaucrat. Capital punishment has thus become a commodity dispensed without any redeeming social or communal purpose.

Executions today are isolated acts carried out impersonally—in cold blood—to the detriment of us all. This is not violent justice, as was arguably true of the death penalty in times past, but violence pure and simple. We must recognize this violence for what it is and reject it out of hand. In the process, we will discover that we can live with our worst offenders, though some, perhaps even many, must spend their remaining days behind prison walls.

Executions Past

Ancient Executions: Public, Passionate Violence

Executions were once public, passionate events. The earliest executions were acts of spontaneous, explosive violence. Stonings, no doubt, had a savage character to them even as they united the community against the criminal. Later executions primarily featured hanging and took a more formal, restrained cast, though the crowds at hangings could be quite festive. The word *gala,* for instance, derives from *gallows,* an association that evokes the scene at many hangings in times past. The death penalty was, paradoxically, a confirmation, and occasionally a celebration, of community values and community life. One might weep for some of the condemned, but the violence inflicted on them met with little or no repugnance.

Executions in antiquity, particularly during biblical times, served largely religious ends. People lived in fear of provoking God's wrath, which was thought to take the form of natural catastrophes ranging from plagues to famines and droughts. The offender sinned against God; through punishment, especially capital punishment, people sought to expiate the sin and thus appease God. In the words of the authoritative *Encylopaedia Judaica,* "the original and foremost purpose of punishment in biblical law was the appeasement of God. . . . By taking 'impassioned action' to punish violators of His laws, expiation is made to God and God's 'fierce anger' turned away from Israel."[1] Impassioned action was taken not only against murderers, who destroyed creatures made in God's image, but also against anyone displaying sacrilegious or immoral or even uncivil behavior, all of which offended God and thus were grounds for execution because they put the community at risk of supernatural sanction. Executions were originally authorized by a religious leader (for example, by Moses or Aaron) and later by a religious court (the Sanhedrin), though sometimes offenders were executed on the spot, reflecting the righteous anger of the community.[2] In each case, the aim was the same: "So you shall purge the evil from the midst of you."[3]

Most commonly, executions during the biblical era took the form of stoning. In the early biblical period, before the settling of Palestine, when the Hebrews were essentially a nomadic desert people (roughly 2000–1200 B.C.), stonings were rather unceremonious and probably brutal. A stoning might begin with a simple ritual gesture—for example, the harmed party or a witness to the crime might place a hand on the head of the offender to mark him for execution. "In an orderly proceeding the witness was to cast the first stone. . . . [I]f others were necessary to produce death, the bystanders hurled them."[4] When the occasion permitted, the offender might also make a final statement, presumably asking forgiveness from God and perhaps also from the community. Later Jewish law described a more elaborate execution ritual involving two witnesses, though the essentials remained unchanged. The offender, standing on an elevated scaffold, would formally confess, then one of the witnesses would push him from the scaffold, and the other would drop the first stone on him. "If he still lived, all present stoned him."[5]

Given the vast number of capital crimes, executions were probably quite common, especially during the early biblical era, when adjudicatory procedures were informal. (The word of credible witnesses, without other evidence, was enough to convict someone of a capital crime.)[6] The impression to be gained from the Bible, which includes accounts of a number of stonings, a few of them impromptu, is that those executed in this manner somehow came to terms with this terrifying punishment, bearing their fate with some semblance of dignity. And terrifying those executions must have been. Following the lead of the witnesses, the citizens would arm themselves with stones and surround the offender, perhaps also taunting and ridiculing him before launching their onslaught of bruising rocks; they would stop only when the offender's bloody and lifeless form lay buried under the stones. In this manner, the community would act as one, cleansing itself of the guilt of the criminal and putting things right with God.[7]

Capital punishment in ancient Greece, particularly during the Bronze Age (3000–1000 B.C.), was essentially the same as that practiced by the Hebrews during the biblical period. "Stoning was the earliest form of community punishment among the ancients, for stones were the most natural and the most readily obtainable means of defense or attack."[8] Like the Hebrews, the Greeks restricted stoning for the most part to crimes that affected the community as a whole.[9] And among the Greeks, as among the Hebrews, the earliest stonings were unplanned outbursts of "violent indignation" that were "gradually sanctioned by custom and became a regular mode of punishment."[10] Likewise, the legally sanctioned, more refined stonings of later Greece closely resembled those practiced among the Hebrews of the corresponding biblical period.

> When the offender came within four cubits of the place of execution, he was stripped naked, only leaving a covering before, and his hands being bound, he was led up to the fatal place, which was an eminence twice a man's height. The first executioners of the sentence were the witnesses, who generally pulled off their clothes for the purpose: one of them threw him down with great violence upon his loins: if he rolled upon his breast, he was turned upon his loins again, and if he died by the fall there was an end; but if not, the other witnesses took a great stone, and dashed it upon his breast as he lay upon his back; and then, if he was not dispatched, all the people that stood by threw stones at him till he died."

It is worth noting that even after stonings were planned—that is, after they had become an authorized form of punishment following a primitive script—they could still degenerate into mob scenes. In one variant of stoning as planned punishment, known as the "rebel's beating," a mob would use hands, staves, and stones to beat the offender to death.[12]

Medieval Executions: Ceremonial Violence

Near the end of the ancient period, executions became for a time less common and less violent. The heights of civilization reached in classical Greece and republican Rome (500 B.C.–A.D. 44) made executions seem barbaric. (The link between civilization and the death penalty will be examined in the next chapter.) The Imperial Age of Rome (A.D. 14–337), however, saw a resurgence in executions. This time was famous for the arenas in which Christians, criminals, and errant slaves were thrown to the lions before hordes of cheering spectators. And after the Fall of Rome, in the early medieval period, sometimes called the Dark Ages (500–1000), executions became a fact of daily village life. Executions in imperial Rome had had an element of pageantry to them, however coarse and brutal those executions may have been. By contrast, early medieval executions in many ways hearkened back to the more primitive executions of antiquity.

Life in medieval Europe was a parochial and impoverished existence, particularly during the earlier years (the Dark Ages). Invasions from without and disorder from within were constant threats. Disease ran rampant; mortality rates were high.[13] The precariousness of the times may have bred an angry, fearful, punitive psychology. In any case, punishment was distinctively arbitrary and harsh, a state of affairs "regarded with apathy by the public." Punishment was seen "as one of the chances of fortune, or one of the many crosses laid on mankind by Heaven; a misfortune that might befall anyone, and which must, therefore, be borne patiently."[14]

And publicly. Adjudication during the early medieval period was a bare-bones, almost spontaneous public procedure often involving the entire community. In Nuremberg around the year 1000, for example, it was the prosecutor's job to observe the crime and capture the criminal. His proofs were physical—stolen goods retrieved from the criminal or parts of the bodies of murder victims (for example, a finger, which the prosecutor himself had to forcibly remove). Having chased down the criminal, secured the evidence, and "fastened [it] to the culprit's back," the prosecutor, loudly announcing the crime, would drag the offender (often literally) to the authorities and call for a trial. The trial would be "held publicly in the market place, and anyone who chose could follow the proceedings." Throughout, there was minimal formality and precious little decorum. If condemned, the accused would be executed by the aggrieved party, "who strung up the criminal on any suitable tree or post."[15] A slow and ignominious death by strangulation would ensue before the eyes of the townsfolk.

By the later Middle Ages, adjudication had become more formal and dignified. In the Nuremberg of 1400, for example, torture administered discreetly in prison cells produced confessions, obviating the need to place stolen goods or expropriated body parts in evidence before the public. "Trials no longer took place in the market square, but in a special hall within the Rathaus [city hall], after the accused had been privately examined." Rules of evidence and procedure were increasingly elaborate. As in the early medieval period, punishment followed swiftly. The practice of allowing citizens to carry out executions, however, was abandoned. Such was now "considered to be incompatible with the dignity of the court that had pronounced judgment; it also brought undesirable odium on the accuser." Executions were therefore assigned to an official of the court, usually the Zuchtiger, the man in charge of torturing suspects. By the close of the Middle Ages (1500), the Nuremberg court and its executioner behaved with considerable decorum and even civility:

> Orders were given to produce the prisoner in court. The executioner knock-
> ed at the door of the condemned cell, entered, apologising for the intrusion,
> bound the prisoner's arms, cast a white cloak about the victim, and led him
> between two chaplains to the Judgment Hall. Here the Bannrichter [judge]
> enquired of the Schöffen [jury] whether the judgment passed were in
> conformity with the law. Having received assurance of this, he ordered the
> court clerk to read out the sentence, after which the condemned man was at
> once led out to execution.[16]

From beginning to end, the Middle Ages were a time of periodic famine and almost constant scarcity, particularly of the bread and ale that were the staples of the peasant diet.[17] Still, this period was given to occasional excesses in the form of grand banquets and elaborate pageantries in honor of special events—including executions. (As Barbara Tuchman reminds us, "outward magnificence" in entertainment was much valued during the Middle Ages.) The contrast was striking: "Amid depopulation and disaster," observed Tuchman, "extravagance and splendor were never more extreme."[18] During those few moments in which their sun shone, people made hay, eating, drinking, and being merry virtually in front of their suffering fellows. Thus, in Nuremberg as the medieval period drew to a close, "guests at the sumptuous banquets and entertainments given in the splendid Hall of the Rathaus were not troubled by compassion for the poor wretches lingering, often enough under sentence of death, in the dark cells only a few yards below."[19]

Some of those poor wretches were destined for executions that were entertainments in their own right, gaudy pageantries of violence and prolonged, agonizing death. In such instances, a formal parade, replete with dignitaries in full dress, would convey the condemned to the place of execution, often the town square. Feelings would run strong and find immediate, if generally restrained, expression. The condemned was required by custom to forgive the executioner, who was considered God's agent. The prisoner might openly and sincerely embrace his killer. Spectators, though not directly involved in the execution, would be anything but passive observers. They might cry out in anger. Occasionally, an unruly mob would storm the scaffold. They would be repelled, sometimes at the cost of individual lives, by the gallows guards. The condemned would speak (sometimes shout) his piece to the crowd, usually closing with a declaration to the assembled citizenry that he had repented and was ready to meet his Maker. The crowd would respond, depending on the particulars of the case, with piety or ridicule. With God and Man appeased in their fashion, the criminal would be killed.[20]

With a vengeance. One procedure was to hang the person, cut him down before he died, and then disembowel him or draw and quarter him—that is, disembowel him and cut him in four—while he was still alive. Another method was known as breaking on the wheel. "The prisoner's arms and legs were propped up on a wheel-like platform and were broken in several places by the use of a heavy iron bar. The mangled remains were then turned rapidly, scattering gore about until the unfortunate victim was dead." Breaking on the wheel was a variant of sawing the victim in pieces, "a popular medieval execution." With this type of execution, "the victim was usually hung up by his feet and sawed in two vertically by the executioner."[21]

Such might be the fate of a common criminal. A more grievous offender, such as a traitor or assassin, would be drawn and quartered in a most protracted and painful way, then beheaded for good measure. The grisly details of execution, including what was to be done to which parts of the miscreant's body, were sometimes specified in law. One such statute, of old if not venerable lineage, read as follows when applied to a group of traitors:

> Ye do respectively go to the place from whence ye came; from thence to be drawn upon a sledge to the place of execution, to be there hanged up by the neck, to be cut down while ye are yet alive, to have your hearts and bowels taken out before your faces, and your members cut off and burnt. Your heads severed from your bodies, your bodies divided into quarters, your heads and bodies respectively to be disposed of according to the king's will and pleasure; and the Lord have mercy upon your souls.[22]

In other scenarios for the execution of grievous offenders, molten wax would be poured in the offender's open wounds, and the flesh of his arms and legs torn with hot iron pincers. All the while, onlookers might exhort the executioner to greater violence. At the proper moment, just before death, the good confessor would commend the criminal's soul to God. Indeed, all the condemned might hope for at this juncture was escape into the hereafter.[23]

Executions of the Inquisition

Nowhere is medieval pomp and circumstance, and the complaisance with which violent executions were viewed, better illustrated than in the autos-da-fé—literally, "acts of faith"—of the Inquisition. At these public events, criminals, and especially heretics, were executed en mass. Autos-da-fé were more religious pageantries than mere civil ceremonies, providing an occasion "by which men gave a public and splendid proof of their warm zeal for religion." An auto-da-fé would be publicly announced thirty days in advance and would be scheduled to coincide with such momentous events as the coronation or marriage of a king or the birth of a royal child, "in order that they might be the more solemn and more authentic."[24] The pageantry would but thinly disguise the raw violence of the executions in which it culminated.

The pageant would begin with a remarkable procession. One such procession in Madrid, a pageant unto itself but typical of these affairs, has been described as follows:

> A hundred coal-merchants, armed with pikes and muskets, marched front, because they furnished the wood which was employed in the punishment of those who were condemned to the flames. Next followed the dominicans, preceded by a white cross. The Duke of Medina Celi appeared next in order, bearing the standard of the Inquisition according to the hereditary privilege of his family. This standard was of scarlet damask; upon one side was embroidered a naked sword in a crown of laurel, upon the other the arms of Spain. Next was borne a green cross bound with black crepe. Several grandees and other persons, familiars of the Inquisition, marched after it, dressed in cloaks adorned with black-and-white crosses, and edged with gold lace. The procession was closed by fifty halberdiers or guards of the Inquisition, clothed in black-and-white robes, commanded by the Marquis of Povar, hereditary protector of the Inquisition in the Kingdom of Toledo.[25]

The procession, having passed the royal palace, would end at a grand stage, on which the auto-da-fé proper would take place. Replete with amphitheaters, balconies, platforms, and altars, the stage, stationed in the town square, was built expressly for the occasion. Dignitaries of the Inquisition, of the town, of the church, and of the kingdom would be arranged on the stage according to their prestige. Victims would be displayed on a platform in the lower center of the stage, closest to the crowds.

At the appropriate moment, the victims would be marched onto the higher levels of the stage and paraded before the king, then placed on the left side of the stage on a plain platform. This sad procession, in Madrid and elsewhere, was led by "twelve persons, male and female . . . with ropes around their necks, and torches in their hands, and carrochas or caps of pasteboard, three feet in height, upon their heads, on which their pretended crimes were represented in various manners." Others followed, some fifty or more in number, wearing special cloaks of varying colors, often with representations of flames and the devil painted on them.

An elaborate ritual would then unfold on the stage, featuring many masses and special events—a marriage or coronation ceremony, for example—and lasting an entire day or more. Finally, the sentences of the condemned would be read, which alone would take hours. Those sentenced would proceed, one by one, into prominently displayed cages, "in order that they might be seen distinctly by everybody." A final mass would be said; the grand inquisitor would grant absolution, not pardon, to those who repented. The king would retire. At this juncture,

> the criminals . . . were delivered over to the secular arm, and were carried upon asses to the distance of three hundred paces without the gate [of the town]. They were executed after midnight. The obstinate were burned alive, the repentant were strangled before they were cast into the fire.[26]

The crowd, at once terrified and edified, would disperse. The spectacle of violence, devoid of compassion for the poor souls caught up in it, would thus come to an end.

Early Modern Executions: Refined Ritual, Subdued Ceremony

After the Middle Ages, executions gradually became more tame, though perhaps no less grisly. In the early modern period, roughly the sixteenth through the eighteenth century, public punishments became, in the main, less grossly violent than their biblical or medieval predecessors. Sensibilities had evolved considerably. Disemboweling and beheading were common and unremarkable in the Middle Ages. It was the custom to display the head of the condemned to show the crowd in no uncertain terms that the order of the court had been carried out. By the close of the eighteenth century, however, executions of this sort were rare, revolting spectacles. Even traitors were typically spared disemboweling, though disemboweling followed by beheading was the punishment specified in law, and long observed in custom, for such offenders. When traitors were merely beheaded in early modern London, the crowd would be visibly repulsed:

> When the first stroke of the axe was heard, there was a burst of horror from the crowd, and the instant the head was exhibited there was a terrifying shriek set up, and the multitude ran violently in all directions, as if under the influence of a sudden frenzy.[27]

An even more telling example of the change in sensibilities during this period was the introduction of a cap to "conceal the obscenely contorted features" of the hanged man, as well as to give "a certain privacy and decency in public death."[28] Garden-variety hangings of ordinary criminals during the early modern period, though both public and violent, were a far cry from the stonings of antiquity or the public tortures of the Middle Ages.

The English Experience

Perhaps following the lead of the infrequent yet spectacular inquisitional executions of the medieval period, early modern executions were also carefully staged, if comparatively modest. England provides a case in point. Executions were to be proper and dignified undertakings, marked by the ringing of church bells, special prayers for the condemned, and the final dropping of a handkerchief by the prisoner to signal his readiness to die. The condemned would normally go to the gallows in his best clothes, often making speeches marked by contrition.[29] Afterwards, the prison warden might schedule an official repast to mark the close of the execution ceremony. The governor of Newgate, for example, sent out invitations to a private party following each execution: "We hang at eight, breakfast at nine."[30] All very proper.

One explicit aim of these ceremonial executions, no doubt true to some degree of all public executions in all cultures, was education of the citizenry. English citizens, including school children, were encouraged to observe the condemned in their cells (the prisoners were exhibited for this purpose) and to attend their executions to see firsthand the fate of those who had gone bad and therefore "come to a bad end"—the end of a rope.[31] Executions in rural areas of England during the early modern period appear to have been undertaken with appropriate decorum, meeting with the approval of schoolmasters, parents, and other authorities.

In London, however, the crowd could be quite raucous, with drunken revelry the normal state of affairs. Violence among the spectators was disturbingly common at these executions. (This violence might include a grim battle for the corpse, waged by the deceased's loved ones against the minions of anatomists seeking bodies for medical research.) For their part, condemned prisoners were often as drunk as the spectators, having imbibed freely at the traditional pub stops along the route to the execution site. Some of these prisoners were also nursing hangovers from parties held in their honor on the eve of their executions. A perhaps extreme yet instructive case is that of Renwick Williams, known as the Monster of London, who was executed during the late eighteenth century. His last evening on death row was anything but a solemn testimony to the wages of sin.

> The Monster sent cards of invitation to about twenty couples among whom were some of his alibi friends, his brothers, sisters, several of the prisoners, and others. . . . At four o'clock, the party set to tea; this being over, two violins struck up, accompanied by a flute, and the company proceeded to exercise their limbs. In the merry dance, the cuts and entrechats of the Monster were much admired. . . . About eight o'clock, the company partook of a cold supper, and a variety of wines, such as would not discredit the most sumptuous gala, and about nine o'clock departed, that being the usual hour for locking the doors of the prison.[32]

For the London crowds that came to Williams's hanging and those of others, executions were gala affairs. On occasion, the executioners, themselves inebriated, joined the party. One drunken executioner made a concerted effort to hang the prisoner's confessor, who made the mistake of positioning himself too near the condemned man on the scaffold! Others pandered to the baser desires of the crowd, performing their jobs like actors in a music hall, even bowing deeply before the cheering masses.[33] The condemned were expected to do their part as well, which amounted to dying with panache and upholding their family name. One mother is reported to have called out to her son as the noose was being tightened around his neck, "Son, I hope you will die courageously like your father."[34] Some public education!

Graeme Newman explains these patently irreverent executions as the result of social dislocations, manifested in an extreme form in London, accompanying the demise of the medieval period and the emergence of the modern.[35] Unseemly gallows behavior proved quite persistent and, indeed, may have become an English tradition in its own right. The spectacle of an hysterical English crowd watching a man hang did not really change until executions were moved indoors during the latter half of the nineteenth century. Be that as it may, in early modern London, it is fair to say that in regard to executions, a pearl of ceremony was cast before an often unruly crowd of swine.[36]

The Continental Experience

On the whole, executions were considerably more restrained and dignified in the continental Europe of the early modern period than in England.[37] On the Continent, ritual came more successfully to channel feelings and suppress spontaneity. Executions were held on a stage, with spectators cast in a more circumscribed (and certainly more sober) role than their English brethren. The condemned, as well, were given less room for personal expression, both in their final hours and in their dress and deportment on the scaffold. Executions were meant to have a certain purity, and even beauty, as ceremonies unto themselves. They might have evoked feelings, especially of sadness, but these sentiments generally did not spill over and affect the conduct of the executions in any direct way.

Petrus Spierenburg, whose observations on early modern executions in Amsterdam are most illuminating, recounted the execution of one Hendrina Wouters, described as "the darling of eighteenth-century stagers of beautiful executions." Having been tortured on the rack, she confessed to the crime of murder and was sentenced to death. She proved to be a most cooperative subject of the court.

> She thanked the judges for their merciful sentence, saying she deserved a more severe penalty. On Friday, when her death sentence was announced, she bade farewell to her husband and two children. Bystanders burst into tears. The preacher was very content. Although, while professing to be a Catholic, she proved unable to say the Lord's Prayer, he declared that she would pass away as a child of God. On the justice day he concluded his prayer by expressing the wish that it might have impressed the sinner and the spectators. He asked the Lord's blessing to descend upon her and the judges. Then Hendrina begged forgiveness once more. She remained humble and kept her eyes down. Approaching the cross, she expressed no fear but became even more cheerful. The executioner broke her arms and legs, but she kept on praying until she received a cut in her throat.[38]

Though flagrantly violent, Wouters's execution was considerably more formal and restrained than those of her biblical or medieval counterparts.[39]

The Threshold of Accepted Violence

As a general rule, eyewitness accounts of executions in times past bespeak a familiarity with violence that is "largely unhampered by feelings of repugnance."[40] The threshold of accepted violence is lower in later times, reflecting more refined sensibilities that were sometimes violated (as with early modern beheadings). But more important, at each juncture of history up to the early modern period, people show a considerable capacity for observing crude acts of violence without being repulsed by them. One sees sadness at Wouters's impending plight, which suggests an element of compassion absent in earlier executions, but the general civility of the proceedings implies that her execution does not trouble the executioner or the crowd. There is certainly no apparent repugnance at her bloody fate. There are no reports of public revulsion at the sight of stonings (or crucifixions, another common mode of execution) during the biblical era or in other periods in antiquity. Nor is there evidence of revulsion at the sight of the gross bodily tortures that accompanied medieval executions.

Artistic renderings of execution scenes on the Continent during the early modern period depict executions and their aftermaths as entirely normal and unremarkable.

> A few pictures from the seventeenth and eighteenth centuries show the Volewijk in winter. Men and women are skating on the frozen Y. Along the shore of the Volewijk there are *koek-en-zopie-tenten* (stalls with cakes and drinks). The customers do not even seem to notice the gallows behind them. A few others walk at the foot of the gallows and point at the corpses. No one looks embarrassed by the sight.

These decent, eminently civilized people "saw the corpses" of the condemned and quite clearly "did not care."[41] It was as if the bodies of the condemned were so many carcasses of beef hung out to dry.

Their London counterparts during this period lived in what was colloquially known as the City of Gallows, with bodies gibbeted—hung up in chains and left to rot in the open air—at every major crossroads. This was considered standard fare by the English, if not by visitors from the Continent. "No matter by what approach the stranger then entered London, he had the fact of the stringent severity of English criminal law most painfully impressed upon him by a sight of the gallows."[42]

Actual executions, however, both on the Continent and in England, were a different matter entirely. "Then the crowd came specially to watch the spectacle and did not want to miss a minute."[43] The violence of execution was taken at face value: A public killing was exciting and worthy of interest; residual bodies were not. Executions occurred; public attention rose and fell, not in response to the tragedy of life lost but in response to the drama of life taken. The bodies of the dead may have lingered, but life in the community went on.

Notes

1. "Punishment," *Encylopaedia Judaica,* 16 vols. (Jerusalem: Keter, 1971), 13:1386.
2. T. Sellin, *The Penalty of Death* (Beverly Hills, Calif.: Sage, 1982), esp. Chap. 1.
3. Deut. 17:7.

4. J. Hastings, ed., *Dictionary of the Bible,* 5 vols. (New York: Charles Scribner's Sons, 1898–1905) 1:527.
5. *The Interpreter's Dictionary of the Bible,* 4 vols. (New York: Abingdon Press, 1962) 4:447.
6. Later, evidentiary requirements became so strict as to preclude the use of the death penalty. See Sellin (n. 2), 15.
7. The connection between crime and impurity, with punishment serving as a means of cleansing for the community, survived in modified form virtually up to the modern period. During the early Middle Ages, for example, offenders would be dragged on a leather slide to the place of execution so that their feet would not touch and hence pollute the ground. In the late Middle Ages, and even during the early modern period, condemned criminals would be driven in a cart, their coffins beside them, so that at no time would they touch the earth. This practice, Newman tells us, was part of the "officially worded death sentences used in Germany and Switzerland during the middle ages. . . . [R]equiring the criminal to be kept from the earth until hanged thrusts him into the gulf between heaven and earth. The earth is saved from the criminal's demonical powers." G. Newman, *The Punishment Response* (Philadelphia: Lippincott, 1978), 37.
8. I. Barkan, "Capital Punishment in Ancient Greece" (Chicago, 1936), 41. In the ancient world, stoning was a natural, simple, and public method of execution. Other methods sharing these attributes to lesser degrees, generally reserved for more specialized offenses, included drowning, burying alive, beating to death with sticks, and immolation, or burning to death. For an account of the nature and import of executions by these various means, see G. R. Scott, *History of Capital Punishment* (London: Torchstream Books, 1950).
9. Barkan (n. 8), 53.
10. Ibid., 41.
11. Scott (n. 8), 19.
12. Ibid., 20.
13. D. Kagan, S. Ozment, and F. M. Turner, *The Western Heritage* (New York: Macmillan, 1979), 251.
14. A. Keller and C. V. Calvert, *A Hangman's Diary: Being the Journal of Master Franz Schmidt, Public Executioner of Nuremberg, 1573–1617* (Montclair, N.J.: Patterson Smith, 1973), 2.
15. Ibid., 29.
16. Ibid., 34, 38, 37.
17. Kagan, Ozment, and Turner (n. 13), 290.
18. B. W. Tuchman, *A Distant Mirror: The Calamitous Fourteenth Century* (New York: Knopf, 1978), 12, xvii.
19. Keller and Calvert (n. 14), 2.
20. See Scott (n. 8) and A. Mencken, *By the Neck: A Book of Hangings* (New York: Hastings House, 1942).
21. H. E. Barnes, *The Story of Punishment: A Record of Man's Inhumanity to Man* (Montclair, N.J.: Patterson Smith, 1972), 242.
22. W. O. Douglas, *An Almanac of Liberty* (New York: Random House, 1954), 17.

23. This type of execution for grievous offenders was comparatively common in the Middle Ages. Isolated examples of this punishment can also be found in the early modern period. Notable among these is the case of Damiens the regicide, executed in Paris in 1757. See M. Foucault, *Discipline and Punish: The Birth of the Prison* (New York: Pantheon, 1977), 3–5.
24. Scott (n. 8), 26.
25. Ibid., 28.
26. Ibid., 30.
27. L. Radzinowicz, *A History of English Criminal Law,* 5 vols. (New York: Macmillan, 1948), 1:26–27.
28. J. Atholl, *Shadow of the Gallows* (London: John Long, 1954), 108.
29. Radzinowicz (n. 27).
30. See Newman (n. 7), 144.
31. Atholl (n. 28), 73.
32. Radzinowicz (n. 27), 1:167.
33. Ibid., 1:188–189.
34. Atholl (n. 28), 75.
35. Newman tells us that it was during this period, "one of the most sanguine in all English history," that

> the feudal, medieval rhythm of life—the unhurried, detailed work of the master craftsman, the leisurely raising of sheep and spinning of cloth, the quiet tilling of the earth—was deeply disturbed. The merchants, traders, and industrialists were beginning to take over. The people were being thrust headlong into the business of production. To make matters worse, the ordinary people were constantly embattled by wars, civil and international. The civil war, though fought with dignity, nevertheless was a war. And wars cannot circumvent the horrors of death. As if this were not enough, the people of England were visited frequently by terrible plagues—the worst one being the black death of 1666, followed soon by the Great Fire of London. Death was all around them at the time when the social and economic life of the country began to throb. All the basic fibers of English life had been subverted. . . . And in the crowded city of London the specter of death and killing loomed larger than ever. It is little wonder that by the time the eighteenth century was under way, the ordinary Londoner, soon to become known as one of the "working class," found himself gazing dumbfounded or yelling hysterically with the crowd at the foot of the gallows.

    See Newman (n. 7), 130, 135.
36. See Radzinowicz (n. 27).
37. The orgies of execution that came in the wake of the French Revolution were a notable exception to this observation. These mass guillotinings were bloody spectacles, and the crowd, reeling from the infamous Reign of Terror of Robespierre and incensed at the political scapegoats paraded before them, might even cry out to see the heads of more infamous victims. The crowd's

appetite for gore was not insatiable, however, and after the first few be-headings, their ranks would thin out. Be that as it may, this episode of raw public violence was quite unusual, both for France and for the continental Europe of the early modern period. See O. Blanc, *Last Letters: Prisons and Prisoners of the French Revolution, 1793–1794* (New York: Farrar, Straus & Giroux, 1987).

38. P. Spierenburg, *The Spectacle of Suffering* (Cambridge: Cambridge University Press, 1984), 65, 66.
39. Wouters's execution was a sanitized version of breaking on the wheel as it was practiced in the Middle Ages.
40. Spierenburg (n. 38), 94.
41. Ibid., 91.
42. Radzinowicz (n. 27), 1:200.
43. Spierenburg (n. 38), 91.

CHAPTER 2

Executions Present

The Twentieth-Century American Experience

The End of Public Ritual

Executions at the turn of the twentieth century were not substantially different from those carried out some four hundred years earlier, at the beginning of the modern period. This was particularly true in rural areas in the United States. The ritual had been streamlined; bodies were no longer left hanging for all to see (and smell), at least not for long. And again one saw ceremony, this time characterized by a certain bucolic simplicity. Conducted in woods and pastures, these executions were unobtrusive, almost natural. In general, the condemned betrayed no profound emotions. The crowds, still quite large at that point in history, were sometimes loud and coarse but more often were subdued in their reactions. Occasionally, some of the observers would display sadness for the condemned, many of whom were black.

Philippe Aries recounted the hanging of a young black man in Georgia in 1890. Though comparatively recent, the execution is striking for several reasons. First, the man was killed almost immediately on conviction. Second, he was executed in public, before a crowd of spectators. Third, the crowd displayed an easy familiarity with violence and death, though an unadorned hanging was, historically speaking, fairly tame. Fourth, the condemned man, formerly a servant, was attended by his master, who "prepare[d] him for death and . . . play[ed] the role of confessor" even as the condemned man stood on the scaffold. Finally, the man went to his death with simple resignation, eating his last meal with relish, just moments before his execution, then mounting the scaffold with a deliberate step. "His bare feet did not tremble." His manner was "calm," "natural," and "completely dignified." His farewell was simple and direct: 'I'm all right now,' and very firmly, 'Good-bye, captain . . . good-bye everybody.' "[1]

Describing a similar execution, that of one Asbury Dixon, a black man hanged in 1902 in the town of Snow Hill, Maryland, August Mencken called it one of "the quiet little hangings [that] made a pleasant break in the monotony of farm life." On the eve of his execution, Dixon, his family, and his fellow prisoners congregated freely in the jail, singing religious hymns. Dixon sang "with a fervor and solemnity unsurpassed by any of them." His young son, Tema, "much interested in the singing of hymns and the farewells of the other prisoners to his father," tired, then fell asleep in his father's cell. The jailor let the boy stay, leaving him to sleep the night "in his father's arms." The parting of father and son the next morning was a wrenching experience for the jailor as well as for the man and his boy. Still, that morning Dixon seemed resigned to his fate; the jailor, too, went about his duty without any visible emotion. Dixon ate heartily, smoked a cigar, and then was driven by carriage to the site of his execution. On the scaffold, surrounded by a sizeable crowd, he delivered a farewell speech in the time-honored tradition of public executions. Dixon did not embrace his executioner (as did some of his medieval counterparts) or articulate a ritual confession (as did the early modern Wouters), but he did acknowledge the error of his ways, speak of receiving forgiveness from the Lord, and say a gentle goodbye to the onlookers.[2]

Prison Executions: Private, Bureaucratic Procedure

Public executions would be held in some states well into the twentieth century; there were public executions in Mississippi, for example, in the 1940s.[3] But public executions have been the exception, not the rule, during the 1900s. After the turn of the twentieth century, most executions in America took place within penal institutions. Some of these executions, however, particularly those occurring at the turn of the century, had a semipublic character to them. Interested citizens were allowed to enter the penal institution and observe the proceedings. Like their more public counterparts, these executions were treated as utterly natural and unremarkable events.

The execution of Willie Francis, though relatively recent, is in many ways a case in point.[4] (This case is famous because the first attempt to execute Francis failed, but that is not important here.) Conducted in a rural Louisiana jail in the mid-1940s, this execution was marked by an air of casual informality. The room in the jail holding the electric chair was full to overflowing with local citizens; the streets outside the jail were crowded as well. The instrument of execution was a portable electric chair, installed in the jail on the morning of the execution by a prison captain and an inmate on assignment from the state penitentiary. Both the officer and the inmate were reportedly drunk, which almost certainly explains why the chair failed to kill Willie Francis.

Willie's demeanor on the day of his execution was calm and collected, even relaxed. Earlier that day, his head had been shaved by a fellow prisoner. Though at first uneasy during this procedure, Willie came to trade jokes with the prisoner as well as with the sheriff and deputy in attendance. "Everybody was being so nice to him," Willie was reported to have thought, "that for a while dying didn't seem like such a bad thing." Though he later stated he was fearful, Willie indeed acted as if dying weren't such a bad thing. At one point, he was led near the electric chair and docilely started to seat himself of his own accord. He was stopped by the sheriff, who ushered Willie into a cell in an adjoining corridor for his last words with a priest. It was apparent to everyone on the scene that Willie was "fully resigned to his fate." Moments later, Willie was summoned by the sheriff.

> Willie looked at the sheriff, who said nothing but instead gave him a slight nod. Not fully understanding what to do, Willie left the cell, walked across the hallway, back into the execution room, and sat down in the chair. This time no one stopped him.[5]

The execution failed for technical reasons (the chair was not properly grounded), and the botched effort gave rise to a spate of litigation about whether or not a person could be lawfully "executed" twice. But the execution itself was only remarkable in its curious blending of pastoral sentiment with modern technology. Willie's second bout with the chair, roughly one year later, was orchestrated with more formality and, by modern lights, more professionalism. The chair worked, and Willie died.

The easy informality of executions like that of Willie Francis are a thing of the past. Gradually over this century, executions came to take on a new meaning and a new, impersonal form. (This appears to have occurred at different times in different parts of the country, presumably because of variations in the pace of modernization.) Increasingly, executions were seen as acts of violence that were likely to harden the public and demean the condemned. Accordingly, executions became both less frequent and less public. They were moved into penal institutions, sometimes initially to jails (as seen in the Francis case) but eventually to prisons. Within prisons, executions typically were performed at first in the center of the prison yard, which accommodated sizeable crowds; later, they were conducted in remote corners of the yard, thus restricting the viewing audience. Finally, executions were moved inside prison buildings, generally to the basements of death rows, which in turn were housed deep within the prison compound.[6]

Efforts were made to make executions as tame as humanly possible—and, thereby, it was hoped, decent and humane. In practical terms, this meant that executions were to be quick, painless, minimally disfiguring, and private. In particular, one scrupulously avoided anything that would draw a condemned prisoner's attention to an impending execution, such as a preview of the execution apparatus. Such an experience, by "unnecessarily sharpen[ing] the poignancy of the prisoner's apprehension," would in turn cause "those last torturous minutes to be even more unbearable."[7] In the process of trying to spare prisoners such suffering (and no doubt to lessen the discomfort of prison staff as well), executions became strained, hidden, hurried undertakings. To paraphrase a mid-twentieth-century executioner, one stayed out of sight and worked as quickly and quietly as one could.[8]

Present-day executions could hardly be more different from executions in the past. Executions today are always conducted in secluded areas within prisons. Only a limited number of official spectators attend; these witnesses maintain a discreet silence, and many are reportedly shaken by what they see. (Air-sickness bags are standard equipment in some witness rooms.) Neither death nor killing is any longer a familiar part of life. Killings by officials are especially rare events, and are drained of their emotional import by secrecy (hardly anyone sees them) and euphemism (hardly anyone calls an execution a killing). Speed and efficiency, too, dampen the emotional resonance of the proceedings. Executions are over within a matter of minutes. (By contrast, in early modern London it took upwards of two hours to get from the prison to the scaffold.) In extreme cases today, executions take as little as *nine seconds* from when the prisoner leaves his cell.[9] Observers of executions past would hardly know that a killing had occurred, or that a fellow human being had died. It is perhaps unsurprising, then, that now and again prisoners would escape from lynch mobs and run straight into the arms of the official executioner. Relating one such story, a correctional official in Georgia observed,

> The point is that a good executioner's better than a mob. The guy knew he was gonna die. He chose between a professional and a bunch of bloodthirsty crazies. I would have done the same thing: at least a professional's gonna get it over with fast.[10]

Today's executions are highly bureaucratic jobs with clearly delineated roles, responsibilities, and procedures. All behavior is spelled out by the prison authorities and occurs in the context of rigidly enforced bureaucratic routines. Of course, most prison work, indeed most work in general, is bureaucratized. But the execution of prisoners is an extreme case, and for good reason. Killing and dying are elemental activities, and so we thoroughly "encase" them, as it were, within sterile but comforting bureaucratic procedures. The process is ritualistic, by virtue of its mechanical precision, but bureaucratic executions are not true rituals. Rituals, like bureaucratic procedures, allow people to disengage from their normal roles. But with true rituals, this disengagement occurs in the service of a larger undertaking—some form of cleansing or celebration—that has larger communal meaning. The bureaucratic execution is an end in itself, recognizing only its own internal logic.

Citizens not officially connected with an execution play a restricted, impoverished role in these proceedings. As in times past, crowds may assemble during executions, though today's crowds are small by historical standards. (The large, coarse crowd outside Florida's Starke Prison for the 1989 execution of Ted Bundy was atypical, though many execution crowds in times past dwarf even this assemblage, which approached two thousand.) People may mill about outside the prison gates, sometimes protesting or applauding the executions taking place within, but they have no real awareness of what is going on. Certainly they have no meaningful involvement in the execution process (the staff carrying out executions pay little attention to these protesting groups). Loved ones are also on the periphery of modern executions. The family and friends of the condemned have limited opportunities to visit their loved ones. They are not involved in the execution or even, with rare exceptions, present at them.[11] Neither, again with rare exceptions, are the families of the victims involved in any way with the execution process.

Even the condemned are curiously removed from today's executions, present more in body than in spirit. The condemned spend years on death row awaiting their fate, not, as in the past, a mere few days or weeks. (A corollary of our modern concern for humanely administered executions is our desire to allow inmates to explore every avenue of appeal before we execute them. This greatly lengthens the prisoner's stay on death row.) During their lonely and barren confinement, the condemned die a slow psychic death, so numb submission to the executioner has replaced calm acceptance of one's fate.

Today we have an elaborate and largely clandestine bureaucracy to carry out death sentences, and we use technologically sophisticated modes of execution. The changes are telling. Slowly but inexorably we have distanced ourselves from the reality of the death penalty. We now kill efficiently and above all impersonally—"without anger or passion," to use Max Weber's fine phrase—like so many functionaries in the business of justice.[12] The contemporary execution procedure is unlike any premodern procedures—even those followed in executions at the turn of this century. Though modern executions are obviously violent in that they entail the forcible taking of life, the technical process is quick, clean, and precise, and perhaps even free of physical pain.[13] Such, then, is the nature of progress. We have come a long way from the public slaughters of the past.

Modern Executions and the Illusion of Humaneness

Or have we? Though remarkably restrained by historical standards, today's executions are purely destructive undertakings. They neither appease God nor involve or affirm the community. Instead, the execution procedure smacks of a mechanized, assembly-line nihilism. Byron Eschelman, a former chaplain at San Quentin and a participant in many executions, makes this point in a strident yet compelling way:

> Society is expert at cold-blooded, unemotional, businesslike, professional killing. The death penalty is routine, ritualistic, even-tempered, assembly-line annihilation. The state becomes a legal "Murder, Inc.," serving respectable citizens who pay taxes to get the job done.[14]

There is even a kind of "countdown for death" detailing the condemned prisoner's last hours, as though his execution were a mere technical drill.

The official countdown of the final hours of inmate Cain (an unfortunate pseudonym), part of San Quentin's official execution schedule during Eschelman's tenure there, embodies the modern execution procedure.

Count Down for Death[15]   Friday, May 8   Death in ten hours.

S	M	T	W	T	F	S
						89
					X	X
X	X	X	X	X	X	9
10	11	12	13	14	15	16
17	18	19	20	21	22	23
24	25	26	27	28	29	30
31						

When	Where	Who	What
A.M.			
1:00	Holding Cell Area	Death Watch Officers	Maintain regular entries on the log sheet.
3:00	Holding Cell Area	Watch Lieutenant	Makes routine checks with the death watch officers during their shifts.
4:00	Holding Cell Area	Watch Lieutenant	Telephones count to control center.
6:15	Holding Cell Area	Death Watch Officers	Ask Cain what he wishes for breakfast.
7:00	Employees' Dining Room	Supervising Cook and Correctional Sergeant	Prepare and deliver breakfast for Cain and the death watch officers.

When	Where	Who	What
7:15	Holding Cell	Chaplain	Offers religious services and counseling. May remain until after the execution if Cain asks him to, or may return after 9:00.
8:00	Death Cell	Watch Lieutenant	Checks and dispatches log sheet to warden.
8:10	Gas Chamber	Chamber Operator and Chemical Operator	Arrange necessary chemicals and test the chamber.
9:00	Employees' Lounge	Citizen Legal Witnesses	Sign official register.
9:30	Holding Cell Area	Chamber Operator	Unrolls strip of green rug leading from cell to doorway of gas chamber.
9:40	Administrative Area	Associate Warden Custody	Drives sedan with warden and associate warden administration about 150 yards from Administration Building to entrance of witness area.
9:45	Holding Cell Area	Warden and Associate Wardens	Accept last wishes and messages from Cain.
9:52	Holding Cell	Lieutenant	Unlocks Cain's cell; asks him to remove all of his clothing, including slippers. Cain dresses only in new blue jeans and a white shirt.
9:55	Holding Cell	Chief Medical Officer and a second doctor	Affix stethoscope on Cain's chest with sterile tape, rubber tube extending through shirt front.
9:55	Employees' Lounge	Correctional Lieutenant	Escorts official witnesses and institutional staff to entrance of gas chamber witness area.
9:58	Witness Area	Associate Warden Administration	Signals for entrance of witnesses. Correctional officer no. 1 stationed to left of chamber; correctional officer no. 2 on right inside iron railing. Medical technical assistant on raised steps available for first aid to witnesses.
10:00:30	Holding Cell	Lt.-in-Charge of Execution, Death Watch officers, and Chamber Operator	Escort Cain from cell to chamber. Strap Cain to Chair B, which is the nearest to the connection for the stethoscope hose.
10:01:30	Observation Area	Correctional Officer	Closes steel door and spins tight the locking wheel.

When	Where	Who	What
10:02:30	Observation Area	Warden	Orders executioner to proceed.
		Chamber Operator	Removes safety pin from lever. Depresses mechanical action. Cyanide gas generates in chamber.
10:03	Gas Chamber	Cain	Unconscious.
10:13	Observation Area	Medical Officer	Confirms death of Cain.
10:15	Observation Area	Warden	Passes report of time of death to associate warden administration through porthole in door.
10:17	Observation Area	Chamber Operator	Starts exhaust pumps to clear chamber of gas.
10:21	Observation Area	Associate Warden Administration	Informs official witnesses of time cyanide pellets dropped and time of death.
10:25	Administrative Office	Warden	Returns by car and tele-phones office of governor.
10:30	Observation Area	Official Witnesses	Sign affidavit as they leave observation area.
10:35	Warden's Office	Warden	Meets press.
P.M.			
1:00	Gas Chamber	Hospital Crew	Remove body from chamber to prison morgue. Finger-print.
2:00	Hospital	Medical Officer	Completes death certificate.
3:00	Administrative Office	Secretary	Prepares notice to court, transmitting affidavit of death.
4:00	Control Center	Control Sergeant	Subtracts one from institutional count.
4:15	Administrative Office	Records Officer	Assembles case folder for deposit in archives.
4:30	Warden's Office	Warden	By request, sends letter confirming execution of Cain.

No community, not even the impoverished community of the prison, could draw emotional sustenance or larger meaning from such a pseudoritual, which is as lifeless as the corpse it is meant to produce. Nor can the condemned find support or purpose in these proceedings. Execution procedures in earlier times, however brutal, at least allowed the offender "abundant opportunities to establish for himself a public character" and to die with a "display of courage and dignity."[16] This is no longer the case. Indeed, the point of the modern bureaucratic execution procedure is to suppress any real-life human reactions on the part of the prisoners or their executioners. Human reactions would interfere with the efficient administration of the death penalty.

The impersonality of the modern death penalty makes it distinctively brutal. Admittedly, this is a curious proposition. We explicitly seek humane executions. Whereas in times past we physically assaulted the condemned as a community or selected executioners brutal enough to kill them before our eyes, today we select personnel for execution teams who are, among other things, civil and accommodating to the needs of the prisoners during their last hours. To be sure, we do not pick such men, nowadays referred to as deathwatch or execution team officers, entirely out of the goodness of our hearts. Their interpersonal skills promote a decent sort of social control and facilitate the smooth execution drill that is the hallmark of the modern death penalty.[17] Perhaps the prisoners sense that there is an element of duplicity in this, however well-meaning it may be. Though most of the condemned appreciate the attention of the deathwatch officers, both they and the officers remain emotionally aloof from one another. The result is a civil but impersonal proceeding that gives company but not comfort to the condemned (see Chapters 6 and 7).

Executions today are disturbingly, even chillingly, dispassionate. If you doubt this, listen to Caryl Chessman's fictional rendering of a modern execution. Himself a death row inmate, Chessman vividly depicted the pain of a lonely, anonymous death, a death predicated on one's personal insignificance. Though fictional, even melodramatic, his account is authentic. Chessman knew, as we all know, that death is a profoundly personal experience. He knew as well that today's condemned prisoner suffers the ignominy of an impersonal death inflicted by faceless bureaucrats. This prisoner is reduced to the status of an object and disposed of according to a schedule.

Your waiting is over.

Three of the executioner's assistants come for you. The cell door is unlocked, opened. You're told quietly, impersonally, "It's time."

It's time to die, to be executed.

You stand there for an instant, unmoving. Perhaps you take a last drag on your cigarette, drop the butt, step on it. Three pairs of eyes watch you.

"Go to hell!" you can scream defiantly. "I'm not going! Do you bastards hear me? I'm not going!"

They hear you. But you're going nevertheless. They'll take you by force if necessary. They have a job to do.

You can whimper. You can cry out to God to help you, to save your life. But don't expect a miracle. He won't intervene. So ask only for the strength to die like a man.

You can shrug. You didn't think it would come to this, but it did. And here you are, at the end of life's road, about to take that last short walk.

Automatically, your legs move. You're walking, mechanically—out through the death watch cell entrance, around a bend in the short hallway, through a doorway. And there it is. The gas chamber. No stopping now. No turning back. You're hustled into this squat, octagonal, glass and metal-sided cell within a room. Its elaborate gadgets don't interest you. Quickly you find yourself seated in the chair. The guards strip you down. Their movements are swift and sure, smoothly rehearsed. The stethoscope is connected.

There! The job is done.

"Good luck," says the guard captain in charge.

Then you're alone. The guards have left. The metal door has closed. The spoked wheel on the outside of that door is being given a final turn.

Everything is in readiness! This is the dreadful, final moment. While the physical preparations were underway, while you moved, it wasn't so real. Activity blocked full realization. It was like watching a gripping scene in a movie, where the camera had been speeded up and the action had carried you along with it, irresistibly. You had only a blurred awareness that it was leading to this. But now that you're physically immobilized, there's a jarring change. The camera slows. You see; you absorb; the scene unfolds with a terrible clarity. For an instant, time is frozen. Your thoughts and sensory impressions are fragmented, each one stabbing at you like a needle.

The warden is at his post. So is the executioner and the attending physician. On the opposite side of the chamber, behind a guard rail less than four feet from where you sit, stand the official witnesses, their eyes riveted on you through the thick glass. In a matter of minutes, you'll be dead. They're here to watch *you* die.

The executioner is signalled by the warden. With scientific precision, valves are opened. Closed. Sodium cyanide eggs are dropped into the immersion pan—filled with sulphuric acid—beneath your metal chair. Instantly the poisonous hydrocyanic acid gas begins to form. Up rise the deadly fumes. The cell is filled with the odor of bitter almond and peach blossoms. It's a sickening-sweet smell.

Only seconds of consciousness remain.

You inhale the deadly fumes. You become giddy. You strain against the straps as the blackness closes in. You exhale, inhale again. Your head aches. There's a pain in your chest. But the ache, the pain is nothing. You're hardly aware of it. You're slipping into unconsciousness. You're dying. Your head jerks back. Only for an awful instant do you float free. Your brain has been denied oxygen. Your body fights a losing ten-minute battle against death.

You've stopped breathing. Your heart has quit beating.

You're dead.

The minutes pass. The blowers whirr. The ammonia valves are open. The gas is being driven from the cell. The clerical work is being done.

That's your body they're removing; it's your body they take to the prison morgue. No, don't worry about that cyanide rash on your leg.

If you have no one to claim your body and you're not of the Jewish or Catholic faith, you'll be shipped off to be cremated. You'll come back to the prison in a "jar." You'll go to Boot Hill.

If your body is claimed, a mortician will come for it. He'll take you away to a funeral parlor, prepare you for burial, impersonally. Services? Well, that's up to your people. Then burial. The end. But not really the end.

An aged mother may be weeping silently. She carried you in her womb. She gave you birth. And your life came to this.

"Mommy," a little girl may ask, "where's Daddy?"

Cruelly, a playmate may tell a small son, "Your old man died in the gas chamber!"

A young wife is dazed, numb.

This is your legacy to them.[18]

Chessman had seen the execution process at work when many of his fellow condemned were taken to their deaths. He coped with the threat of his own execution, according to a psychiatrist who interviewed him on a number of occasions, "by thinking of himself as the attorney in the case rather than as the condemned man." When this stratagem failed, as it did periodically, Chessman would talk with his psychiatrist "about the feelings of torture that he experienced waiting for death. At times, he felt that he could no longer tolerate the pain, the anxiety, and the fear. At such times, he expressed a wish to get the suffering over with."[19] Chessman never dropped his appeals, but his appeals did finally run out. After twelve years on death row, Chessman took his last walk.

As Chessman's fictional account implies, and as I will attempt to prove in Part II and especially Part III of this book, executioner and condemned alike are dehumanized in today's executions. They are morally dead—dead as persons—even as their bodies move to the cadence of this modern danse macabre. Each participates in a peculiarly subtle and insidious form of torture that prepares them for their respective roles in the execution process. This is not justice but rather, in Camus's wise reckoning, administrative murder.[20] To be sure, these arrangements make executions easier and more palatable. Indeed, given our modern sensibilities, there may well be no other way we can execute a person. But at bottom these dehumanizing procedures hide a reality that we must face head on—namely, that the death penalty is utterly out of step with our current standards of decency and has no place in our justice system.

Civilization and the Death Penalty

The reasons for the change in the administration and ultimately in the meaning of the death penalty are rooted in the civilization of punishment.[21] Civilization proceeds unevenly, sometimes undergoing dramatic setbacks (witness the primitive quality of life after the fall of the Roman Empire), but in general civilization advances over time. In each subsequent age, people's awareness of and empathy for the humanity of others increases, expanding to include even deviant others. There is, then, a growing distaste and even revulsion for punishments that feature the public infliction of pain and finally a rejection of punishments that involve the infliction of any visible bodily pain at all.[22] Thus our modern, highly civilized sensibilities reject violence, especially public violence, as a means of punishment.

It is reasonable to suppose that when a culture or civilization is at its height, its members' emotional bonds to one another and their awareness of their shared humanity are strong. One salient result of this is that criminal sanctions are both less harsh and less readily used. This is true relative to the standards of the times, in that people reject as cruel the punishments they have inherited from their ancestors. This is also true objectively. Violence per se becomes, to varying degrees, objectionable, and is reduced as much as possible given the available means of execution. No clearer example can be found than that of classical Greece. Solon reigned during a period of great civilization. Though he inherited Draco's incredibly arbitrary and brutal system of law, in which virtually all crimes were capital offenses, he rejected this draconian code and replaced it with one of the more progressive criminal codes of any historical period. The death penalty was rarely administered at all, and incarceration was rarer still.[23] Moreover, when executions did occur in classical Greece, the method used was ingestion of hemlock, a comparatively painless poison that was self-administered by the condemned in a private and supportive milieu. The prototypical execution of the time was that of Socrates, who chose the hour of his death, conversed freely with his disciples until the end, and died in their comforting presence.[24]

Of a piece with the retreat from inflicting physical pain in punishment is the move away from spontaneous, face-to-face forms of bodily punishment. Typically, the violence of executions is muted by ritual, which functions as a sort of psychic buffer, separating the community from the condemned. (Executions in classical Greece are an extreme and perhaps unique case. The execution ritual is self-administered in private, obviating the need for an executioner and obscuring the underlying violence of the process.) Finally, as is true today, capital punishment becomes an isolated, ritualistic, mechanical event unto itself. In this context of remote and rigidly orchestrated bodily punishment, the community is profoundly removed from the proceedings, and even the participants in the process have virtually no human contact at all. It is a paradox of the modern death penalty that, having come to more fully appreciate the humanity of those we punish, we must suppress our awareness of that humanity, indeed suppress that humanity itself, if we are to carry out executions. Hence, we first kill the person, the moral entity, by a process of dehumanization. Then we kill and dispose of the body. This can be a smooth and efficient procedure, but never a just one.

With the civilization of punishment has come a gradual recognition of the finality of death. The death penalty is now seen as a final and irrevocable sanction.[25] The finality of death heightens the awesome and awful reality of the death penalty and, in turn, heightens our need to distance ourselves from the punishment process. However painless and impersonal the penalty of death may become—and with lethal injection this sanction may have become as impersonal and painless as it can conceivably be—execution is increasingly perceived as an annihilation of the person.

This is a uniquely modern perception. In earlier times, people shared the comforting belief that the death penalty, though surely violent, left the truly final matters in God's hands. We did His work, observing recognized ritual forms. He, and often the condemned as well, understood and approved (and, when necessary, forgave). Today we can take but cold comfort in the death penalty, if we take any comfort in it at all. The extreme nature of such a sanction gives us added impetus to distance ourselves from executions, even to the point, as we see today, of using bureaucratic procedures that psychically and morally numb us to the reality of the death penalty.

The evolution of the death penalty might be summarized as follows. Killing criminals, particularly in public, came to be seen as a revolting spectacle as people began to appreciate the humanity of those being killed, and hence to empathize with the humiliation and degradation wrought by their punishment. In response, executions became more tame, with savage communal stonings giving way to increasingly restrained and impersonal execution ceremonies and rituals. Thus, the killing of Hendrina Wouters in early modern Europe, though flagrantly violent by modern standards, was quite civilized compared with earlier executions, and the hanging of Asbury Dixon in twentieth-century America was so civil as to hide the violence of the death penalty. Subsequently, executions were physically hidden from the public by moving them behind the walls of penal institutions, until finally, today, executions take place only in remote prison cell blocks, beyond the ken of all but a handful of official observers. Eventually, the violence of execution came to be hidden even from the participants themselves. This was done by bureaucratizing executions, thereby dehumanizing the various participants and muting their moral sensibilities. Of course, executioners know that they kill people, though some of them do not like to be called executioners. They are so caught up in the procedural concerns that mark the modern execution drill, however, that the violence of executions is effectively hidden from their awareness.

In the past, we were in the main less aware of our shared humanity and mortality, and so the enormity of executions escaped us. Violence against others, especially outcasts, was unremarkable. We could execute criminals spontaneously and without remorse. Even planned executions could still be casual or cordial or even festive, because the participants did not recognize the awful finality of the proceedings. As we came to sense our shared humanity and mortality, and thus to recognize the violence of the death penalty, executions became morally and psychologically problematic events. Public execution rituals became less accepted and were gradually replaced by private procedures. Executions today carry this evolution to its logical conclusion: We have replaced meaningful ritual with mechanical ritualism. The result is a bureaucratic execution procedure that abrogates our humanity under the guise of justice.

Notes

1. P. Aries, *The Hour of Our Death* (New York: Vintage, 1982), 28.
2. A. Mencken, *By the Neck: A Book of Hangings* (New York: Hastings House, 1942), 34.
3. See C. Goins, "The Traveling Executioner," *American Mercury* 54 (217): 96 (January 1942).
4. A. S. Miller and J. H. Bowman, *Death by Installments: The Ordeal of Willie Francis* (New York: Greenwood Press, 1988).
5. Ibid., 10, 8, 8.
6. R. G. Murdy, "Brief History of Capital Punishment in Maryland," *Report of*

the Committee on Capital Punishment to the Legislative Council of Maryland (1962), Sec. 1, pp. 1–4.

7. Royal Commission on Capital Punishment, 1949–1953. Report presented to Parliament by Command of Her Majesty (September 1953), 253.

8. R. G. Elliot, *Agent of Death: The Memoirs of an Executioner* (New York: Dutton, 1940).

9. Royal Commission on Capital Punishment (n. 7).

10. M. Lesey, *The Forbidden Zone* (New York: Farrar, Straus & Giroux, 1987), 135–136.

11. In Florida, one of the official witnesses is selected by the prisoner, who may ask a relative to attend the execution. In Georgia, five witnesses can be selected by the prisoner.

12. M. Weber, *The Theory of Social and Economic Organization* (New York: Oxford University Press, 1947), 340.

13. We normally think of modern execution methods as physically painless. Certainly they appear to be, but appearances can be misleading. Barnes, for example, has cited evidence from earlier in this century that casts doubt on the presumed painlessness of electrocution, which is still the most common method of execution in use in America. See H. E. Barnes, *The Story of Punishment: A Record of Man's Inhumanity to Man* (Montclair, N.J.: Patterson Smith, 1972), 243. And Supreme Court Justice Brennan is of the opinion that sufficient evidence exists to declare electrocution a cruel and unusual punishment, in violation of the Eighth Amendment. See the Brennan dissent from denial of certiorari in Glass v. Louisiana, 471 U.S. 1080 (1985). In that same dissent, Brennan cited evidence that criminals executed in the gas chamber also seem to suffer great pain. In addition, some contemporary anesthesiologists question whether or not lethal injection is as painless as it would appear, contending that it might produce a slow death by suffocation. In Chaney v. Heckler, 718 F.2d 1174 (1983), the court referred to "known evidence concerning lethal injection which strongly indicates that such drugs pose a substantial threat of torturous pain to persons being executed" (1177). The court noted that, when using the mixture of barbiturates and paralytics required by law, "even a small error in dosage or administration can leave a prisoner conscious but paralyzed while dying, a sentient witness of his or her own slow, lingering asphyxiation" (1191). In contrast, the British Royal Commission on Capital Punishment has made a convincing case for the comparatively quick and ostensibly painless death produced by hanging, at least as it was practiced in this century in England (n. 7).

14. Quoted in *Death Row: An Affirmation of Life,* ed. S. Levine (New York: Ballantine, 1972), 167.

15. A. L. Smith and R. M. Carter, "Count Down for Death," *Crime and Delinquency* 15 (1): 77–92 (1969).

16. These observations were made by Lofland following a comparison of contemporary American execution procedures with those used in England in the eighteenth and nineteenth centuries. See H. Bleackley and J. Lofland, *State Executions Viewed Historically and Sociologically* (Montclair, N. J. : Patterson Smith, 1977), 308, 321.

17. G. R. Scott, *History of Capital Punishment* (London: Torchstream Books, 1950).

18. C. Chessman, "Trial by Ordeal," in *Death Row: An Affirmation of Life*, ed. S. Levine (New York: Ballantine, 1972), 15–17.

19. I. Ziferstein, "Crime and Punishment," *Center Magazine* 1(2):84 (1968).

20. A. Camus, "Reflections on the Guillotine," in *Resistance, Rebellion, and Death* (New York: Knopf, 1969).

21. Elsewhere I have discussed the civilization of punishment at some length. See R. Johnson, *Hard Time: Understanding and Reforming the Prison* (Pacific Grove, Calif.: Brooks/Cole, 1987), 45–50. For an unusually thoughtful discussion of this subject from a philosophical perspective, see J. H. Reiman, "Justice, Civilization, and the Death Penalty," *Philosophy and Public Affairs* 14(2):115–148. (Spring, 1985).

22. Psychological pain, too, becomes less tolerable as a form of punishment. Where once we aimed to inspire terror among those sentenced to confinement, now incarceration most powerfully evokes shame. Often, we will accept mere contrition or simple submissiveness from a prisoner as evidence that he is being adequately punished. See Johnson (n. 21).

23. Note that in late republican and Augustan Rome—that is, Rome at the height of its civilization, corresponding to classical Greece—"voluntary self-banishment," or exsilium, "became a legal institution, when magistrates were strictly ordered to allow the condemned person time to escape before executing the capital sentence." See *The Oxford Classical Dictionary*, 2nd ed. (Oxford: Clarendon Press, 1970), 426.

24. By the standards of the time, and perhaps even by contemporary standards, execution by hemlock was humane. See I. Barkan, "Capital Punishment in Ancient Greece" (Chicago, 1936), and J. Gorecki, *Capital Punishment: Criminal Law and Social Evolution* (New York: Columbia University Press, 1983). Hemlock kills by a process of refrigeration that proceeds

> from the lower extremities upward. . . . The head is taken with dizziness, the mind becomes obscured, the sight is warped, the eyes roll haggardly, the knees weaken, the throat is pinched, and the extremities become numb. Death comes as a swoon when the circulation and respiration are abated. (Barkan, 75–76)

> Executions were private. "Only the prosecutor . . . had the right to witness close at hand the punishment of the victim," to spare him the "insults of enmity" (81). Like Socrates, persons condemned to die could have the supportive companionship of others, whether colleagues, friends or family, during their last moments (75–76).

25. See, for example, A. Camus (n.20).

PART II

Waiting to Die
A Study of Modern Death Rows

Death Row is a unique environment. Its monotony and repetitious predictability create to varying degrees a ritualistic sensory deprivation environment: the constant beige flat hard steel, the endless rows of rivet heads protruding like the tiny helmets of buried soldiers in a battlefield cemetery, the constancy of iron bars, the grey concrete. Rather than being bombarded as in any other contemporary twentieth century American environment, the eye wanders seeking stimuli, escape. Death Row creates a withdrawal of the senses, an inward turning, a necessity to self-stimulate, to remain centered, to keep from slipping off into bizarre fantasies of persecution and dull-eyed madness, to keep the mind intact.

Stephen Levine
Death Row

The place was a dungeon, full of men who were as good as dead.

Michael Lesy
The Forbidden Zone

I fear that death row means a gradual killing of my humanity, which is more painful than any execution can ever be.

Death row prisoner

CHAPTER 3

Death Row
Conditions of Confinement

Today's condemned prisoners spend years on death row. They live in a segregated area of the prison, often in close proximity to the instrument of their death. During the deathwatch, when a prisoner is only hours from execution, he is guarded by men who are also his executioners. Allowed only the barest existence, particularly during those final hours, condemned prisoners are warehoused for death. It is, after all, only the body of the condemned that must be delivered to the executioner, and though prisoners who have been certified insane cannot be executed, their state of mind short of that extreme condition is irrelevant. The essence of death row confinement was captured by a condemned prisoner who observed, "A maggot eats and defecates. That's all we do: eat and defecate. Nothing else. They don't allow us to do nothing else." Such an existence, he maintained, amounts to a "living death."[1]

Condemned prisoners are permitted to do more than simply eat and defecate in solitary confinement, but the powerful perception persists among the condemned that they cannot do much more than that. The psychological impact of death row confinement is such that most condemned prisoners gradually waste away as human beings. By the time they reach the deathwatch, the condemned lead lives not much richer than that of a maggot. In short, though a bit exaggerated, our prisoner's description is basically correct. Death row is indeed a living death, a place where the body is preserved while the person languishes and ultimately dies awaiting execution.

This is no new discovery. Albert Camus knew it some thirty years ago and concluded from it that capital punishment amounted to death with torture.

> As a general rule, a man is undone by waiting for capital punishment well before he dies. Two deaths are inflicted on him, the first being worse than the second, whereas he killed but once. Compared to such torture, the penalty of retaliation seems like a civilized law. It never claimed that a man who gouged out one of his brother's eyes should be totally blinded.[2]

Once we have examined more fully the psychology of capital punishment—the waiting, killing, and dying, as seen by both prisoner and staff—I shall attempt to confirm and extend Camus's assertion about the torturous nature of life under sentence of death, then examine the implications of this position for the justice of the death penalty.

To address these issues more fully than was possible through existing research, I interviewed death row inmates, death row officers, execution team officers, and others (for example, the prison warden) involved in executions. The setting for my research was a Southern state (which remains unnamed to protect the identities of the staff, especially those serving on the execution team). The state provides a reasonably representative view of the death penalty in the United States today. It has a sizeable population of condemned prisoners (about fifty) exposed to a normal contingent of officers who maintain a level of security that is typical of contemporary death rows. In addition, the state conducts executions regularly (roughly one a year). As is the case in most other states with an active death penalty, executions are carried out by a trained team of correctional officers.

What I found in my research confirms that the cumulative confinement experience of condemned prisoners—from death row to the deathwatch and, finally, to the death chamber—is profoundly dehumanizing, resulting in nothing less than the literal moral death of the person, who is reduced to a compliant object of execution. Accordingly, we begin our examination of the psychology of capital punishment where the killing and dying begin: on death row.

Death Row Confinement in Historical Perspective

Separate confinement for the condemned, away from the masses of criminals awaiting lesser punishments, is a relatively recent practice, probably beginning with the early modern period, when prisons, then known as "bridewells" (after a London jail), became more common. During that period, some condemned prisoners appear to have been treated fairly decently for the short interval between sentencing and execution. In early modern Nuremberg, for example, prisoners were held in a condemned cell for three days, during which they were "allowed a liberal table, provided by charitable people, and visitors had free access to [them]."[3] Wealthy or notorious English offenders of this period might throw themselves a farewell party on death row. (The Monster's Ball, detailed in Chapter 1, is a case in point.) All the while, officials would openly go about the business of preparing for the execution. "Gallows were noisily tested, graves openly dug, the condemned assessed face-to-face for the drop appropriate to his weight, build, and neck defects, and his coffin brought casually into view."[4] Executions were public (see Part I). No effort was made to hide their grisly violence.

Vestiges of these practices still remained at the turn of the twentieth century. Though conditions of confinement were uniformly spartan and executions were generally private, there was still an openness among the participants about the killing and dying at the heart of the death penalty. On Sing Sing's death row at the turn of the century, the condemned were quite directly exposed to executions and their aftermaths.

> The execution chamber was immediately adjoining [the condemned prisoners' cells], and the little green door which led to it and death was in plain view of the condemned prisoners awaiting execution. The last short walk took the prisoner past the cells of some of these awaiting execution, and all

could hear the hum of the deadly motor and even the noise made by the drills and saws used in the autopsy immediately after the execution.[5]

Tame by historical standards—Hendrina Wouters withstood much worse, as we saw in Chapter 1—these executions were nevertheless out of step with modern sensibilities. Indeed, they "tended to drive even the strongest mind insane and resulted in desperate efforts being made to effect an escape."[6]

In 1922 a new death row was built in Sing Sing, known formally as the Condemned Cells. A distinctive feature of this death row was that it afforded the prisoners some insulation from the sights and sounds of death. Still, the Sing Sing prisoners called their new home "the slaughterhouse." They lived there in solitary confinement under obsessive custody. There were to be no farewell parties in the slaughterhouse.

Sing Sing's death row was a remarkably secure custodial environment. The prisoners spent all but fifteen minutes of each day locked in their cells. "While locked in the cell, no condemned prisoner [could] see another," though conversation was possible. Prisoners were "dressed in," meaning that, on arrival, they were assigned "clothing . . . of such quality that it [could not] easily be used to make a rope to be used in an attempt at suicide by hanging."[7] Only one prisoner succeeded in taking his life in Sing Sing's Condemned Cells.[8]

A concerted effort was made to prevent makeshift weapons from falling into the prisoners' hands. In their cells, prisoners wore felt slippers instead of shoes; during their brief periods of recreation, they wore special shoes with soft insteps, which made them less formidable weapons. Eating without knives and forks, instead using comparatively harmless spoons, prisoners were also denied the use of pepper, which could be used to temporarily blind an officer. The prisoners were shaved and even manicured by the officers. Cells contained "no movable object" but the prisoner, who moved only rarely and not far. "In fact," stated Warden Lawes, "the condemned prisoner [was] in the same position as a rat caught in a wire-caged trap."[9]

Sing Sing was not in any way unusual. (Life on San Quentin's death row, for example, followed a virtually identical pattern.[10]) The psychology of life in this and other wire-caged traps reflected the desperate situation of the prisoners. The condemned were chronically tense and deeply despondent. Facing reasonably swift and certain execution—the wait then was at most a matter of months—these prisoners were evidently a dangerous and unstable lot, requiring close confinement to hold them safely. In the words of one prisoner,

> The men in death row have nothing to lose except the hope of a commutation. In the mood of despair that gripped us all, tempers were short, nerves frayed. It was enough to put one prisoner within striking distance of another for murder to be done. It was enough to leave a prisoner alone for seconds, if he meant to take his own life. Neither of these possible occurrences was acceptable to the authorities, if only because they implied that a prisoner still held within himself certain liberties they couldn't touch. If you could kill yourself, or the man in the next cell, it meant that you didn't belong to them entirely. And from the moment the gates shut behind you, everything was

calculated to give you the opposite impression: that you were their property.[11]

That such a regime actively reduces the person to so much state property, to be dispatched in the execution chamber, is a central theme of this book.

Current Conditions on Death Row

Conditions on most death rows have changed little since the officials of Sing Sing built their new and improved wire-caged trap. Perhaps this is to be expected. Death rows are located in prisons, and prisons are meant to be painful, depriving environments. Indeed, "one of the striking things about prisons is that we make no bones about the fact that we intend them to be uncomfortable."[12] Death row is not managed like the rest of the prison, however, and condemned prisoners are not treated like regular inmates. Always, "the condemned live with the barest services, the minimum contact, the slightest concern."[13] As I have observed elsewhere,

> Death row is the most total of total institutions, the penitentiary most demanding of penitence, the prison most debilitating and disabling in its confinement. On death row the allegorical pound of flesh is just the beginning. Here the whole person is consumed. The spirit is captured and gradually worn down, then the body is disposed of. A century ago prisoners were subjected to the discipline of silence. Today on death row, this silence may prove endless.[14]

Death row is the extreme case of the pain and deprivation of imprisonment, the prison's prison.

The peculiar silence of death row stems from the empty and ultimately lifeless regimen imposed on the condemned. These offenders, seen as unfit for life in even the prison community, are relegated to this prison within a prison and held— sometimes even today in virtual solitary confinement—for periods measured in years rather than days or months. Typical maximum security prisoners spend about eight to twelve hours a day in their cells; typical death row prisoners spend twenty to twenty-two hours a day alone in theirs. Death row prisoners leave their cells to shower (often handcuffed) and to exercise (in a restricted area, sometimes fittingly called a "recreation cage"). If one has visitors, he leaves his cell to receive them. But visits occur under heavy guard, are restricted in frequency and duration, and become increasingly rare as a prisoner's stay on death row continues. There may be an occasional trip from the cell to the law library for the self-proclaimed "writ writer," or inmate lawyer. Otherwise, condemned prisoners remain in their cells. They are, with few exceptions, ineligible for prison jobs or correctional programs, or even the usual forms of prison recreation, such as sports and movies. Deemed beyond correction, they are denied access to even the meager privileges, amenities, and services available to regular prisoners.

In general, the custodial routine of death row varies little from state to state. A nationwide survey of death row living conditions conducted in 1979 revealed that

> most DSIs [death sentence inmates] cannot work at prison jobs, cannot attend education classes, clubs or religious services, have much less op-

portunity for exercise and recreation and much less adequate facilities and equipment [than regular prison inmates]. DSIs have little human contact. . . . Many are shackled for trips within the prison. Most eat in their cells and are separated from visitors by barriers. . . . [T]he lives of DSIs are grim. . . . Perhaps more important than any single deprivation is the fact that the impact and effect of each restriction is exaggerated because of the more general deprivation of being kept in cells most of every day and isolated from almost all contact with other human beings.[15]

Detailed descriptions of individual death rows, whether civilian or military, holding hundreds of prisoners or only a handful, bear out these observations. The death rows of Florida's Starke Prison, a civilian death row with a population approaching three hundred, and Fort Leavenworth Penitentiary, a military death row with a population of fewer than ten, are virtually indistinguishable. Each is located in the prison's segregation unit, and each conveys the impression that one is "deeply embedded in the prison—lodged, figuratively, in its bowels—shut off from light and liberty."[16] The tomblike ambience of the physical setting complements the empty existence of its inhabitants.

- In Florida, each condemned man is housed in a separate 6 × 9 foot cell, from which [three] departures are scheduled each week. Two of these are for showers, when the man is handcuffed and permitted to walk a short distance down the tier to a special shower cell. The third exit is [for] exercise . . . in an enclosed blacktopped area. No visits to the prison library, chapel, or gynmasium are permitted. . . . No education or work opportunities are available to the prisoner, and opportunities for counseling are extremely limited. . . . Most of the day is spent reading, watching television, and talking with one another.[17]

- On death row at Fort Leavenworth the cells were typical segregation cells and in fact were alongside and connected to the maximum security cells. The difference was that in front of these six cells was a steel caged area. This steel cage encompassed all six cells and provided the exercise room for the inmates. Death row inmates never left the confines of the caged-in cells except to shower, and they were placed in leg-irons when so engaged. Once a day for one hour each prisoner was permitted to exit the cell into the caged area to exercise. The rest of the death row inmate's time was spent in his cell.[18]

In a recent federal case, the court described in detail the conditions of death row confinement in the state of Tennessee in the mid-1980s. The plaintiff, one Mr. Harries, had lived on death row for a number of years.

Mr. Harries lives in a six by eight foot cell, which contains a toilet with a wash basin in the toilet well. A bunk bed is provided for his use, which takes up about one-third of the cell. Lighting in the cell consists of one sixty-watt light bulb; additional lighting is available by use of an electrical hook-up, but this must be done at the inmate's expense. There is no window in Mr.

Harries' cell and ventilation within his cell consists of blowers drawing out stale air. According to Mr. Harries, the ventilation is so poor that cigarette smoke stains his cell walls and toilet odors frequently make it difficult for him to sleep. Also, fumes from the respondents' [prison officials'] use of oil-based paints [for the walls and such] result in difficulty in normal breathing. . . . The ventilation problem is exacerbated when the humidity increases due to steam created from the showers of inmates. . . .

Mr. Harries is confined in his cell for twenty-three hours per day. Respondents permit him to exercise during the day for forty to forty-five minutes and to shower daily for ten to fifteen minutes. . . . The exercise area is too small for running and the number of inmates in the yard restricts them from walking. Moreover, even when the inmates are outside to exercise, the grate that covers the exercise area restricts the sunlight from shining through. While the respondents have provided a set of weights for inmates, many are unable to use them. When the weather does not permit inmates to go into the small exercise area, during the winter or when it rains, no exercise is afforded to inmates. Thus, according to Mr. Harries and other death-row inmates, it is not unusual for inmates not to exercise for a week or more during such times. . . . At all other times, including the taking of his meals, Mr. Harries remains within his cell. The temperature in Mr. Harries' cell averages, according to the respondents, between eighty and eighty-five degrees Fahrenheit. . . . A stipulation jointly submitted by counsel for the respondents and Mr. Harries indicates that the temperature within his cell on July 11, 1984 was ninety degrees. . . . [T]he stipulation indicates that the temperature within Mr. Harries' cell may reach uncomfortable and potentially life threatening limits. . . .

Turning to the area of food service to [death row] inmates, it is undisputed that prior to the commencement of this lawsuit, food served to inmates was cold. . . . The court . . . is concerned about the credible assertions of Mr. Harries that he discovered part of a mouse in his food. . . . [Finally,] inmates receive no religious services or counseling from respondents and the respondents prohibit any such services from outside sources.[19]

Mr. Harries, though a prisoner of death row in the 1980s, might just as well have been held in Warden Lawes's Condemned Cells at Sing Sing during the 1920s. The court concurred in this assessment, finding the conditions of Mr. Harries's confinement to be offensive to contemporary standards of humaneness. As a result of this litigation, reforms are being developed.[20]

Death Row Reforms: The Illusion of Change

Some contemporary death rows are more accommodating than those we've reviewed, having been liberalized as a result of legal consent decrees developed by reformers and correctional administrators.[21] A few of these settlements have been quite successful, though they have typically been piecemeal rather than comprehensive efforts. Some reforms have reduced cell time, sometimes also increasing the amount of recreation time prisoners have while out of their cells. Other reforms have expanded prisoners' opportunities for contact visits. The most comprehensive death row reforms were achieved in Texas.

On January 3, 1986, Texas initiated a "death row activity plan" that groups death row prisoners into two categories: "work-capable" (roughly 40 percent of the prisoners) and "death-row segregation" (roughly 60 percent of the prisoners). Those deemed capable of working are assigned a "meaningful job" as prison jobs go, primarily as laborers pulling four-hour shifts in a garment factory located near death row. Moreover, officials are "to provide a reasonably balanced range of recreation, work, programming and other out-of-cell activity" to work-capable inmates. Regular death row inmates, though still essentially segregated, also benefit. They are allowed "three hours of out-of-cell time five days a week" and are given access (in their cells) to "religious and educational programs." The frequency and length of visits remain restricted for all of Texas's condemned prisoners, however, and physical contact with visitors is prohibited altogether. The reactions of the prisoners are mixed but generally favorable. Though some of Texas's work-capable prisoners compare themselves to slaves in death camps—their labor is unpaid, and they may one day be put to death—others stress that the reforms break up the monotony of the day and offer small but important freedoms. A few prisoners hope that, should their death sentences be commuted, their work experience will help them make parole.[22]

Reforms of death row confinement conditions are laudable on purely humanitarian grounds. Such reforms, in Texas and elsewhere, are also practical, given that today's condemned prisoners face years of confinement. Solitary confinement may have been defensible as an across-the-board policy when prisoners faced a few weeks or months or even a year or two on death row. But when the stay on death row stretches, as it does today, to five, ten, or even fifteen years, such confinement becomes at best an oppressive, last-ditch option for unmanageable prisoners.

After careful study of the pertinent consent decrees, John Carroll and I concluded that these reforms, though likely to please some prisoners and satisfy the courts, "will only nominally improve the quality of daily life on death row." It is our view that

> a few hours of exercise and of the company of one's fellow prisoners are no doubt to be preferred to solitary confinement, but years of the circumscribed existence that is death row will certainly remain a numbingly boring and ultimately debilitating experience. After all, only so much can be said and done by prisoners who share the essentially eventless limbo world of death row, no matter how much time they spend out of their cells and no matter how diverse the hobbycraft programs or work experiences that are available to them. Contact visits [where available] will help to relieve the isolation and boredom of life on death row, yet they are, in the final analysis, but brief interludes in this lonely regime of confinement.[23]

Death row, by its very nature, remains a prison within a prison, delimited by the violent sanction it serves.

Case Study of a Failed Reform

The study on which this book is based, conducted over a three-year period from 1987 to 1989, involved in part a reformed death row. (The focus of my study was the execution process, examined in Part III.) What I found in this study, conducted after my collaboration with Carroll, confirmed our earlier conclusion that the quality of life under sentence of death is subject to only slight improvements.

The site for the study was a death row housed in a Southern prison. I interviewed at length twelve officers, eight men and four women, each of whom was designated a trained and experienced security technician. The interviews were focused,[24] covering the nature and quality of work on this death row, but there was no predetermined set of questions. Each officer was asked to describe his or her assignment on death row, and the interview proceeded from there. The aim of the interview was to learn how the officers perceived their work, and this was aided by allowing them to determine what aspects of the job they viewed as salient. I then met for about an hour with sixteen condemned prisoners housed in one area of death row (my access to the prisoners was limited by the prison authorities). My discussion with the prisoners did not constitute a genuine interview. It was more like a gripe session, but a useful one in that their concerns dovetailed with those of other prisoners interviewed more systematically. Finally, I reviewed all pertinent documents pertaining to the organization and management of the death row environment. Though this part of my research is at best tentative and exploratory, I came away with strong impressions of the environment.

The prisoners on this death row are afforded considerable liberties. They are allowed out of their cells in groups of up to eight men to spend time in a common dayroom, sometimes for as long as five hours a day; they are served meals outside their cells in the dayroom; they have opportunities for as much as ten hours a week of outdoor exercise; they are offered group religious services; and visits are regularly permitted, with prisoners sometimes allowed physical contact with their guests. Some inmates are allowed within limits to work; all have access to an educational counselor. A psychological counselor is on call three days a week. The courts would surely approve these arrangements. Yet for all these reforms, this death row is still oppressive, with a social climate not much different from that of Warden Lawes's Condemned Cells.

Let me explain. This death row, like all death rows, is formally defined—and aptly described—in the prison's institutional operating procedures (IOPs) as "a special housing unit set aside for the strict control and maximum security management" of condemned prisoners. There is a tight chain of supervision and command; all activities on death row must be approved in advance in writing, and staff are monitored regularly. Only certified officers, specially trained as security technicians, can work there. Vigilance is stressed; security is demanded. Cell searches, for example, are done three times a day, once on each shift. The IOPs read as follows: "During cell searches, inmates are required to be removed from the cell in restraints, searched, and held on the tier under the supervision of a certified officer." I observed a number of these searches and can attest that the procedure is thorough and intimidating. By any measure, the level of control on this death row is high.

Prisoners are housed in semicircular configurations of cells, called pods, each containing two tiers of eight cells. Each pod has a dayroom that abuts the cells and offers indoor recreation, mostly cards and television. The dayroom is enclosed within bars. These bars are interrupted by a cement-and-glass control booth, located half within and half without the dayroom. Each booth holds one officer, known as a pod control officer, who opens and closes all cell doors as well as all doors leading to and from the housing pod. All prisoners in the dayroom are within easy view of the pod control officer at all times. This officer can also speak with the inmates by means of an intercom system. Another officer sits in a hall just outside the pod, alongside the bars, and is able to observe and interact more directly with the prisoners.

The prisoners, then, spend a number of hours each day out of their cells in a dayroom, under the gaze of the pod control officer and interacting, if they so choose, with the hall officer. It is fair to say that these dayrooms are, in essence, large communal cells that function as extensions of the prisoners' individual cells. Each group of condemned prisoners, while in their cells or in the dayroom, is securely segregated from the general prison inmate population. In one prisoner's words, "We have absolutely no contact with general population prisoners." The same can be said for condemned prisoners in other areas of death row. Each pod functions as a death row within the larger death row, set apart from the rest of the world.

Prisoners periodically leave death row and go to other locations within the prison. When they do so, they move under heavy security. It is as if they drag the death row regime behind them, shackled to it by the chains that bind their hands and feet during these excursions. As dictated in the prison's IOPs,

> Inmates shall be placed in restraints prior to leaving the cells. The restraints shall consist of handcuffs and safety chain. The inmates shall be thoroughly searched by frisk upon exiting and entering the cell. Strip searches can be conducted if the officer in charge has reason to believe an inmate has a weapon or personal contraband.

Typical destinations within the prison include the medical section and visiting area. In each instance, security procedures are stringent: "Upon arrival at the back door of the Medical Department," for example, "leg restraints shall be placed on the inmate. The inmate shall remain in leg restraints at all times while being treated, unless otherwise requested by the attending medical employee." For visits, which are preceded and followed by strip-searches, "hand restraints may be removed at the discretion of the Chief of Security, but at no time will hand restraints be removed without the use of leg restraints."

Inmates also leave death row proper for outdoor exercise, in this case in small groups. The recreation area is a large outdoor cage topped with barbed wire and housing a basketball court. Since, here, the prisoners are only a few fences away from freedom, security procedures are elaborate. As specified in the IOPs, a ranking officer and four correctional officers go to the

> pod area to begin pulling inmates for recreation. The lieutenant or sergeant will position himself by the pod control room. The correctional officers working in teams of two will go to the cell door of the inmate coming out for

recreation. The lieutenant or sergeant will communicate to the pod control room officer which cell door to open and when. The correctional officers will restrict their activities to one tier at a time. The pod control room officer will not be allowed to open more than one cell at a time.

Each inmate will pass the clothes that he will be wearing to the recreation yard through the food slot to the officer for inspection. Each inmate will be handcuffed through the food slot. . . . [T]he inmate will come out of his cell in his shorts. Under the supervision of two correctional officers, the handcuffs will be removed, and the inmate will be allowed to dress. The inmate will be recuffed with his hands behind him and ordered to the dayroom area where he will be supervised by the lieutenant or sergeant.

The prisoners are then escorted to the recreation area. An officer "shall remain outside the recreation yard and shall maintain radio contact with the tower and the building."

It is nowhere recorded in the official IOPs, but this death row is haunted by an escape that occurred a few years back. At that time, security procedures were poorly articulated, and little attention was paid to the implementation of those procedures that were in force. As a result, six inmates returning from outdoor recreation (then unrestrained) were able to take a hostage, gain access to the control area, leave the death row building, and commandeer a truck that was allowed off the prison grounds because the inmates were able to convince the gate officer that they had a bomb in their possession (it was a TV wrapped in a blanket). That was a correctional nightmare, though fortunately no one, officer or civilian, was hurt during or after the escape. To some degree, the security concerns at this prison are a legacy of that escape. But security is a salient concern on all death rows. If this death row differs from its fellow death rows on the matter of security, the difference is one of degree, not kind.[25]

As on all death rows, the officers who work here rank security as their main concern, with prevention of escapes as their top security problem. Security is a virtual obsession with the death row commander. Working on death row is, in his words, a "battle of minds," and the lines of conflict, in his eyes, are clear: "They want out; we must keep them in." In this continuing battle of wits and wills, no one can afford to be casual or relaxed. Or friendly. As specified in the IOPs,

All staff assigned to work in the Death Row Unit(s) . . . shall avoid any personal discussions. Employees *must not* be too familiar or discuss personal items of interest with the inmates. Employees must conduct business and activities on a professional basis and be observant at all times and be knowledgeable of all duties.

There is no such thing as small talk here. The death row commander warns his staff to "speak cautiously, and always ask yourself 'why' when someone is talking to you—what is he *really* after?"

A Death Row by Any Other Name . . .

This death row, like its unreformed counterparts, is seen by both the keepers and the kept as cold, lonely, and often frightening. For their part, the inmates bemoan the constant pressure, the feeling of being hemmed in and harrassed by their keepers, their vulnerability to the guards, and the threat of personal debilitation. In their far-ranging grievances, they echo concerns uncovered in more systematic research on prisoners of solitary-confinement death rows. One prisoner, who has spent some nine years on this death row, may have captured the tempo of life on this environment when he observed,

> Not a day passes that I do not fight just to get out of bed. And in the late hours of the night, it takes much strength just to keep a grip on my sanity. I have spent many hours at my window, standing on my toilet at the air vent, pleading with men who were considering suicide. . . . I have been on that very edge myself.

Our reformed death row thus emerges as, in this prisoner's words, "a psychological nightmare that very few survive." I heard nothing in my session with the prisoners to belie this claim. A comprehensive assessment of the psychological nightmare that is played out on our nation's death rows, affecting both the prisoners and, to a lesser degree, the staff, is the aim of the next chapter.

Notes

1. R. Johnson, *Condemned to Die: Life under Sentence of Death* (Prospect Heights, Ill.: Waveland Press, 1989), 116.
2. A. Camus, "Reflections on the Guillotine," in *Resistance, Rebellion, and Death* (New York: Knopf, 1969), 205.
3. A. Keller and C. V. Calvert, *A Hangman's Diary: Being the Journal of Master Franz Schmidt, Public Executioner of Nuremberg, 1573–1617* (Montclair, N.J.: Patterson Smith, 1973), 36.
4. H. Bleakley and J. Lofland, *State Executions Viewed Historically and Sociologically* (Montclair, N.J.: Patterson Smith, 1977), 288.
5. L. E. Lawes, *Life and Death in Sing Sing* (New York: Sun Dial Press, 1937), 161.
6. Ibid., 162.
7. Ibid., 162, 163.
8. In absolute terms, suicides are more numerous on today's death rows, but since the number of condemned prisoners and their length of stay on death row have increased greatly, it is unclear whether the rate of suicides is higher or lower than in times past.
9. Lawes (n. 5), 164.
10. C. T. Duffy with A. Hirshberg, *Eighty-Eight Men and Two Women* (New York: Doubleday, 1962).
11. I. Zimmerman with F. Bond, *Punishment without Crime* (New York: Clarkson N. Potter, 1964), 119–120.
12. R. Johnson and H. Toch, eds., *The Pains of Imprisonment* (Prospect Heights, Ill.: Waveland Press, 1988), 13.
13. B. Jackson and D. Christian, *Death Row* (Boston: Beacon Press, 1980), 28.
14. Johnson (n. 1), 121.
15. J. F. Else, E. Kudsk, and J. Meyer, "Living Conditions of Death Sentence

Inmates in the U.S." (unpublished paper, 1981; available from J. F. Else, School of Social Work, University of Iowa, Iowa City, Iowa 52242). John Conrad and I conducted an informal survey of death row living conditions during 1983–1984. Our impression was that little had changed on our nation's death rows since the Else et al. report.

16. Johnson (n. 1), 43.
17. M. L. Radelet, M. Vandiver, and F. Berardo, "Families, Prisons, and Men with Death Sentences: The Human Impact of Structured Uncertainty." *Journal of Family Issues* 4(4):595–596 (December 1983).
18. P. Dumm, personal communication following a visit to Fort Leavenworth's death row, spring 1983. I have it on the authority of current military personnel that procedures have remained unchanged since then (Maj. J. Tyler, personal communication, summer 1989).
19. Groseclose *ex rel*. Harries v. Dutton, 594 F. Supp. 949 (1984), 959, 960, 961.
20. Stressing the bleak physical milieu, the long periods of cell time and attendant idleness, and the absence of any type of attention to the unique psychological stresses faced by the condemned, the court held Tennessee's death row to be in violation of the Eighth Amendment prohibition of cruel and unusual punishment. However, on appeal the circuit court subsumed this litigation under Grubbs v. Bradley, 552 F. Supp. 1052 (1982), a prior prison-conditions suit covering the entire Tennessee prison system. In *Grubbs,* the court had taken a narrow view of the Eighth Amendment, holding that "the mere fact that inmates may tend to degenerate as a result of incarceration is not actionable." Only "serious physical or psychological deterioration [that] is inevitable" violates the cruel and unusual punishment clause (1124). The presumption is that "core" protections afforded by the Eighth Amendment pertaining to "food, clothing, shelter, sanitation, medical care, and personal safety" would have to be violated to produce serious and inevitable deterioration (1122).

    In this circuit court's rendering, the Eighth Amendment would seem to require us to preserve the body of the prisoner—which is to be fed, clothed, maintained in clean and hygienic conditions, and held safe from harm—while allowing us to ignore the person. Though death row confinement conditions in Tennessee are not, under this standard, in violation of the Eighth Amendment, reforms were nevertheless considered necessary both on death row and throughout the prison system. Accordingly, a special master was appointed to supervise reforms of the entire Tennessee prison system, including death row.
21. A summary of these reforms can be found in R. Johnson and J. L. Carroll, "Litigating Death Row Conditions: The Case for Reform," in *Prisoners' Rights Sourcebook: Theory, Litigation, Practice,* ed. I. Robbins (New York: Clark-Boardman, 1985), 8.3–33.
22. Ibid, 8.11–12. For a more detailed discussion of this reform effort, focusing on the work experience of the prisoners, see J. R. Sorensen and J. W. Marquart, "Working the Dead," in *Facing the Death Penalty: Essays on a Cruel and Unusual Punishment,* ed. M. L. Radelet (Philadelphia: Temple University Press, 1989), 169–177.
23. Johnson and Carroll (n. 21).

24. I have used focused interviews in prior research. See, for example, Johnson (n. 1), 11–15, and R. Johnson, *Culture and Crisis in Confinement* (Lexington: Lexington Books, 1976), esp. 31–34. For a general discussion of focused interviews, see R. Merton and P. Kendall, "The Focused Interview," in *The Language of Social Research,* ed. P. Lazarsfeld and M. Rosenbert (New York: Free Press, 1955).

25. Security levels on death rows in Texas and Alabama, neither of which has experienced an escape, are essentially the same as those reviewed above. See Sorensen and Marquart (n. 22) and Johnson (n. 1).

CHAPTER 4

Living and Working on Death Row

At its best, life on death row amounts to long hours of "dead time," as the inmates are wont to put it, spent in either single or congregate cells. That such an existence is a psychological nightmare hardly requires elaboration. With only rare exceptions, condemned prisoners are demoralized by their bleak confinement and defeated by the awesome prospect of death by execution. Worn down in small and almost imperceptible ways, gradually but inexorably they become less than fully human. At the end, the prisoners are helpless captives of the modern execution drill.

The dehumanization condemned prisoners experience is in no way reduced by recent reforms of some death rows. In no instance in even the most extensively reformed death row are condemned prisoners prepared in any way for the ordeal they must face. And as executions occur with increasing frequency, a trend that has gathered momentum since the advent of the death row reforms discussed in the preceding chapter, there is every reason to believe that conditions of confinement on death rows will become more rather than less restrictive.

Preliminary evidence from an American Correctional Association (ACA) survey of death row conditions, conducted in 1987, suggests that this is indeed the case. There is, according to the ACA survey, a definite trend toward increased security on death rows, as well as toward maximum separation of individual prisoners.[1] A return to a standard regime of solitary confinement is a real possibility.

Moreover, none of the recent death row reforms affects the deathwatch, the period that culminates death row confinement and ends in the execution of the prisoner (see Part III). This period continues to be one of virtually unmitigated solitary confinement under conditions of total security. As we shall see, the stress of life under sentence of death reaches its zenith during the deathwatch.

Living on Death Row: The Psychology of Human Warehousing

The bleak quality of life on all death rows, reformed and unreformed, reflects their common goal: human storage. This goal dictates that condemned prisoners be treated essentially as bodies kept alive to be killed. This concern for preserving the body without regard to the quality of life reaches an extreme in suicide prevention efforts that amount to treating the person like a piece of meat.

Philip Brasfield, for example, reported that a suicidal prisoner on death row in Texas, where Brasfield himself was also confined while under sentence of death, was

> placed in a straightjacket that was left open at the back to secure him to a bare mattress on the bunk. In addition, handcuffs were placed on his wrists. A crash helmet much like a motorcyclist would wear, was placed on his head and there he lay for weeks, helpless, alone, and drugged. The care and feeding he received was from the inmate porters. At times, he'd call for assistance for over an hour before a guard would open the door and untie him so he could urinate.[2]

Similar procedures apply to inmates whose mental health problems present trouble. On the reformed death row I studied (see Chapter 3), an inmate testified to these procedures:

> Should any individual with psychiatric problems present a problem [to staff], his cell will be stripped of all belongings (including clothing and hygiene items), and he is subject to be chained to the cell's bare steel bunk. This has happened to me, personally, and I have seen the same happen to other men.

Yet another example of preserving the body but ignoring the person was related to me by Alvin Bronstein of the American Civil Liberties Union's (ACLU's) National Prison Project. One of his condemned clients required triple-bypass heart surgery but refused treatment. Officials allegedly urged the prisoner to undergo surgery so he could be alive for his execution, at one point asking Bronstein to argue their case with his reluctant client. Bronstein declined. The prisoner subsequently died of a heart attack.[3]

Daily procedures on death row embody the storage premise quite explicitly. "Neat and efficient," in the words of Jackson and Christian, these procedures are tellingly described in terms that objectify the prisoners. For instance, Jackson and Christian tell us that

> death row inmates get showers one at a time. The noun takes a verb form: "I'm going to shower the row now," the guard says. "I'm opening one-row cell 13 to shower Jones." One is "being showered" rather than "taking a shower." The option is the guards', always. The same thing happens with recreation; it becomes a verb: "I'm going to recreate group three now," the guard says, meaning he will let one-quarter of the men on the row out of their cells and into the small dayroom.[4]

The immediate result of such efficient storage arrangements is a radical reduction in the prisoner's privacy. Indeed, prisoners typically claim that on death row one has no privacy at all! In the words of Caryl Chessman, who spent twelve years on San Quentin's death row before his execution in 1962,

You have no privacy. Day and night, you're watched closely. Having claimed it, the state is jealous of your life. Every possible safeguard is taken to prevent you from cheating the executioner—by digging, cutting, or assaulting your way to stolen freedom; by self-destruction; by fleeing to the world of the insane. You've come to the wrong place if curious eyes and the probing beams of flashlights make you uneasy.[5]

A present-day death row prisoner seconded Chessman's observations, reminding us that nothing essential has changed on the row:

They read your mail. Take a visit, they're standing over your shoulder. They know everything you're saying. You shower and they're watching you. At night they're shining flashlights in your cell. You never have a free moment.[6]

Regular prisoners are permitted to develop an informal society and, to some extent at least, police themselves.[7] But the margin for failures of control on death row is exceedingly narrow. The prisoners are watched closely, though not continuously, and without apology.[8]

Held powerless on death row, condemned prisoners also come to feel powerless—that is, alone and vulnerable. Many—as many as seven out of every ten[9]—deteriorate in measurable ways. All are to some degree weakened and demoralized. Those condemned prisoners who reach the deathwatch, examined in Chapters 6 and 7, are subjected to constant surveillance and complete loss of privacy. Made susceptible by their death row confinement, they collapse under the substantial pressure of the deathwatch. In the final analysis, they are reduced to dehumanized objects that are mere pawns in the modern execution process.

Powerlessness

Close confinement combined with almost constant surveillance renders death row inmates powerless to alter or influence their daily existence in any meaningful way. Their lives are monotonous and lonely, and they are predictably bored, tense, and depressed. Chronic irritability and periodic lapses in personal control can leave prisoners feeling alienated from themselves. The prisoner comes to see himself as essentially a stranger in a strange land.[10] Powerlessness and its emotional sequelae, established in the *Harries* case as key factors in the cruelty of Tennessee's death row (see Chapter 3), affect prisoners of all death rows. The reason is straightforward: All death rows are, at bottom, sterile, eventless, oppressive environments that demoralize their inhabitants as a direct function of the setting's emphasis on custodial repression.

The experience of powerlessness is magnified on solitary-confinement death rows, in which warehousing for death takes its most blatant, unvarnished form. The barren dimensions of the condemned prisoners' lives on such death rows are evident in the empty diversions they employ to occupy their time. In the prisoners' words,

- I have got so bored at times, I used to hook cockroaches together, sort of like they was a team of mules, to drag a matchbox around on the floor to pass time. I mean that may sound weird to you or somebody else, and it might be. Matter of fact I just flushed a little frog down the shit jack the other day that I had back there [in my cell]. It came up through the shit jack. I kept him back there a couple of weeks and I kicked roaches and things to feed him. Just any little old thing. . . . To more or less keep your mind off the damned chair and the things that you're seeing around you. Anything to occupy your mind.

- I got a big dictionary. I look in there and I read—just look at words, I can't even pronounce the words I be looking at, you know, but I read the meaning to them. I like doing stuff like that. It's hard to stay at that thing, you get sleepy—without moving—you can't stay up but an hour at a time, you have to lay back down. I can't seem to settle down in my cell. Like, I spend 23½ hours in there and I can't ever come to peace with myself. It irritates me all the time.[11]

Long hours in the cell are a source of psychological pressure and emotional turmoil. All prisoners experience some pressure; for some, the experience is almost disabling. For example,

I sit in that cell, you know, and it seems like I'm just ready to scream or go crazy or something. And you know, the pressure, it builds up, and it feels like everything is—you're sitting there and things start, you know, not hearing things, things start to coming in your mind. You start to remember certain events that happened, bad things. It just gets to a person. I sit up at night, you know. You just sit there, and it seems like you're going to go crazy. You've got three walls around you and bars in front of you, and you start looking around, you know, and it seems like things are closing in on you. Like last night, when I sit in there and everything's real quiet, things, just a buzzing noise gets to going in my ears. And I sit there, and I consciously think, "Am I going to go crazy?" And the buzzing gets louder; and you sit there and you want to scream and tell somebody to stop it. And most of the time you get up—if I start making some noise in my cell, it will slack off. And it sounds stupid, I know, but it happens. . . . [S]ometimes I wonder if I don't get it stopped, I'm going crazy or something. . . . And you know, maybe tonight when I lay down it's not going to break when I get up and try to make some noise.[12]

Against the suffocating vacuum of the cell, a chance to place a simple order at the commissary can be an exhilarating, liberating experience—a small freedom so sweet it accentuates the bitter constraints that envelop one's life on death row.

They have one day which is a store day. That one day actually is to these people on death row like Christmas and all they actually get is cigarettes and candy or cookies, and that's actually become to be a thing like Christmas. I've surveyed it from watching the guys and everybody gets excited and they are actually more happy on Tuesday when they get that little package. But you see this is actually what we have been reduced to as far as being men, trying to be a man, finally enjoying a little thing like a cookie. To me it's actually absurd, this actually affects me to that point and there is no way out of it, there is no way to rebel against it.[13]

Prisoners on reformed death rows generally have more autonomy than those on solitary-confinement death rows. (I say generally because reformed death rows go through periodic lockdowns, during which the prisoners are kept in solitary confinement as punishment. On the reformed death row I studied, one such lockdown lasted a full five months.) These prisoners normally have the company of their dayroom companions to fall back on, and this can, no doubt, be a source of comfort, giving them a sense of a more normal and at least minimally autonomous daily life. Contact with other prisoners, however, can be a double-edged sword. One's fellows can be a source of pressure, harassment, and sometimes violent victimization, all of which add to feelings of helplessness. As a case in point, on our reformed death row, one man was brutally attacked by a fellow prisoner in the dayroom. The victim was paralyzed for life.

Even congenial conversations in dayrooms (for those on reformed death rows) or with men in neighboring cells (for those in solitary confinement) offer only limited opportunities for autonomous action or emotional support. Eventually, one says and does all that one can say and do in the compressed world that is death row. One's social life, as it were, becomes numbingly redundant and oppressive in its own right. It is worth recalling that Sartre's notion of hell was being confined for eternity with people one despises. For at least some prisoners, especially on reformed death rows, the fact that they have "no exit" from the other condemned prisoners may make their confinement a kind of hell.

The enduring difficulty is that on death row—any death row—everything remains the same. "It's continuously having the same walls, the same bars, the same papers, the same books," said one condemned prisoner. "Nothing changes. Only the outside, the light. We have day and we have night, we have day and then we have night." People become fixtures, as unchanging as the schedule. A paradoxical dependence is bred; routines come to hold in check the very resentments they produce. "If something changes, it's like a shock to you," observed one inmate. "You'll hear them yelling and screaming and everything else."[14] With the inexorable return of routine, the inmates retreat once more into the familiar, however impoverished it may be.

Loneliness

Though familiar, the routine on death row offers little real comfort—to the prisoners, that is. For the staff, routine can become an end in itself, a means of distancing themselves from the prisoners. Too often, the staff become insensitive to the human tragedies unfolding among the condemned; they seem unwilling or unable to offer meaningful support. "Caring," observed one group of researchers studying death row officers, "is simply not part of the job."[15] "Nobody is going to help you," confirmed an inmate. "Nobody is going to give you a kind word. Nobody is going to ask you, 'How's it going, how's your day? Is everything coming out okay?' You're totally ignored." Nor do other prison officials fill the emotional void. Like the occasional citizen's groups that tour death rows, "they just look in the cage and they go away."[16] Though these are almost surely overstatements on the part of the inmates—some officers and officials say they care, and try to show it—they indicate widely and firmly held perceptions of the social reality on death row. Almost to a man, condemned prisoners feel abandoned by the prison staff, denied simple human compassion, treated "as if already dead."[17]

Feeling abandoned by the prison staff often goes hand in hand with feeling abandoned by the world. The custodial regime not only insulates guards from prisoners, it also isolates prisoners from the moral and social community of the outside world. Inmates suffer "a symbolic isolation that comes from living with the fact that 12 members of your community have determined that you are a worthless person who should no longer be permitted to exist." Prisoners may feel "so isolated that it is nearly impossible to share a religion with those on the outside." As time passes and they gradually exhaust their appeals, prisoners may feel further removed from the world of the living. One reason is that fewer people are apt to write or visit in support of a lost (or losing) cause.[18] Another is that failed appeals mark progressive stages in the killing and dying process, "pull[ing] layers of legal legitimacy over a corpse that hasn't quit moving and complaining yet."[19]

Their isolation on death row contributes to the weakening and often the dissolution of the prisoners' relationships with their loved ones. In one condemned man's words, "While most people rely on their families for their major source of support, it is not at all uncommon for this resource to be unavailable to death row prisoners."[20] One reflection of this sad fact is an empty visiting room. "On the death row visiting day," Jackson and Christian tell us, "the room is usually empty. It is rare for even two death row inmates to get a visit at the same time."[21]

Visits are a precious but rare—and precarious—commodity in the eyes of the condemned. Visits are not matters of right but rather privileges that can be—and, in fact, regularly are—suspended at the discretion of prison officials.[22] Officials discourage visits through a variety of restrictive rules and regulations. For example, visits can take place only on certain days and for limited periods of time. This creates logistical problems for the prisoners' loved ones. And though no physical contact is allowed during typical visits, the staff nevertheless carefully monitor all visits. What is worse, after all visits, inmates are shackled and subjected to thorough body searches, even when the visits involved no physical contact. For some prisoners, the pain and humiliation engendered by such treatment outweigh the pleasure of the visit. One prisoner could barely suppress his rage when describing his experience with visits.

> Your people come to this place. You go down and you sit down for an hour or whatever you stayed and you get your mind away from this place. And just as soon as you come in after having enjoyed yourself for a little bit, just as soon as you get up from out there and walk in here, they strip you, look up your asshole and in your mouth and strip search you and handcuff you behind your back and drag you back up that hall. Well, you see, they just broke your whole fucking visit. You would have been better off, in a way, if you'd just stayed in your cell and if you could have slept through that

hour. . . . . I mean that's the kind of attitude that leaves you with after they fuck with you. Knowing your people drove and went through all this trouble to come see you, to give you an hour or something. Then they have taken the fucking time to figure out a way to fuck it up for you.[23]

Condemned prisoners tend to see the death row regime as a calculated and gratuitous assault on their humanity. For them, the physical setting is punitively spartan; rules and regulations are means to inflict pain.[24] The intrusive procedures associated with visits do much to fuel the prisoners' angry perception that their keepers mean them harm.

Aside from humiliating searches, the rules regulating visits with condemned prisoners make these encounters strained and potentially divisive. Visiting arrangements for Florida's condemned, under which visitors are continuously observed, have been found to impede the flow of information and emotional support between families and condemned prisoners, "thereby sustaining rather than alleviating feelings of isolation and uncertainty."[25] The visiting routine on Alabama's death row frustrates any attempt at congenial conversation. The visiting situation in Alabama, as I stated after observing visits there firsthand, is more akin to a wake than to a supportive family gathering.

> The priorities on [Alabama's] death row seem almost unforgivable in regard to visits. The routine surrounding visits might be compared with the preparations for a funeral. Noncontact visits, in particular, seem peculiarly reminiscent of the viewing at a wake. The inmate sits alone in an enclosed chamber, neatly dressed and carefully groomed, almost as if on display for his loved ones. The need to shout across the barrier separating the inmate and his visitors precludes intimate conversation and results in awkward interludes of silence. Visitors speak as much among themselves as with their prisoner; they appear nervous and out of place. The prisoners, too, seem ill at ease.[26]

It is hard to be natural when yelling to loved ones or when officers are looking over your shoulder, perhaps eavesdropping as well. In turn, truncated conversations and awkward interludes of silence can leave people feeling confused and lonely: What did she *really* mean by this pause or that phrase? The prisoner, on returning to his cell, is left to wonder. And worry.

The empty existence on death row may, in any case, render prisoners mute during visits. They and their loved ones live in utterly different worlds, with little or no common ground to draw on to sustain communication (though more accommodating visiting conditions would certainly improve matters). Unrewarding visits reflect and reinforce the prisoners' basic sense of alienation. The custodial milieu of death row thus tends to corrode relationships. As a result, most condemned prisoners describe themselves as abandoned by the free world and left to their own devices to endure their confinement.[27]

Vulnerability

Held powerless under conditions of indifference and neglect, prisoners tend to resent their guards, who are the nearest at hand to blame for their helpless and lonely state. Prisoners also come to feel vulnerable to harm by their keepers. Alone and defenseless when in their cells, living at all times in harsh and deprived conditions, convenient objects of contempt, condemned prisoners feel vulnerable to abuse from their keepers. Condemned prisoners are usually held in the most secluded quarters of the prison—a condition that, absent effective supervision of the guard force, invites, indeed almost authorizes, abuse. Their stark vulnerability may be apparent from the moment prisoners set foot on death row. One prisoner put the matter like this:

> The biggest fear is when you walk onto this place. I've seen one man walk out there and he stood right there and he broke down and cried. I've seen more come in here and live three days and start praying. I've seen them come in here and cuss the day they was born because of fear. I've seen grown men come in here and get down and pray like kids. And cry.[28]

Condemned prisoners see death row as a law unto itself, one based on the premise "Might makes right." As one prisoner observed, "They can do anything they want to you. Who's going to stop them?" Power, many say, emanates from the butt end of the baton or billy club that is often standard equipment for death row officers. This weapon, sometimes tellingly called an axe handle by the prisoners, can function as both a symbol of violence and an instrument of social control. As one prisoner observed,

> You have to more or less watch what you say to these guys because if they want to get you back, they could easily do that. You're on your way out to the yard, the guy could say as soon as you get out of the center—around that little bend—where the rest of the guys couldn't see you, they could easily claim "well, he turned around and hit me," "he turned around and I thought he was attacking me," or "he pushed me." And one whack with one of those axe handles up against your head, if you're not going to be dead, you're going to be insane for the rest of your life. And then you're not going to be able to help no one. . . . I am really afraid of that. I'm trying to hold on to my own common sense, you know, because I feel that is one of the main factors that I do have that is still mine. My knowledge that I can think and my ability to learn and do my own research on my own case. I feel that if I got hit with one of those sticks, I wouldn't have that much sense. So, I live in constant fear of that actually all the time."[29]

Abuse, including violence, may also be implicitly authorized in the training of death row officers. Colin Turnbull's research revealed that death row officers' training emphasized "combat duty" and made "no attempt to help the guard approach the extremely difficult task of maintaining appropriate human relations [with condemned prisoners]."[30] The profound suspiciousness of the officers on the reformed death row I studied, a suspiciousness demanded by their superior officer, promoted a combat mentality among many of these officers. Informal socialization on the job, moreover, is apt to alert the guards of any death row to the potential dangers of their work, reinforcing the apparent value of a cold and even pugnacious stance with the inmates. One prisoner put this matter plainly:

They got us one sorry motherfucker right here and that's the only way I know how to put it. One of the most sorriest motherfuckers right here that could be working in a penitentiary. Now he comes to work and sits his ass down right up there, and sits there and tries to figure out a way to fuck somebody back there on death row. And he's the one that shows the others how to do us. . . . It's just like father teach son—that's their routine. When a guard comes here, instead of giving him [formal] training and everything and teach him how he should cope with these things in prison and stuff, they bring him right up here, put him under one of the worst sons-of-bitches there is here. Then father teach son. Then it's just a very short period of time until they have built up this attitude and they look at you the same way he does. . . . Now I been in down here since way back. So a whole lot about the outside, I don't know nothing about it. But about these sons-of-bitches, I do. And that's why I say, when a guy come into here and he say, "Well, there goes a good guard." Shit. It won't be three days before he's just as sorry as the next motherfucker.[31]

Many condemned prisoners believe that their keepers, with or without provocation, would resort to violence.[32] Indeed, some prisoners' fear of violence from their keepers merges with their fear of execution. One prisoner, visibly afraid, had this to say:

When you're on death row and you're laying down in your cell and you hear a door cracking, you'll think of where it comes from. When you hear it crack. And when you hear the keys and everything, when something like this happens, the keys come through here: I'm up. I'm up because you don't know when it's going to take place. The courts give you an execution date, that's true. But you don't know what's going to take place between then and your execution date. You don't know when you're going to be moved around to the silent cell over here. That's right down the hall, what they call a waiting cell. You don't know when you're going to be moved down there. And this keeps you jumpy, and it keeps you nervous, and it keeps you scared.[33]

Such fear, which borders at times on raw panic, may be more prevalent among condemned prisoners than one would imagine. It bespeaks the profound vulnerability these prisoners feel, and the deep distrust they have for their keepers.

A Living Death

The cumulative impact of death row, as noted by the court in the *Harries* case, is an "overall sense of defeat."[34] Hopelessness is the condemned prisoner's cellmate. In one prisoner's words,

You can hear its empty sound in the clanging of the steel doors, in the rattle of chains, in the body searches, in the lack of privacy, in the night sounds of death row, and you can see it in the eyes of the guards who never really look at you, but are always watching to see that you do not commit suicide.[35]

The *normal* reaction in such an environment, observed the noted psychiatrist Seymour Halleck, who testified as an expert in the *Harries* case, features "depression and lethargy."[36] (Harries himself showed signs of psychological deterioration that a number of experts attributed to the conditions of his confinement on death row, an attribution supported by a body of empirical research and accepted by the court.)[37] Prisoners of other death rows bear out this observation, describing death row as a "living death" and themselves as the "living dead."[38] As one prisoner poignantly observed, "You need love and it just ain't there. It leaves you empty inside, dead inside. Really, you just stop caring."

Death row prisoners, to restate Halleck's point, give up on life as we normally know it. They exist rather than live. That existence, however, can be deceptive to outside observers, even to correctional officers and officials on the scene. For on a social level, death row prisoners, and, to a lesser extent, their keepers, create a make-believe world premised on denying the reality of the death penalty. Prisoners talk tough and act cool, posturing even within the cells that cage them, desperate to deceive themselves and those around them. Humor, in particular, is used to bolster a facade of manliness, as well as to distract attention from inner doubts and turmoil. But denial is a psychological gambit that always comes home to roost. As one prisoner of a solitary-confinement death row put it,

> The row ain't serious; it's a lot of funny things happening on the row. Everybody seeing who can be the funniest, you know. So, I contribute in that there, too. I figure if I contribute in that, that will keep me going halfway. But I figure now when things really get hard and everybody stops joking, that's when you are going to see about ten people just bug out from the jump. All of us are going to bug out sooner or later.[39]

Things "get hard," to complete the prisoner's point, when someone is executed—as happens these days with increasing regularity. These executions would seem to be both the logical and the psychological culmination of death row confinement.

Working on Death Row

Tension and Fear

The condemned prisoner's life on death row is grim. The lot of those who guard death row is singularly unrewarding as well. Work on death row is, in fact, a stressful and often frightening assignment that lends itself to indifferent and even abusive treatment of the condemned prisoners. Death row guards are enjoined solely to preserve the corpus of the condemned—to feed them in their cells or in common areas, to conduct them to out-of-cell activities, to watch them at all times. In large measure, the officers are reduced to intrusive waiters and unwanted escorts. Moreover, the death row guard's role is in some respects an impersonal and hence symbolically dehumanized one: The officer's character as a distinctive person, though not stripped from him, is rendered largely irrelevant to how he carries out his work as a death row officer. Unsurprisingly, like the prisoners, the guards are bored and tense much of the time. Some even report being depressed by their circumscribed, thankless jobs.

Relations between guards and inmates have been described as either overtly hostile, with harassment and counterharassment a common form of exchange,[40] or impersonal, with little or no contact.[41] Still, the condemned and their keepers usually accommodate one another to some degree, and a few death row officers are even able to transcend the limitations of their role and develop normal, if superficial, relationships with death row prisoners. Nonetheless, death row officers are, at best, professional custodians; they may be tactful and even courteous, but not "chummy."[42] "They don't make friends," said one prisoner of such guards, "they just do their job and go home."[43] Tension is high, affecting officers and inmates alike.

Neither is fear of violence restricted to inmates. Officers, too, feel vulnerable as they go about the work of guarding condemned prisoners. Officers regularly cite the dangers posed by the prisoners as justification for the custodial restrictions on death row. Guards are quick to point out that condemned prisoners are men of proven violence with little to lose in trying to escape. It is widely believed that because the prisoners face execution and often live in the most depriving environment the prison has to offer, they feel free to attack or even kill guards. What more can we do to them? worried officers ask. The guards thus come to fear the potential violence of their captives just as the prisoners fear the potential violence of their keepers. Too often, shared fears give way to mutual hate.[44] The peace on death row can seem precarious indeed.

Fears harbored by officers may be especially pronounced on reformed death rows, because the inmates are out of their cells in small groups and hence are a more potent threat. The security-related concerns of many of the officers on our reformed death row appeared to be rooted, at least in part, in fear.

For some of these officers, my interviews revealed, fear lurks in the background. Said one officer, "You know in the back of your mind who you're dealing with, what they are, but still you don't bring it to the surface." Other officers spoke of conscious fears. The prisoners, they believe, are violent men bent on escape. These officers work under constant pressure. As one said, "They will hurt you to get away. You've got to watch them all the time. You know if these guys get a chance, you're gone. They'll kill you. They've all killed before." In the words of another officer, "There was always that thought in my mind, 'If they ever get out of here, I'm as good as dead.' I feel they don't have anything to lose. If we get in their way, they just get rid of us quick." Security procedures are in place to restrain the prisoners and protect the officers, but they fail to reassure. Assessed against a backdrop of fear, regulations appear flawed. "If they want to escape, they can," said one officer with an air of futility. "Somebody's going to slip up somewhere along the line."

The officers' fears are not indiscriminate. There are periods of high risk and hence high anxiety, though different officers expressed different concerns. For one, it was "taking inmates to recreation" that required extreme caution. For another, "Counts are scary. I worry there'll be one hiding 'round the corner and I'll have to go and find him." According to a third, "Open areas bother me. I'm uncomfortable working in the open area [in the hall] near the control station." One officer, though calm on the surface, found almost *any* occasion a source of fear because he was intimidated by the prisoners' crimes. He readily admitted that some prisoners were less fierce than one would expect, given their crimes, but he took no comfort in this. "You can't judge a book by its cover. You've never seen him mad."

A troubling and pervasive sign of fear is that officers see themselves as potential hostages. "The inmates constantly threaten to take hostages," said one officer. Some of it is joking, he acknowledged, but the risk of one day becoming a hostage "is very real." That fearful eventuality preoccupies a number of officers, who envision scenarios that would result in their being taken hostage. A common fear is that a harried, and thus distracted, control officer will open the wrong door at the wrong time, unleashing a group of inmates on a defenseless hall officer. The officers respond to such intimidating contingencies with a grim fatalism, taking the attitude that they should do what they can to control their own lives and let other matters sort themselves out.

> Anybody can get attacked or taken hostage at any time. But I just have a job to do, and I just go ahead and do it and hope that nothing will happen. I just try to do my job, be alert and observant, and nothing should go wrong. If it does, I'll just have to deal with it.

As another officer put it, "You know who you're dealing with, *what* you're dealing with, but you have to deal with it as it comes. You do what you have to do in the line of your duties, your job. You focus on what you're doing."

Fear can directly affect the way officers do their jobs. A common but dangerous temptation, born of fear, is to appease prisoners to gain their cooperation. (Inmates do not note or mention officers' use of this approach, perhaps because they see such officers as friendly to their immediate interests.) One officer stated the premise underlying appeasement quite baldly: "Anybody facing death, they gotta be danger-ous. If he calls and he needs something, you got to try to get it for him." Such officers are said by their colleagues to bend or even ignore the rules "to keep it calm in there and to make their day go by." Other officers are said to get "too personally involved." They "play" with inmates rather than controlling them, and are "slap happy" and "sloppy" in following procedures. These officers, according to their colleagues, say to inmates, " 'You're my buddy.' Slap 'em on the back and say, 'You're my partner. I know you're not going to hurt me because we're stick buddies.' This is no place to play. If you get that far gone, I think you better get out." Obsequious guards make their fellow officers nervous. The problem for the staff, and for the weaker inmates they must protect, is that appeasement corrodes the officers' authority and undermines control, lowering the general level of secur-ity. "We're supposed to be a team," complained one officer, "and what happens to them happens to me." If a colleague trembles visibly, he is useless as an officer. What is worse, his presence emboldens the more predatory prisoners, which in the long run spells trouble for officers and inmates alike.

Some officers go to the other extreme and become overbearing and abusive. This response, as we have seen, is salient in the minds of the prisoners. As Radelet et al. observed, "Relations with the correctional officers are fragile, with one hostile guard easily able to overshadow relationships with those who are more humane."[45] A major reason for this fragility is fear. Ever on the defensive, abusive officers are quick to take personal offense and quick to intimidate and harass prisoners in retaliation. Under conditions of solitary confinement, officers of this type may have the upper hand because prisoners are locked in their cells. They may even set the example for other officers to follow.[46] On less restrictive death rows, however, abusive officers are more apt to be seen by their colleagues as a liability.

Contrary to appearances (and inmate perceptions), these abusive officers are not gratuitously hostile. Rather, condemned prisoners are a trial for them, taxing their limited self-control. Though the prisoners are, in the view of most officers I interviewed, reasonably well behaved on a day-to-day basis, the officers pointed out that the prisoners are not easy to be around. They characterized the inmates as impatient, touchy, demanding, and given to wide mood swings that sometimes end in tirades. Such, said the officers, is the pressure of life on death row. To get into a "cursing match" with the prisoners is tempting, noted one officer, but he resists because to do so "would put me at their level." Unfortunately, this officer felt that some of his colleagues regularly lower themselves to the level of the prisoners, becoming defensive about their authority and abusive with prisoners. Wherever these officers go, this man maintained, they stir up trouble.

> We have some hard cases. I could have everything calm, but this one guy wouldn't be there but two seconds and he'd rile 'em up so. When he left, you could hear the inmates down the hall, he'd rile 'em up so. . . . Just some small remark or something he'd know would get 'em riled.

Since trouble is seen as contagious, given the pressure of life on death row, abusive officers are as much of a problem as their lax colleagues. In the one instance, abuse may provoke an incident. In the other, timidity may invite trouble. Either way, other officers—and the prisoners—suffer.

The fears of the prisoners and guards, though quite real, are not necessarily realistic. It is by no means clear that death row guards would be eager to harm their captives if the opportunity arose. Certainly the officers cannot simply enter prisoners' cells and carry them off to the execution chamber on a whim. (Fearful prisoners can acknowledge this last point intellectually, by the way, but not emotionally. They still feel starkly vulnerable.) Nor is it clear that condemned prisoners, most of whom face years of legal appeals and therefore have reason to hope for reprieve, are desperate enough to callously harm or kill a guard to escape the executioner or to exact revenge.

But the fear persists on this and other death rows, with harmful consequences. A prisoner of a solitary-confinement death row described the consequences as follows:

> There seems to be too much security. There seems to be an abnormal amount of fear in the guards simply because we have a death sentence and that makes it hard for us to have the same courtesies that we should—that other inmates have. For example, the guards are so afraid of us where they won't get close to us or they won't come up and talk to us when we need something done seriously. It could be a medical problem or something. And because of this fear in the guards, we don't get the assistance we need like

other inmates do. . . . You can easily tell it's fear in the officers and other employees of the institution. Just because we have this death sentence, people are so afraid of us that they don't want to get close to us and because of this very thing we just don't get what I would say [is] the compassion that we need or the assistance that we need. Sometimes it's hard to find the right word, but I know that it is something that we don't get that every man, regardless of his condition, should have.[47]

The main casualty of fear, then, is simple human compassion, the absence of which contributes to the distinctively cold interpersonal climate on death row.

Human Services

Yet fear need not contaminate all encounters on death row. Implicit in the above-quoted prisoner's insightful observations about the corrosive effect of fear is the hope that individual officers and inmates can, through more open interaction, come to know one another and use that knowledge to suspend, or at least place in perspective, the stereotypes that divide them. That hope sometimes bears fruit. On the reformed death row I studied, three officers, admittedly a minority, suppressed their fears and went about their jobs as responsible correctional officers. Two of these officers were women. Like good officers of either gender in any correctional setting, they saw themselves as figures of authority whose job was to help the inmates cope with the pains of imprisonment.[48] In their view, condemned prisoners, like all other prisoners, are entitled to a range of basic human services, and these officers provided those services as a matter of course.

One officer ticked off by rote some examples of human services provided on death row: "You must provide phone calls, supplies, commissary, legal and personal calls [call the switchboard for them], toilet paper, soap, towels. The list goes on. . . ." Paradoxically, security is on that list of services, even on death row. For these officers, security means more than merely preventing escape. It also means protecting the inmates and the officers. In one guard's words,

This is a security job: to keep them protected while they're here and to keep them from getting out. Anytime they go anyplace within the building or outside it, they have to have waist chains, leg irons, and all this stuff. So you have to act as a buffer between them and the inmates who are "free." So it's a form of protective custody. You have to protect them from the other inmates because they can't protect themselves.

Condemned prisoners need protection from each other as well. Stress builds up on death row, and men under pressure sometimes act out. Violent men sometimes act out violently, so fights are one periodic symptom of stress on death row with which the officers must deal. Such fights are usually broken up on command. When they are not, the regular death row officers do not enter the dayroom, where they might be taken hostage, but instead call in a twelve-man tactical team, which restrains the prisoners. In this way, both the inmates and the officers are protected.

Sometimes officers go a step beyond efficient provision of services. In the words of one such officer, they "develop a friendly-type relationship" with the prisoners. Having come to empathize with the prisoners in their difficult situation, they are moved to respond to the prisoners' legitimate concerns. "It may be a simple thing to you and me, but if it's something that's pressing them, then they want it done today. They don't have a lot of business. The least thing that comes up is important."

These more responsive officers occasionally find themselves in a helping role. Interactions may start with a request for a basic commodity, such as toilet paper, and end in an informal counseling session.

> The man may start a conversation which eventually brings out a problem they're struggling with. For example, problems with girlfriends. They ask me because I'm a female. Or [problems with] kids or cooking, things they know I know about.

At other times, such officers may simply offer a friendly word to lift a prisoner's spirits. "Sometimes you just smile to cheer them up sometimes. Sometime they're looking sad, you say, 'What's wrong? It's not that bad. Cheer up.' " The fact that prisoners may not tell them what's wrong or visibly cheer up is a disappointment—none of the officers claimed success as informal counselors—but it does not discourage the officers from trying to be of help. Their job, they say, is a thankless one. These officers behave as they do to satisfy their own personal and professional standards, not to win praise or recognition from the prisoners.

Such officers are explicitly aware of the limits of a human-service role on death row. Quite consciously, they try to be friendly without becoming friends, to be responsive without kowtowing. They don't appease; they simply care enough to serve and protect. In their view, the ideal officer "doesn't get too close but gets close enough to deal with them and accept them for who they are." If a guard gets too friendly, prisoners "can ask you for favors, and you can get caught up in things." The objective is to be a concerned professional—that is, "to deal with them on a one-to-one basis but not get emotionally involved with them." These officers see themselves as correctional professionals who must go about their work in a civil and responsive but fundamentally businesslike way.

Us and Them: The Divisive Role of Executions

Executions cast a long shadow over death row and impose a stark limit on the degree of emotional involvement that is possible between officers and inmates. As one prisoner on a solitary-confinement death row observed, "We know within ourselves that no matter how courteous a guard tries to be to us, we know what he will do in the end. And so that right there makes us guard against them."[49] Contrary to the view of this and, indeed, most condemned prisoners, death row officers normally are not involved in executions; the execution team is assembled from officers who have had little or no contact with the prisoner prior to the deathwatch. Still, complicity is obvious in that the death row officers expressly hold the prisoners for the purpose of execution. Some of the guards of our reformed death row recognized this complicity; others did not. In any case, the prisoners hold each and every officer accountable. "You can feel the tension in the air after an execution," observed one officer. "I think they are angry at anybody with a [correctional] uniform."

Anger is not the only emotion to follow in the wake of executions. Prisoners may also feel a sense of loss. Some condemned prisoners, on this and other death rows, develop among themselves a primitive notion of community.[50] The execution of one of their fellows is therefore a loss. Their sense of loss accentuates feelings of powerlessness and vulnerability; it reaffirms in no uncertain terms the lonely fate that awaits the condemned prisoners. The complicated mix of sentiments evoked by the execution of their fellows can seem overwhelming and inexplicable; only rage at the death row officers, the culprits once removed from the execution team, offers relief. In the words of one prisoner,

> I wanted to understand why Mike was being taken from me, but it was impossible. Each day I have to interact with the same guards who came to the unit and took him from me. These guards were the same guards who were telling me, "Joe, Mike is a good man. *They* shouldn't kill him." Each time I heard a guard say that, I could feel the anger churning within me. What they were saying made no sense to me. I wanted to scream, "NO!" I wanted to tear down the prison walls and make *them* stop. I hated them. . . . Before that day four other friends had been executed: men whom I ate with, talked with, played with, argued with—men whom I came to know as friends and shared a life bond with. Men whom no matter what their crimes, I *could not* see as anything but human beings . . . men whose tears I saw, whose flesh I touched, whose pain I still feel. I still know the hopelessness, I am still with the guards who took them away to be executed, and I am still trying to understand.[51]

Some of the death row officers, too, develop a sense of community with at least some of the prisoners. The executions of these prisoners are a loss for the staff as well. Parting with prisoners one has come to know and like can be at once touching and depressing. An officer on our reformed death row, supervising a prisoner's last visit with his family, reacted in a revealing way.

> The reality of that last family visit really made me feel bad. His daughter didn't even know him. It was depressing to be there. . . . It's supposed to be part of the job, like being a doctor or something. You lose a patient and that's just it, but it's not that easy. You never forget this type of thing, but you can put it behind you.

For this officer, one "loses" a prisoner to execution. Like any genuine loss, it doesn't come easily.

To be sure, officers on this and other death rows more typically remain aloof from condemned prisoners or even treat them abusively. They do not see executions as emotionally wrenching events, nor do they take pleasure in them. They behave as they do, in part, to avoid the emotional hurt that involvement with prisoners would bring. "You can't be buddy-buddy," said one officer, "you've got to keep it business." This business is a matter of life and death, killing and dying. Death row officers, however, are not simply waiting to kill the prisoners, whatever the prisoners may feel. In many ways, the officers, too, are pawns in the death penalty drama. The officers know that condemned prisoners either have their sentences changed by appeal or commutation, in which case they never see them again, or the prisoners are executed. In either case, but particularly when prisoners are executed, most officers feel it is better not to have known them well.

More concretely, one officer told me that he kept his emotional distance from the condemned because he might be the one to escort them to the death house. The death house, which in the state under study is located in another prison, is where the executions occur. There another group of correctional officers takes over, conducting the deathwatch and carrying out the execution. It is to the experience of these officers, our modern executioners, that we now turn.

Notes

1. C. A. Nesbitt and R. L. Howard, *Management of Death Row Inmates: An Examination of the Issues* (Laurel, Md.: American Correctional Association, 1988). See especially Chap. 3, p. 8, and Chap. 5, p. 4. The ACA disseminates this monograph only to prison officials and their consultants. A shorter version is available to the public. See *Managing Death-Sentenced Inmates: A Survey of Practices* (Laurel, Md.: American Correctional Association, 1989).
2. P. Brasfield with J. M. Elliot, *Deathman Pass Me By* (San Bernardino: Borgo Press, 1983), 91–92.
3. A. Bronstein, personal communication.
4. B. Jackson and D. Christian, *Death Row* (Boston: Beacon Press, 1980), 14.
5. C. Chessman, "Trial by Ordeal," in *Death Row: An Affirmation of Life,* ed. S. Levine (New York: Ballantine, 1972), 4.
6. Jackson and Christian (n. 4), 94.
7. See G. Sykes, *The Society of Captives* (New York: Atheneum, 1966); J. Irwin, *Prisons in Turmoil* (Boston: Little, Brown, 1980); and R. Johnson, *Hard Time: Understanding and Reforming the Prison* (Pacific Grove, Calif.: Brooks/Cole, 1987).
8. B. Schwartz, "Deprivation of Privacy as a 'Functional Prerequisite': The Case of the Prison," *Journal of Criminal Law and Criminology* 63 (1972):235–236.
9. I and Professor Stanley Brodsky of the University of Alabama independently found 70 percent of Alabama's condemned prisoners to be showing signs of deterioration. My finding, based on content analysis of interviews, was that "7 of every 10 prisoners diagnosed themselves as suffering physical, mental or emotional deterioration in what was typically portrayed as the interpersonal vacuum constituting the human environment of death row." See R. Johnson, "Life under Sentence of Death," in *The Pains of Imprisonment,* ed. R. Johnson and H. Toch (Prospect Heights, Ill.: Waveland Press, 1988), 132. Brodsky found a 70 percent deterioration rate for this same population using objective personality tests. Brodsky's results are reported in depositions pertaining to Jacobs v. Britton, No. 78–309H et al. (S.D. Ala., 1979).

Other studies have described the problem of deterioration as common among condemned prisoners but have not provided statistics on the prevalence of symptoms. See R. Johnson, *Condemned to Die: Life under Sentence of Death* (Prospect Heights, Ill.: Waveland Press, 1989) (Chap. 6 contains a fuller ethnographic description of deterioration among Alabama's condemned than that found in the article cited above); Jackson and Christian (n. 4), 174–189 (examining Texas's death row); L. West, "Psychiatric Reflections on the Death Penalty," *American Journal of Orthopsychiatry* 45 (1975):689–700 (covering death row prisoners generally); H. Bluestone and C. L. McGahee, "Reaction to Extreme Stress: Impending Death by Execution," *American Journal of Psychiatry* 119 (1962):393–396 (covering death row prisoners at Sing Sing); and J. Gallemore and J. Panton, "Inmate Responses to Lengthy Death Row Confinement," *American Journal of Psychiatry* 129 (1972):167–172 (covering death row prisoners in North Carolina). In 1968, Congress heard testimony on the problem of deterioration among the condemned. See U.S. Congress, Senate Committee on the Judiciary, *To Abolish the Death Penalty: Hearings before the Subcommittee on Criminal Laws and Procedures,* 90th Cong., 2nd sess., March 20 and 21 and July 2, 1968, S. 1760.

10. C. M. Lambrix, "The Isolation of Death Row," in *Facing the Death Penalty: Essays on a Cruel and Unusual Punishment,* ed. M. L. Radelet (Philadelphia: Temple University Press, 1989), 199.

11. Johnson, *Condemned* (n. 9), 48, 48.

12. Ibid., 49.

13. Ibid., 51.

14. Jackson and Christian (n. 4), 232, 226.

15. M. L. Radelet, M. Vandiver, and F. Berardo, "Families, Prisons, and Men with Death Sentences: The Human Impact of Structured Uncertainty," *Journal of Family Issues* 4(4):596 (December 1983). For many regular prison guards, caring, expressed as a concern for delivering human services and thereby ameliorating the stresses of confinement, is a central feature of their work. See H. Toch, "Is a Correctional Officer, by Any Other Name, a 'Screw'?" *Criminal Justice Review* 3 (1978):19–35; R. Johnson and J. Price, "The Complete Correctional Officer: Human Service and the Human Environment of Prison," *Criminal Justice and Behavior* 8(3):343–73 (1981); L. Lombardo, *Guards Imprisoned: Correctional Officers at Work* (New York: Elsevier, 1981); and R. Johnson, *Hard Time* (n. 7), Chap. 8.

16. Jackson and Christian (n. 4), 90, 19.

17. Brasfield (n. 2), 80.

18. Lambrix (n. 10), 198, 200, 200.

19. Jackson and Christian (n. 4), 31. See also Lambrix (n. 10).

20. Lambrix (n. 10), 199.

21. Jackson and Christian (n. 4), 15. See also Johnson, *Condemned* (n. 9); Radelet et al. (n. 15); and B. Eshelman, *Death Row Chaplain* (New York: Signet Books, 1972).

22. M. Vandiver, "Coping with Death: Families of the Terminally Ill, Homicide Victims, and Condemned Prisoners," in *Facing the Death Penalty: Essays on a*

Cruel and Unusual Punishment, ed. M. L. Radelet (Philadelphia: Temple University Press, 1989), 133.

23. Johnson, *Condemned* (n. 9), 54.
24. Ibid., 50.
25. Radelet et al. (n. 15), 605.
26. Johnson, *Condemned* (n. 9), 115.
27. Ibid., Chap. 1; Radelet et al. (n. 15); Jackson and Christian (n. 4), 100–109.
28. Jackson and Christian (n. 4), 78.
29. Johnson, *Condemned* (n. 9), 70–71, 71.
30. C. Turnbull, "Death by Decree: An Anthropological Approach to Capital Punishment," *Natural History* 87 (1978):54.
31. Johnson, *Condemned* (n. 9), 65.
32. Ibid., Chap. 4.
33. Ibid., 74.
34. Groseclose v. Dutton, 609 F. Supp. 1432 (D.C. Tenn. 1985), 1436.
35. J. M. Giarratano, "The Pains of Life," in *Facing the Death Penalty: Essays on a Cruel and Unusual Punishment,* ed. M. L. Radelet (Philadelphia: Temple University Press, 1989), 195.
36. *Groseclose* (n. 34), 1436.
37. See n. 9.
38. Johnson, *Condemned* (n. 9); Jackson and Christian (n. 4).
39. Johnson (n. 9), 112, 96.
40. Ibid., Chap. 3.
41. Radelet et al. (n. 15); Jackson and Christian (n. 4).
42. Toch (n. 15).
43. Personal communication from a death row inmate, as part of an unpublished survey of death row living conditions conducted by John Conrad and myself (1984).
44. Johnson, *Condemned* (n. 9), 69.
45. Radelet et al. (n. 15).
46. Johnson, *Condemned* (n. 9), 69.
47. Ibid., 60.
48. Lombardo (n. 15); Johnson, *Hard Time* (n. 17).
49. Johnson, *Condemned* (n. 9), 64.
50. Ibid., Chap. 7.
51. Giarratano (n. 35), 194–195.

PART III

In Cold Blood

A Study of Modern Executions

Now it is a terrible business to mark out a man for the vengeance of men. But it is a thing to which a man can grow accustomed. . . . And the horrible thing about public officials, even the best . . . is not that they are wicked . . . not that they are stupid . . . it is simply that they have got used to it.

G. K. Chesterton.

I can take or leave executions. It's not a job I like or dislike. It's a job I've been asked to do. I try to go about every job in the most professional manner I can. If they would stop the death penalty, it wouldn't bother me. If we had ten executions tomorrow, it wouldn't bother me. I would condition my mind to get me through it.

Execution team officer

CHAPTER 5

Death Work

A Modern Execution Team

The execution of Gary Gilmore, carried out in 1977, marked the resurrection of the modern death penalty. The event was big news and was commemorated in a best-selling nonfiction novel by Norman Mailer, *The Executioner's Song,*[1] later made into a movie. The title is deceptive. Like others who have explored the death penalty, Mailer told us much about the condemned but very little about the executioners. Indeed, if we examine Mailer's account more closely, the execution-er's story is not only unsung, it is also distorted.

Gilmore's execution was quite atypical. His was an instance of state-assisted suicide accompanied by an element of romance and played out against a backdrop of media fanfare. Gilmore, unrepentant and unafraid, refused to appeal his convic-tion (under a then-untested capital statute). He dared the state of Utah to take his life, and the media repeated the challenge until it became a taunt that may well have goaded officials to action. A failed suicide pact with his lover staged only days before the execution, using drugs she delivered to him during an exceptionally intimate visit, added a hint of melodrama to the proceedings. Gilmore's final words, "Let's do it," seemed to invite the lethal hail of bullets from the firing squad. This nonchalant phrase, at once fatalistic and brazen, became Gilmore's epitaph. It clinched his outlaw–hero image and found its way onto tee shirts that confirmed his celebrity status.

As befits a celebrity, Gilmore was treated with unusual leniency by prison officials during his confinement on death row. He was, for example, allowed to hold a party on the eve of his execution, during which he was free to eat, drink, and make merry with his guests until the early morning hours. As we have seen, this was not unprecedented: Notorious English convicts of centuries past would throw farewell balls in the prison on the eve of their executions (see Chapter 1). For the record, Gilmore served Tang, Kool-Aid, cookies, and coffee, later supplemented by contraband pizza and an unidentified liquor. Periodically, he gobbled drugs obligingly supplied by the prison pharmacy. He played a modest arrangement of rock music albums but refrained from dancing.

Gilmore's execution generally, like his parting fete, was decidedly out of step with the tenor of modern executions. Most condemned prisoners fight to save their lives, not to have them taken. They do not see their fate in romantic terms, and they do not host farewell parties of any sort. Nor are condemned prisoners given medication to ease their anxiety or gain their compliance. The subjects of typical executions remain anonymous to the public and even to their keepers. They are very much alone at the end.

The focus of my research, in contrast with Mailer's account, is on the executioners themselves as they carry out typical executions. In my experience, executioners—not unlike Mailer himself—can be quite voluble, and sometimes quite moving, in expressing themselves. I draw on their words to describe the death work they perform in our name.

Death Work and Death Workers: Defining Parameters

Executioners are not a popular topic of social research, or even of conversation at the dinner table or at cocktail parties. We simply don't give the subject much thought. When we think of executioners at all, we typically imagine men of disreputable, or at least questionable, character who work stealthily behind the scenes to carry out their grim labors. We picture hooded men hiding in the shadow of the gallows, or anonymous figures lurking just out of sight behind an electric chair or firing blind, outside a gas chamber, or, most recently, beyond a curtained partition, lethal injection in hand, in an execution chamber made to look like a hospital room. We wonder who would do such grisly work and how they sleep at night.

This image of the executioner as a sinister and often solitary character is usually wrong and always misleading. To be sure, a few states hire free-lance executioners and engage in macabre theatrics. Executioners may be picked up under cover of darkness at lonely country crossroads; some still wear black hoods. They slip into the prison unnoticed, do their work, then return to their civilian lives. This curious Gothic scenario may give comfort to skittish prison administrators. In one warden's words, "We can honestly say that we didn't do it."[2]

That warden, of course, is spouting sheer nonsense. Correctional officials are *always* involved in executions, even if they themselves do not directly carry out the killing. Broadly speaking, the execution process starts with the prisoner's confinement and doesn't end until the prisoner has been killed. In today's world, this means that death work starts on death row, the bleak and oppressive "prison within a prison" where the condemned are housed for years awaiting execution (see Part II). Death work culminates in the deathwatch, a brief period, usually twenty-four to forty-eight hours long, that ends when the prisoner has been executed.

This final period, the deathwatch, is generally supervised by a team of correctional officers who report directly to the prison warden. The warden or his representative, in turn, must by law preside over the execution. In many states, it is a member of the deathwatch or execution team, acting under the warden's authority, who in fact plays the formal role of executioner. Though this officer may technically work alone, his teammates are apt to view the execution as a shared responsibility. As one member of a deathwatch team told me in no uncertain terms,

We're all as a team . . . together. We all take a part of the killing, the execution. So, this guy that pulled the switch shouldn't have more responsibility than the guy that cut his hair or the guy that fed him or the guy that watched him. We all take a part in it; we all play 100 percent in it, too. That take[s] the load off this one individual [who pulls the switch].

The formal executioner concurred. "Everyone on the team can do it," he said, "and nobody will tell you I do it. I know my team." My research confirmed these claims.

The correctional officers who serve on deathwatch teams are expressly selected and trained to carry out executions. They are executioners, in my view, even when they are assisted by an outsider who is hired to complete the formalities of the execution—to flip a switch or push a button, thus taking the life of a prisoner he may have never even seen. By contrast, the deathwatch team officers must serve, observe, and control the prisoner, then escort him to the death chamber and secure him for execution—if they do not also perform the execution themselves. It is they who are the most active in the conduct of executions; it is they who carry the heaviest psychological burden.

The officers of these deathwatch teams are, for all intents and purposes, our modern executioners. I studied one such team, composed of eight seasoned male officers of varying ranks. (A ninth officer, a woman, seated the witnesses but was not otherwise involved in the execution. The team is very much a man's world.) The team had carried out five electrocutions when I began my research. I interviewed each officer on the team after the fifth execution, following the same general format that I had used with the death row officers.[3] Again, my aim was to elicit and explore the officers' perceptions of their work by allowing them to delineate the execution process as they saw and participated in it. At the start of each interview, I posed open-ended questions about each officer's role in the execution process. These questions, in turn, led to others about how the officer was trained to do his job, about how he felt about and perceived the executions he had helped to carry out, about his observations of the prisoners as their executions drew near, and about the effects on him personally of his involvement with executions. I then served as an official witness at the team's sixth execution and as a behind-the-scenes observer during their seventh, at which point I informally reinterviewed each of the officers.

I also interviewed the warden, the prison's operations officer, and a member of the prison's treatment unit who had advised a condemned prisoner who was later executed. In these interviews, again focused but using open-ended questions, I probed the dimensions of each person's role in the execution process, their perceptions of the individual condemned inmates they had observed, and the effects, if any, their involvement in the execution process may have had on them as individuals. In addition, I interviewed a counselor affiliated with a prison reform organization. The counselor had assisted both of the men whose executions I'd observed, in each case staying with them through all but the final minutes of the deathwatch. I also interviewed a journalist who had spoken with one of the condemned prisoners both before and, by telephone, during his deathwatch. These latter interviews were almost exclusively aimed at reconstructing the experiences of condemned prisoners during their final hours. The results of this research form the substance of this and the following two chapters on the psychology of capital punishment.

The Deathwatch Team

Members of the deathwatch team referred to themselves, with evident pride, as simply "the team." This pride was shared by correctional officials. The warden praised them as solid citizens—in his words, "country boys." (Some of the officers were in fact from urban areas, but they qualified as country boys because of their reliable characters.) These country boys, the warden assured me, could be counted on to do the job of execution and do it well, however unpleasant they might find the experience to be. As a fellow administrator put it, "it takes a certain amount of grit" to serve on the execution team. Continuing, he mused,

> What's the expression? "When the going gets tough, the tough get going." A certain amount of professionalism [is required] there. . . . An execution is something [that] needs to be done, and good people, dedicated people who believe in the American system, should do it. And there's a certain amount of feeling, probably one to another, that they're part of that—that when they have to hang tough, they can do it, and they can do it right. And that it's just the right thing to do.

In the eyes of the warden and other prison officials, an execution is a good man's burden, shouldered stoically for us all.

The official view of an execution is that it is a job that has to be done, and done right. The death penalty is, after all, the law of the land. In this context, "done right" means that an execution should be proper, professional, and dignified. In the words of a prison administrator,

> It was something, of course, that had to be done. We had to be sure that we did it properly, professionally, and [that] we gave as much dignity to the person as we possibly could in the process. . . . You gotta do it, and if you've gotta do it, it might just as well be done the way it's supposed to be done—without any sensation.

In the language of the respondents, "proper" refers to procedures that go off smoothly; "professional" means without personal feelings that intrude on the procedures in any way. The phrase "without any sensation" no doubt expresses a desire to avoid media sensationalism, particularly if there should be an embarrassing and undignified hitch in the procedures—for example, a prisoner who breaks down or becomes violent and must be forcibly placed in the electric chair as witnesses, some from the media, look on in horror. Still, the phrase may also be a revealing slip of the tongue. For executions are indeed meant to occur without any human feeling, without any sensation. A profound absence of feeling would seem to embody the bureaucratic ideal for the modern execution.

There is, to be sure, no room for passion or even for emotion in the professional execution sought by prison administrators. Condemned prisoners are not supposed to be dragged kicking, screaming, or weeping to their deaths. They are meant to go to their deaths with dignified dispatch, if not decorum ("graciously," to quote one of the execution team officers). The point is, I suppose, that an execution should be, or should at least appear to be, a punishment to which one submits voluntarily, if reluctantly, rather than a calculated act of violence one resists at all costs. It boils down to a matter of appearances, and appearances matter to everybody on the scene, particularly the officials. There is, then, an execution etiquette. Part of death work is to make sure that this etiquette is observed.

The view of executions held by the officers of the team parallels that of correctional administrators but is somewhat more restrained. The officers are closer to the killing and dying and are less apt to wax abstract or eloquent in describing the process. Listen to one man's observations:

> I look at it like it's a job. I don't take it personally. You know, I don't take it like I'm having a grudge against this person and this person has done something to me. I'm just carrying out a job, doing what I was asked to do . . . . This man has been sentenced to death in the courts. This is the law, and he broke this law, and he has to suffer the consequences. And one of the consequences is to put him to death.

From where the deathwatch officers sit, the important yet "dirty" job of execution must be done in a workmanlike manner. No one is proud of the blood or the mess, the sights and smells of violent death. As one officer observed, "It's nothin' to be proud of; it's just a job to do, one way or another."

The job of execution offers many opportunities for abuse. The prisoner could, for example, be strapped in the chair in an intentionally demeaning or painful way. But no one on the execution team seeks to inflict suffering on the condemned prisoner. Their reasons are rooted in a practical notion of humaneness: Abuse is not only unprofessional but impractical, because it is likely to trigger resistance. Accordingly, the officers have modified equipment such as the face mask to reduce *both* the prisoner's discomfort *and* the likelihood of shifting or squirming; the team members try to cinch down the body straps gently to avoid causing pain as well as to avoid provoking any struggle from the prisoner. All the officers, like the prison administrators, want a smoothly orchestrated, professional execution. In their view, however, such executions are neither acts of patriotism (as some of their administrative supporters would have it) nor acts of murder (as some of their free-world critics would have it). Rather, executions are, in the team's eyes, lawful and arguably humane penal sanctions. For the men of the deathwatch team, that is enough.

Which is just as well, since only a few members of the execution team support the death penalty outright and without reservation. Having seen executions close up, some of the team officers have lingering doubts about the justice or wisdom of this sanction. What puts these officers off is not so much the violence of execution—violence comes with the territory in the penitentiary. Besides, many of the officers have encountered violence in the military or in the free world. But violence in prison and elsewhere is usually situational and reactive, occurring when there seems to be no alternative. Such violence need not be justified, in the eyes of the officers. Executions are different because they are arranged. When asked, "Does being part of a planned life-taking process trouble you?" two men responded as follows:

- (Sigh) That's a good question. That's a real good question. (Sigh and long pause) It do, in a sense, and it don't. It probably—if it do, it's 'cause every person that's put on this earth, I feel, is created equal, you know, and they [are] put on this earth to do, to handle some type of problems and whatever. They got to live to do that. But my old grandfather had a saying, you know, "Do unto others what you want them to do unto you." So when you kill somebody, you should be killed. . . . [But] the execution, the killing itself, don't bother me. I was in the service eighteen months in Nam. I was on body patrol, far as when they dropped napalm and you went in and picked up dead bodies and stuff, put 'em in body bags. I guess another part of it, I live in a ghetto. I see a lot of life and death over there, you know. It really don't bother me, you know. Even inmates here get killed, you know. I've saved a couple of inmates here who have been cut up real bad as well as taken the dead bodies out from here that been killed. So the killing, it really don't bother me.

• There is turmoil, even for someone that I didn't like per se and might not care if he lives or dies, okay? But the violence doesn't bother me. Out in population, you may have to subdue someone or whatever. Certainly, if you subdue someone improperly, you could give them a lethal blow or whatever. So, then, you know, working on the tower, we have firepower. Okay, push may come to shove and we may have to use it. . . . [But with an execution] I ask myself, "Am I doing the right thing? Is this just or unjust? Do we have the right to take a man's life?"

A number of their colleagues entertain similar concerns. Nevertheless, the members of the deathwatch team can be counted on to do the difficult job of execution, because all of them accept without question the authority of the law and hence conclude that the matter is essentially out of their hands. Somebody's got to do it, say these men in unison and with conviction, because it's the system. And if we're the ones to do it, they continue, at least we'll do it right. One officer put the matter this way:

I've seen it. I know what it is. I've smelled it. I've tasted it. I've felt it. . . . I'm not sure the death penalty is the right way. I don't know if there is a right answer. So I look at it like this: If it's gotta be done, at least it can be done in a humane way, if there is such a word for it. 'Cause I know it can be a nasty situation. Executions have been here for a long time. And for a long time it's been done, you know, unprofessionally and for primitive reasons. The only way it should be done, I feel, is the way we do it. It's done professionally; it's not no horseplaying. Everything is done by documentation. On time. By the book.

Executions by the Book

Arranging executions that occur "without any sensation" and proceed "by the book" is no mean task, but it is a task the execution team undertakes in earnest. The tone of this enterprise is set by the team leader, a man who takes a hard-boiled, no-nonsense approach to correctional work in general and death work in particular. "My style," he says, "is this: If it's a job to do, get it done. Do it and that's it." He seeks out kindred spirits, men who see killing as a job—a dirty job one does reluctantly, perhaps, but above all a job one carries out dispassionately. In his words,

> I wouldn't want to put a man on the team that would like it. I don't want nobody who would like to do it. I'd rather have the person *not* want to do it than have a person who *wants* to do it. And if I suspected or thought anybody on the team really's gettin' a kick out of it, I would take him off the team. . . . I would like to think that every one of them on the team is doin' it, is doing it in the line of duty, you know, carryin' out their duties.

Not all officers are candidates for death work. Only volunteers are sought, and though a fair number step forward, only a few are chosen. The team leader screens the volunteers carefully. He knows the officers at the prison from his long years of service there, and his friendly, down-home country style invites them to admit any difficulties they may experience. Reluctant or squeamish candidates are encouraged to move on to different assignments without fear of sanction or prejudice.

> I would know what type of officer you have been, because I've been working with you and seen the way you conducted yourself. I'd sit down and talk to you and tell you what, what we gonna do and what's expected of you, and ask you, "Do you think you could handle it?" And if you told me you thought you could, why, I'd start training you. And then if I saw a weakness or something, that you're falling back, why then I'd ask you, you know, "Do you have a problem with it?" And then I would take you back and sit you down and tell you, if you did have a problem with it, had anything against it or you thought you had anything against it, you ought to just drop out. And nothing would ever be said. We'd just carry it on through.

Those volunteers who are selected to serve on the team are, by all accounts, the cream of the correctional officer corps. They are seasoned, mature, and dependable officers, level-headed types who have proven time and again that they know how to cope with the daily tribulations of work in the prison. Physically and emotionally strong, they take orders well but can also be counted on to use discretion. Common sense and cell-block finesse enable them to relate to and understand convicts. In the warden's words, these officers "can look condemned prisoners in the eye and tell them 'no' when they have to and not get them upset." Some of the officers credit military combat experience as their baptism of fire. All have proven that they can keep cool and handle the pressure that is endemic to the prison community. The observations of one officer, confirmed by the team leader, substantiate this last point:

> I volunteered because of my [military] service background and my job background here. They were looking at experience, more or less, number one. And they were also looking for (pause) the people who had been through a lot of stress—stress from inside the institution—that could handle stress more. The overall thing was to deal with the stress and pressure. . . .

As long as I've been here, I have been used, more or less, as the person to handle the big problems and straighten them out.

Executions always have the potential to become big problems, so this officer feels he has found a niche on the deathwatch team.

In part to avoid any problems, big or little, the deathwatch team has been carefully drilled in the mechanics of execution. The execution process has been broken down into simple, discrete tasks and practiced repeatedly. The team leader described the division of labor in the following exchange with me:

The execution team is a nine-officer team and each one has certain things to do. When I would train you, maybe you'd buckle a belt; that might be all you'd have to do. . . . And you'd be expected to do one thing, and that's all you'd be expected to do. And if everybody do what they were taught, or what they were trained to do, at the end the man would be put in the chair and everything would be complete. It's all come together now.

So it's broken down into very small steps . . . ?

Very small, yes. Each person has one thing to do.

I see. What's the purpose of breaking it down into such small steps?

So people won't get confused. I've learned it's kind of a tense time. When you're executin' a person, killing a person—you call it killin', executin', whatever you want, the man dies anyway—I find the less you got on your mind, why, the better you'll carry it out. So it's just very simple things. And so far, you know, it's all come together; we haven't had any problems.

This division of labor allows each member of the execution team to become a specialist in one specific task, an expert technician who takes pride in his work. Here's how two officers saw their specialized roles:

- My assignment is the leg piece. Right leg. I roll his pants' leg up, place a piece [an electrode] on his leg, strap his leg in. . . . I've got all the moves down pat. We train from different posts; I can do any of them. But that's my main post.

- I strap the left side. I strap his arms and another man straps his legs and another one puts his head in the cap. But my job is strapping his left arm in . . . . I was trained with those straps. The way those straps is on the chair, see, I have to know, you know, exactly where each thing is.

The implication is not that the officers are incapable of performing multiple or complex tasks but simply that it is more efficient to focus each officer's efforts on one easy task. "Every man I got down there can carry the job," the team leader maintained. "We may cross-train . . . but when it comes down to, to the time a man goes into the chair, everybody does only one thing and that's it."

An integral part of the training is realistic rehearsals, with team members cast as recalcitrant surrogate prisoners, or "dummies," so that the team can anticipate problems and practice the restrained use of force.

We might set up a training, and I might be the dummy, you know, the dummy. And I sit in the chair, they put on the arm straps and stuff, and I might buck, you know, whatever, resist them putting me in the chair. So we can practice this. We go through stuff like this. And we have had one officer that nearly got his arm broke in the practice. . . . We have different people we use for dummy. We might carry a small person through, or a big person, or somebody, you know, trying to basically size the person [the prisoner] up. If you've got a man that's scheduled to go and he's gonna be big, I'd use myself or somebody else big.

Serving as the dummy during execution rehearsals at once demands and promotes trust in one's peers. Imagine the role. Officers march you into the death chamber, strap you in an electric chair, and fasten your arms, chest, and legs. With you pinioned, they affix a cap to your head and cover your face with a leather mask. Electrodes are then connected to the cap and your right leg. All this occurs in an electric chair that, though obviously not activated at the moment, is the real McCoy, capable of shooting 2500 volts of electricity through your body.

The team leader, who routinely plays the role of surrogate prisoner, described the experience as "peculiar." "Well, when I first started, it was peculiar, you know, because when they put the mask on me, you know, you can't really tell what the person is doing. You feel helpless." Another officer on the team, more voluble than his leader, chose the word "weird." He, too, stressed the helplessness he felt when strapped in the chair.

It's kind of weird. You feel totally helpless, you can't move, you can't see, you can't speak. It's total darkness. All you can hear are sounds around you. It's definitely weird. It's kinda like puttin' you in another world. . . . You get a little queasy, I guess from being helpless. You can't fight it. This is total helplessness.

According to the team leader, the officers submit to this procedure out of trust and commitment. "You have to trust your peers. You have to trust people. And like I said, it's a team, and you trust and love one another, so you go on and do it for the team." Each of the deathwatch officers shares the leader's devotion to the team: At some point, each has volunteered to play this trying role, doing so quite consciously out of dedication to the team.

Practice is meant to produce a confident group that is capable of fast and accurate performance under pressure. Time is crucial in the execution trade: The less time spent securing a prisoner for execution, the less opportunity there is for things to go wrong. A smooth execution drill unfolds rapidly and conforms to institutional operating procedures (IOPs). Practically speaking, doing an execution right means, perhaps above all else, doing it fast.

We've got a time schedule for everything that we do. The head man has got to see that everything is going according to the clock. The clock—we're timed on everything. There's a certain time—you gotta go by the IOPs on the thing, and each thing has gotta be done at a certain time. . . . You know everything you've got to do. You just got to, you just got to do it in a certain time, a certain time you got to do this. The schedule is boss. You've got to break it down to the schedule, every last minute.

The rewards of practice are reaped in improved performance. Executions take place with increasing efficiency and, eventually, with precision. "The first one was grisly," a team member confided to me. He explained that a certain amount of fumbling made the execution seem interminable. There were technical problems as well: The generator was set so high that the body was mutilated. The execution chamber stank of burnt flesh, described as having a greasy odor reminiscent of fatty pork. (Air fresheners were subsequently installed throughout the death house.) But that is the past, the officer assured me. "The ones now, we know what we're doing. It's just like clockwork."

Team Cohesion

"We're a Family"

In the execution training, individual tasks are emphasized and the team members are called upon to function as automatons. The team itself, however, is a warm and even intimate primary group, a close-knit group its members can trust at all costs. The team's work environment—the death house—is a home away from home. The officers of the team work together to handle the problems and pressures posed by death work. In their words,

- The team is very close. I guess we're probably . . . closer than any of the officers in here. . . . Comes from working close together. It's real, real close, you know. We really don't have nobody [else] to talk to. And we'll share ideas and things, we'll go off and sit down and just talk and share ideas. How we feel or how it's affecting us. We, I guess, have confidence in one another, trust. Just a good group of people.

- There's more closeness than in any other group I've seen in the system, as far as working together. And one thing we do—we got this thing with the team—we talk to each other. If we got a problem, we go and talk to each other *first* about it before we go off [and get upset]. . . . Everything that we do stays there [and gets worked out], you know what I'm sayin'? That's the way we operate.

- We are very, very close-knit. When we got a problem from an execution, we all go down in the basement, the execution chamber—we call that our home—draw the curtains, and go in the back, and we'll talk. One guy may say, "I don't think I can make it tonight." And we'll sit down and say, "C'mon, what's the problem? Let's talk it out . . ." Then we have to remind him, "the law says that this is what has to be done, and we have to do it."

As one officer succinctly put it, "We're not a team, we're a family. In the prison, we fuss, cuss, and threaten each other constantly. But down there [in the death house], we're a family."

At first blush, such sentimentality may seem strained or fabricated, but it is neither. Individual people may function as cogs and, in groups, may be deployed in mechanical fashion as the sum total of those cogs. But this is almost never the whole story. Such arrangements violate essential human needs for purposiveness in action and relationships with others, needs the team members meet through the primary-group relations that exist among them. Each and every officer comes to see himself as a man among men he likes and admires, working together to complete a critical task in service of the larger social good. The team thus functions as a psychological safe harbor and a moral reference point—which is to say, a source of support and direction as the officers go about the business of death work. In the niche provided by the team, officers feel more confident and assured; the demands of death work become a manageable routine. In one officer's words,

> When I first started, I was nervous. I told them I was nervous. I think they could sense it anyway, but I told them I was nervous. I was scared to death—of my reactions, of how I was gonna react to seeing a man executed. Would I get so excited I might pass out, maybe embarrassing everyone? That would be unprofessional. I didn't know how I'd react. I didn't know once the switch threw whether I'd lose everything in my stomach or not. . . . I didn't [lose control], because I had the family. They were there. They gave me all the support I needed through the first one. Then after that it just became a job. It just became a normal job. You build up your self-confidence so that when the time comes, you just do what you got to do.

"Now," the officer concluded with evident satisfaction, executions "seem like something we do every day."

The Private World of the Execution Team

The team that binds these men as a primary group operates in a world of its own, a world that is tailored to promote and reward the efficient conduct of executions. In a number of ways, the team is actually, and not just symbolically, set apart from the rest of the world during practice sessions and particularly during the deathwatch. For one thing, the death house in which the team carries out its duties is located in the basement of a building on the periphery of the prison compound. Though the death house is within the prison's massive walls, it is removed from the daily ebb and flow of life in the penitentiary.

> You just get down there and you're pretty much left alone. . . . It's physically located in the basement. And even the windows—they have windows, but there's an earth mound outside and you can look up and you only see the bottom of people's feet as they're walking by. (laughing) And you're isolated, you know. People sometimes tend to forget about you, too.

Team members work in pairs during the deathwatch. These pairings (four in all) have evolved into stable partnerships. The formal reason for pairing the officers is to promote security, but the resulting partnerships strengthen each officer's bonds to the whole team as well as to his individual partner. When any given pair of officers is on duty during the twenty-four hours of the deathwatch, the remainder of the team sets up camp in the officers' lounge. This, once again, removes the execution team officers from interaction with the regular prison community.

> We set up a place to sleep, almost a camp here. Because we got to rotate, you know, at night, through the night. When some of us are sleeping in [one area], we can walk and come up here [to another area] and drink coffee and eat, whatever.

These arrangements allow for continuing interaction between partners, reinforcing a sense of teamwork and shared purpose. Particularly as the time of execution draws near, the team uses its camp as a place to build esprit de corps and to get ready—"psyched up"—for the execution.

The team's camp also shelters the officers from potentially harsh scrutiny by outsiders, whether in the prison or from the larger community. Paradoxically, most inmates most of the time are indifferent to the workings of the execution team.

> [Inmates] think that the people that is going to be electrocuted have deserved it. They went through all the process of the courts, and some of them been on death row for five or six years, and they figured they've, they've been fair to them.

Fellow officers, however, can be another matter. They may show jealousy and resentment, approval or disapproval. In any case, the team considers these reactions distracting, and best ignored.

> Your fellow workers back here is more harder on you than maybe the inmates. You know, they give you the ol' silent treatment. Funny vibes you get from them, I don't know. . . . Some of 'em disapprove, and some of 'em pat you on the back. I really learnt don't pay no attention to it. Pay no attention one way or another.

The team also sees the media as a critical audience that must be kept at bay. Reporters are said to lurk outside the prison waiting to interview people involved with the execution, so the officers are content to stay where they are until the execution is over. Then, they know, they will be free to go about their business. "News people are funny," said the team leader. "They'll run over the top of you to get a story. But after the story is over with, they'll, they'll leave just as quick as they come in, you know." Meanwhile, according to another officer, "Being up there together and isolated from everybody gives us a little better feeling."

Physical isolation is complemented by the social isolation of self-imposed secrecy. Team members do not want others to know the details of their involvement in executions. Said one officer, "We look for a person who is very secretive, you know, and can keep things to himself. 'Cause this is very secretive, you know, what my part is and what his part is." Officers do not speak of their activities to outsiders. Their presumption is that outsiders simply wouldn't understand because, in one officer's blunt reckoning, "They hadn't been there." (I became an insider, it would seem, because I offered the officers a chance to speak openly and anonymously about their concerns. From the start, the officers encouraged me to attend an execution to form my own assessment of their operations.) Officers are even hesitant to let members of their families know any details of the execution process or their roles in it: "Well, we, we were sworn to secrecy. When I first got on the team, I wouldn't even tell my wife what I was doing. . . . The deal was, keep it among ourselves. Whatever we say or do down here has got to stay down here, you know." Team members particularly fear that if the person who plays the formal role of executioner were to be identified as an individual, he would be stigmatized by others for what is really a team activity, and perhaps singled out and abused by vengeful convicts.

An Elite Unit

The deathwatch team, set apart physically and by its self-imposed social isolation, quite explicitly sees itself as an elite. As one officer observed, "It's an honor among ourselves to be on the team. I wouldn't go out on the street and broadcast that I'm on the execution team, but I'm proud of it." And rightly so. As befits an elite unit, the team receives privileges and perks. The officers are not paid a separate fee for carrying out executions, but the long hours mean overtime pay. Isolation from the regular prison routine allows small but special freedoms: the extra smoke or cup of coffee when they want it, the chance to mingle with their colleagues and to be their own boss much of the time. (Being isolated in the death house means being on their own a lot.) The camp mentality mentioned earlier lends itself to a suspension of normal work routines. There is a sense that on the deathwatch the officers are liberated from the mundane constraints of daily prison work.

Clearly, the team is an important group engaged in an important enterprise. After all, those who work at matters of life and death are protected from the daily hassles of everyday prison work. Furthermore, a direct line of command connects the team with the warden, which attests to the gravity of the team's task and gives the officers the heady sense that finally they can stand or fall on their collective merits.

> One thing that relieved us of a lot of stress was [that] we worked for the warden. When he activated us, we worked for him; that's who our orders came from. Came, you know, through the team leader and then to us. Anybody else, they couldn't come and, you know, disrupt you. So everybody knew what they had to do, and they just did what they had to do. You know, if you did it wrong, *you* did it wrong. You know what I'm sayin'?

In the prison work environment, one is subject to the conflicting directives and evaluations of various sector and shift commanders, and the rules of the game are often a hodgepodge one negotiates at one's peril.[4] Being on "the warden's team," entrusted with a special and clearly defined mission, is a privilege. "That team works on their own," confirmed the warden. "I never interfere. They know what they're doing. If they can't solve a problem, they'll bring it to me." In correctional circles, this is more than a job. It is almost, one suspects, an adventure.

These gratifying arrangements motivate the team members to do their work well. The officers think of themselves as skilled death-work technicians. Functioning as an autonomous team allows them to focus their technical skills to good result. Away from the madding crowds of the cell block and yard, following an explicit procedure and reporting to a single, supportive boss, the team is free to do well what it feels it does best:

> We think of ourselves as a special team. And I even heard one of [the officers] remark one time—tension got bad in the back and we were having a lot of problems [with the regular prisoners], and he walked up to me and he said, "When are we going to go back down in the basement and do what we do best?" Said, "Hell, I'd rather do the work down there than back here."

A Modern Execution Team

Bonds of solidarity, established and nurtured in the private world of the deathwatch team, are forged in commitment to a common purpose and tested in countless rehearsals. These bonds are the psychological cement that holds the team together under the pressures of death work. "It's really a team when you get down to the last hour, you know. You've got to be in, in conjunction. You've got to be ready to work together, to know this man's gonna be with me when I go down there to the death house." When the officers are called upon to take a prisoner to his death, they all draw strength from the knowledge that they are part of a modern execution team.

Notes

1. N. Mailer, *The Executioner's Song* (Boston: Little, Brown, 1979).
2. E. Johnson, "Some States Prepare for First Executions in Twenty Years or More," *Wall Street Journal,* 6 November 1984, 1. Lesy described the division of labor associated with executions, beginning at the top, with the warden, as a series of psychological "cutouts" that the individuals performing the labor use to minimize or even deny their involvement in executions. See M. Lesy, *The Forbidden Zone* (New York: Farrar, Straus & Giroux, 1987), 135–157. This warden exemplifies Lesy's point. Yet the warden and the officers of the execution team I studied did take responsibility, individually and collectively, for the executions they carried out. They asserted that executions are lawful sanctions, and as agents of the law they have nothing to hide from themselves or others. How they prepared themselves psychologically to carry out their perceived duty is a more complicated matter, often involving elements of psychological denial (especially of the humanity of the victim), but they did not deny or downplay their responsibility for executions.
3. For a discussion of focused interview procedures, see Chap. 3, n. 24.
4. L. X. Lombardo, *Guards Imprisoned: Correctional Officers at Work* (New York: Elsevier, 1981).

CHAPTER 6

Deathwatch
The Final Hours

The deathwatch team goes to work during the last hours before a scheduled execution. In the state under study, the deathwatch starts at eleven o'clock the night before the execution and ends at eleven o'clock the next night, when the execution takes place. At least two officers are with the prisoner at all times during that period. "If we thought maybe we had one [who] would commit suicide," stated the team leader, "we'd probably stay with him and sit there for forty-eight hours." The tasks of the deathwatch team are service, surveillance, and control. Their ultimate objective is to keep the prisoner alive and "on schedule"—that is, to move him through a series of critical and cumulatively demoralizing junctures beginning with his last meal and ending with his last walk. When the time comes, they must deliver the prisoner up for execution as quickly and unobtrusively as possible.

Critical junctures during the deathwatch include the prisoner's final visit with loved ones; a last meal; the boxing of the prisoner's personal possessions for distribution to relatives or friends; the shaving of the prisoner's head and right leg (to increase conductivity); a final shower, after which the prisoner changes into a fresh set of clothes for the execution; the transfer of the prisoner to the death cell, which is devoid of personal possessions of any kind; the reading of the death warrant; and finally the prisoner's last walk, to the death chamber and the electric chair. These junctures make up the schedule to which the officers refer as they move the prisoner toward his execution. After studying the general process by which the prisoner is controlled, we will examine how the schedule unfolds to accomplish an execution.

One would expect anybody, particularly a condemned prisoner with a history of violence, to resist execution by turning his rage on his keepers, or, failing that, himself. Officers are alert to these eventualities right up until the prisoner is in the chair. Like their colleagues on death row, the team officers appear to see the prisoner's situation in Hobbesian terms, with self-preservation the prisoner's most basic instinct or right. As Walter Berns has reminded us, it was Hobbes's view that "a man who is justly and legally condemned to death nevertheless retains the right to defend himself; indeed, he retains the right to kill his guards or anyone else who would prevent him from escaping."[1] But resistance is so rare as to be a nonissue. Even on death row, before execution is imminent, most prisoners see resistance as futile, even demeaning. "Either way it go," said one such inmate, "out the cell peaceful like, or you swing at them and hit them in the head and they bust you in the head—they gonna drag me around and strap me in the chair and go and turn on the juice."[2]

Social Control

The typical prisoner is thoroughly defeated—in a word, dehumanized—by the time he commences his last walk. He is beyond resistance. To understand this phenomenon, one must think of the entire period the prisoner spends in confinement awaiting execution, on death row and during the deathwatch, as a continuous social control process. Waiting, worrying, plagued by nightmares that play out the grisly details of execution and by raw anxiety about how he will hold up under the pressure, the prisoner is worn down by the stress of confinement under sentence of death. This stress undermines his integrity as a human being and weakens, if not eliminates, his capacity to resist the will of his keepers.

On death row, the emphasis is on maintaining secure physical custody of the prisoner. Compliance is coerced when it is not forthcoming. By contrast, *social* control is the emphasis in the deathwatch. Shackles and cuffs are available here as they are on death row (see Part II), but modern execution etiquette does not permit a bound prisoner to be taken to his death. The condemned prisoner must be under the social, not physical, control of his keepers; he must submit to the execution routine. The officials' goal, and in the end perhaps the prisoner's as well, is a smooth, orderly, and ostensibly voluntary execution, one that looks humane and dignified and is not sullied in any way by obvious violence.

Keeping the Prisoner Calm

Broadly speaking, the job of the deathwatch officers "is to sit and keep the inmate calm for the last twenty-four hours—and get the man ready to go." Keeping a condemned prisoner calm means, in part, serving his immediate needs. It is paradoxical to think of the deathwatch officers as serving the condemned, but the logistics of the job make service a central obligation of the officers. In the words of one officer,

> Well, you can't help but be involved with many of the things that he's involved with. Because if he wants to make a call to his family, well, you'll have to dial the number. . . . If he wants a cigarette, well, he's not allowed to keep matches, so you light it for him. You've got to pour his coffee, too. So you're aware what he's doing. It's not like you can just ignore him; you've gotta just be with him whether he wants it or not, and cater to his needs.

The officers cater to the condemned because contented prisoners are easier to keep calm and under control. Each and every officer on the team says this is so. But one can never trust even a seemingly contented prisoner facing execution. The deathwatch officers see condemned prisoners as potentially explosive, and literally stay an arm's length away from the prisoners when they hand things into their cells. Quite understandably, the officers are ever alert for trouble in their encounters with these prisoners. In their words,

- You always expect the unexpected. . . . You don't know what, what a man's gonna do. He's liable to snap, he's liable to pass out. We watch him all the time to prevent him from committing suicide. You've got to be ready—he's liable to do anything.

- We are very much concerned about security and him hurting himself. At the least little sign he's gonna attempt to hurt himself, we have to get on in there. . . . We look for mood swings, changes in attitude. Becoming argumentative. Anything out of the ordinary.

- Well, I'm thinking, always thinking. If this happen, what we gonna do? If that happen, what we gonna do? You never relax.

The prisoner is never out of at least one officer's sight, and a light is always burning in his cell. Records are maintained with a scrupulous attention to detail: "We record everything, missing nothing. If he turns over in his bed, we note it. How much he eats, how much coffee he drinks, how many cigarettes he smokes—we record it all." Surveillance is constant, and control, for all intents and purposes, is total.

One officer likened his security role to that of a football linebacker. Always on his toes, he must take in the big picture and be on the alert for any behavior that portends trouble. Another man consciously reads between the lines of his conversations with the condemned in an effort to get a handle on what the man is thinking.

- I'm very security-minded. You have to [be]; you can't be relaxed. It's just like playing football, you know. If you play linebacker, you can't be relaxed, you got to stay on your toes, you got to keep going at all times. . . . The guy might talk about he want to do this, he want to do that. He want this and he want that. He be pacing the floor. You know, you can tell the guy be getting ready to do something. The sound of his voice, you know, the way he talk to you, the way he walk. You watch everything. If you do relax, you get knocked down. You have to watch the whole thing.

- It's just hard. You never know what a man's gonna do when a man is doomed to die. I expect anything from him. I expect him to do anything to get out of this situation. Because he's already backed up to the wall. And the only thing between him and his freedom is me—when I'm down there. So I have to try to keep aware of where he is mentally. Even if it's to take him away from what he's thinking about. I don't want to have to wonder about nothin'. And I don't think he's gonna tell me the truth every time I ask him. I don't expect the truth, but from what he's telling me, he gonna answer my second question. My second question is, "What are you thinking?" Because I know he's thinking about something.

Both officers agree that if they don't anticipate and control any problems, the problems will control them. In particular, they, like the officers on death row (see Chapter 4), fear that a desperate inmate might try to injure or even kill an officer, either out of revenge or simply to delay the execution. The fact that the deathwatch prisoner is almost never out of his cell diminishes this fear, but it lingers as a background concern.

Maintaining Emotional Distance

Relations between the officers and their charges can be quite intense. Watching and being watched are always engaging activities, particularly when the stakes are life and death. These relations are, nevertheless, impersonal; there are no grudges, but neither is there evidence of compassion or fellow feeling. The deathwatch officers are civil but cool, as are most death row officers (see Chapter 4). But the deathwatch team officers—that is, the execution team officers—carry this deportment to the extreme, keeping a profound emotional distance from the men they are about to kill.

And no wonder. The utter and unremitting impersonality of their job symbolically dehumanizes the members of the execution team. This enables the officers, while on the job, to approach executions not as feeling persons but as bureaucrats of violence. The dehumanization these execution team officers experience is far more pervasive that that experienced by their colleagues on death row.

To keep their distance from the prisoner, the execution team officers erect "barriers," to quote the warden, between themselves and the prisoner. The officers concurred with this assessment. To do otherwise, they maintained, would make it harder to execute the condemned prisoner. A more personal relationship with the prisoner might even be a kind of hypocrisy, one officer noted, because one might like him and still have to kill him. The attitude of the officers is thus that the prisoners arrive as strangers and are easier to kill if they go out the same way.

- If they talk to me, I'll try to answer them. But I don't start no conversations. I try to avoid being with them as much as possible. I really don't want to get acquainted with someone, you know, when you're gonna kill him that night. I guess it could be a psychological thing there, you know. If you didn't know him that might make it a little easier. But you could be around a person so long that you might get to know him, you might like him or think pretty much of him, and I really don't want to think that I might like a person, then you got to go on to kill him that night. So, you know, to me it, it's kind of a hypocritical thing, you know, to get to know him.

- I don't like particularly to talk to the men. I just figure we wouldn't, we wouldn't have anything in common to talk about. I'm getting ready to electrocute him, and he's getting ready to die, and we just don't have anything in common. . . . It would be the best if you didn't, didn't know him. It's the best not to know him.

It is, the officers contend, literally "us against them." The officers are a team; he stands apart. The gulf that separates them, the officers might say, is as wide and deep as infinity.

Still, it is hard not to have at least intimations of empathy for a fellow human being in trouble, even if one goes out of one's way to remain aloof from him. The warden, certain that his officers throw up emotional barriers in self-defense, was equally convinced that "they get more personally involved than they will ever tell you or me." He may have a point. Remember, the officers must serve and observe the prisoner, so they are necessarily involved with him to some degree. Final visits, too, can be moving, tearful events, and these occur in the immediate presence of a group of officers. To be sure, the officers are there en masse for the purpose of security, but they cannot fail to note the human drama that is unfolding before their eyes. These encounters may not touch them deeply, but they almost certainly do touch them.

To maintain an emotional distance from the condemned prisoner in the face of such experiences, officers must suppress their natural feelings. This they are trained to do, both as prison officers and as members of the team. In the warden's words, "from the cradle to the grave, correctional officers are told, 'Don't get personally involved,' and that's what they try to do." They become expert at denial, which in the warden's view amounts to "tucking things in the recesses of their minds, where they don't have to deal with it." One effective technique the officers use is to remind themselves of the gruesomeness of the condemned prisoner's crime and the justice of his punishment. Note the following exchange between a team officer and myself:

> We don't see him all that much or talk to 'em, but, I mean, a human being is a human being. But you, the way you get around getting to like 'em, you read the papers and things, and you brush up on the case and just see what this man has done, you know. And when you find out that he drove nails through a woman's, an old woman's hand and nailed her to a chair and set the house on fire with her in it, then you kinda get to saying, "Well, this man here, he can't be no good."
>
> *Even if you have feelings for him, knowing what he did makes it easier?*
>
> I wouldn't have feelings for him; I wouldn't get that close to him. I wouldn't let myself get, get that way.
>
> *So you see it as a problem. You just don't let yourself get close?*
>
> Right, it's a problem. Like I say, you read the newspaper, and you try to find out all the dirty things that he done. (Laughing) So, so you say, "Well, okay, it's okay. It's all right, all right to put him to death."

Officers must psych themselves up during the last hours before an execution, a point I shall return to later. Dwelling on the details of the crime helps them get in the proper frame of mind for an execution.

Calculated Camaraderie

Two specific officers on the team are regularly assigned to guard the prisoner during his last five or six hours, the period during which the critical junctures mentioned earlier take place. These officers are given the delicate but essential job of keeping the prisoner calm and on schedule as the hour of execution approaches. They become more involved with the condemned prisoners than do their colleagues. Indeed, they *seek* relationships with the condemned. But these relationships are calculated and superficial, and are sought for the control they offer. In effect, the *job* of these officers is to establish relations, and they do so *solely* to achieve control over the prisoner. In the end—and until the end—they use this relationship to manipulate the prisoner's behavior so that he will comply with the etiquette of a dignified execution.

These officers work together to keep the prisoner occupied. They pour the man's coffee, light his cigarettes, listen to his stories, laugh at his jokes. Unlike their more taciturn and aloof colleagues on earlier shifts, these officers make a conscious effort to talk with the prisoner. In the words of one of these men,

> It's a critical time. The guys down there, they don't know whether they're going or not until the last minute. And during that period of time, they're constantly going through different mood swings, and I just stay there and try to keep them on an even keel. Whichever way they fluctuate, I go with them. There's me and another coworker of mine; we sit with them for the last hours. We're the only two that's there. And we're able to communicate. So far, we haven't had any problems, anybody getting disruptive right at the end or trying to commit suicide or anything. We just keep them right there and keep talking to them.

The point of these conversations is not merely to pass time; it is to keep tabs on the prisoner's state of mind, and to steer him away from subjects that might depress, anger, or otherwise upset him. Sociability, in other words, quite explicitly serves as a means of social control. Relationships, such as they are, serve purely calculated ends. There may be an element of emotional involvement here, as the warden would have it, but clearly any fellow feeling is secondary to the task at hand, sometimes vividly referred to as "getting the man dead." What dominates here is impersonality—indeed, impersonality at its worst, masquerading as concern for the stranger one hopes to execute with as little trouble as possible.

A more or less constant stream of conversation seems to be at the heart of this enterprise. The impression one gets is that ideally the staff would keep the man talking until the very end, which would come swiftly and without warning. As one officer said,

> Talking to him helps, you know. It moves the time faster, you know. If I see this person going—you know, getting really upset—I just try to talk with him, you know. Just bring up any type of subject not dealing with death, just anything. You don't want the inmate to be looking at his watch, or looking at the clock and saying "Wow, it's almost eleven, it's almost the twenty-sixth and I'm going to die the twenty-sixth." You know, you don't want that. You want it like this: As soon as he come up on that time [for the execution], boom! it's over.

Knowingly or unknowingly, chaplains, lawyers, and visitors may play a role in the denial process. They, too, wish to distract prisoners from the ugly reality that awaits them.

Unintentional Collusion

Relatives and others who call the prisoner, or who accept his calls, serve the useful end of buffering the emotional impact of the execution on the prisoner. Condemned prisoners have access to a telephone in their cells, and they can use it at length. The officers are well aware that conversations, whether with themselves, with visitors, or with callers, keep the prisoner's mind off the electric chair and make it easier for them to keep him calm and on schedule. "I just love it when outsiders stay with the man or talk [on the phone] with the man," the warden admitted. "They take the last-minute heat; it takes pressure off the team." It is almost as if these outsiders were an extension of the team. Indeed, the warden considered one chaplain, who was good at helping prisoners find some mental peace, as an honorary member of the execution team.

The prospect of collusion in relationships between the condemned and their supporters may be especially problematic for attorneys. Attorneys fight to keep their clients alive. Ironically, they do so with a commitment to professionalism that is shared by the warden and the members of the execution team. Once the prisoner's avenues of appeal have been exhausted, however, or when the prisoner has knowingly waived further appeals, professional obligations of attorneys impel them to help their clients die with some semblance of dignity. This means helping prisoners to conform to the official routine, and doing so themselves, so that the execution goes quickly and smoothly. The attorney for John Evans III, who had become demoralized on death row and had relinquished his appeals, described how he dealt with the prison warden.

> I thanked him for his professional attitude and his courtesy. I thanked him for making it easier for John and his family. We shook hands.
>
> I had to wonder at our roles. We were professionals. He was the executioner and I was the defense lawyer. Here we were thanking each other for being so professional. One pro to another. For doing what? Making a hard job bearable? For helping reduce tensions all around? For making it go down easier?
>
> Damn, I thought. This man is going to kill John in about three hours. He is going to pull the switch and shoot electricity through John's head and fry his brains out. That's exactly what he's going to do.
>
> And here I am thanking him for being a pro. What was I doing in all this? Another pro. A respectable cog in this grotesque machinery of butchery. My job was to help provide a clean execution. I should be screaming and shouting. I should make them drag me out of there—create a scene. I should make it as hard and tough and as sick and inhumane as it was. I should be making my voice heard in this ritual of cruelty. I should make these bastards hear my voice and know what the hell they are doing.
>
> And yet my rage gave way to thinking about John and his suffering. I had to serve him. And serving him meant taking my role as set out in the rites of execution. . . .
>
> I had to be strong for John. If it was easier for him to accept his death and make peace within himself, then I would do all I could do to help him."[3]

Evans was executed in Alabama in 1983. In Alabama, the warden serves as the executioner.

The prisoner's supporters may collude in the execution process, as the warden would have it, but at least they are trying to help someone they care about in a time of great need. The role played by the final pair of deathwatch officers is, in contrast, a pseudosocial, strained affair. Yet the prisoner's hunger for human contact is such that even here there are moments of surface congeniality that he may find comforting. In one instance, even the last meal, shared with an officer, was marked by apparently lighthearted banter.

These perverse arrangements are almost certainly mutually exploitative. People are friendly, but no friendships are born; there is laughter but no happiness or joy. Each party has a hidden agenda: The prisoner denies his fate and escapes momentarily into convivial fantasy; the guard moves his man through the execution schedule and closer to his fate. The officers, at least, were clear on their agenda. As one officer made clear in the following exchange with me, the talk and the laughter were all in a day's work:

> People that you think would have problems out of, being the last day, we don't have any problems out of 'em. Half the time me and the individual person be laughing. We just be laughing, you know. The guy's laughing and I'm laughing.
>
> *Do you develop a kind of friendship with the man, do you think, or is that too strong of a word?*
>
> Well, I don't look at it as a friendship thing. I look at it, myself, as an overall job. The man know what he done, and he know what he got to do, you know, and it's my job to get him through it. And I more or less put myself in condition for to get him through them last hours. No matter what it takes. I sit down and eat with him, the last meal, and all that. Anything he want to do, I sit down and do with him. . . . Shoot, one of 'em actually asked what to order and we didn't know what to order so we ordered McDonald's food for 'im. He ate Big Macs and I ate Big Macs, you know. And talk and laugh and whatever, you know.
>
> *So, you're kind of like a companion whose purpose is to get them through this last journey. And in the process (pause), well, in the process, do you develop any friendly feeling for these guys?*
>
> I don't look at it as being a friendly feeling. I just look at it as getting the job done. . . . It's a pleasant conversation, but you still have that sense [that] he's sitting there talking to you but he's thinkin' 'bout this whole matter, you know. He never forget what he's got to do later on, you know.

Neither, one can be sure, does the officer forget.

The Final Hours: Critical Junctures in an Execution

As time grows short, prisoners may ask their guards what, in general terms, awaits them. The prisoners seem to want an overview of the process so that they can prepare themselves for what is to come. They don't want to know the gory details of execution, and the officers have no intention of allowing them to dwell on such troubling matters. To help put the prisoners at ease, though, the officers map out the execution process short of the execution itself. In one officer's words,

> The last five or six hours, guys start asking what's going to happen to 'em and stuff like that—you know, what's going to happen to his property—and

I more or less start running down to him what goes on up until the last fifteen minutes, you know. They appreciate that. I tell them nothing wrong; I'm telling them like it is. More of them worry, "Is my family going to get my personal property?" "Will I be able to talk to my people on the telephone or whatever?" You know, and you explain to them, this is what goes on up until a quarter to eleven. But I never get on a basis of saying, "Hey, you know, this is what's going to happen to you in the chair. . . . This is what goes down at the end." I never get on that basis. If a man start talking about the chair, I change the subject. 'Cause you try to keep them calm, and I don't want, you know, myself, to get them upset.

Exchanges of this sort demonstrate the persistence of denial, even on the threshold of execution. Condemned prisoners use denial as a psychological defense mechanism, first on death row, then during the deathwatch.[4] The prisoners don't want to hear about their executions, at least not in specific, personal terms, and the guards, who also benefit from this denial, don't want to tell them. So the prisoner talks to his executioners about procedures in the abstract and remains calm, even as his private sadness and fear grow apace.

Generally speaking, the mood becomes more somber and subdued during this final period, as the execution draws near. Though, as noted earlier, one prisoner ate a hearty last meal in the ostensibly congenial company of a deathwatch officer, most eat little or nothing at all. At this point the prisoners, in a last-ditch effort at denial, may steadfastly maintain that their executions will be stayed. The pathos of this effort comes through, even in the retelling. One man proclaimed his execution to be "inconceivable." Such bravado is belied by the prisoners' loss of appetite, which reveals deeper doubts and fears and is taken by the officers to be a sign of weakening resistance. "You can see them going down," said one officer. "Food is the last thing they got on their minds."

Next the prisoners must box the meager worldly goods that they have brought with them to their death house cell. They have already given up many of the things that they possessed in their death row cells; items ruled to be either superfluous (no one needs jogging shoes or basketballs in the death house) or potential weapons (hobbycraft items may fall into this category, given the desperate situation of the prisoner) were confiscated and put aside when the prisoner arrived at the death house, in accordance with regulations. The staff, at this point, inventories all of the prisoner's possessions, including those already put aside, records them on a one-page checklist form, packs them in boxes, and marks them for disposition to family or friends.

Prisoners are visibly saddened and even moved to tears by this procedure, which at once summarizes their lives and underscores the imminence of their death. Up until this time, the prisoners have been gradually shedding unnecessary psychological baggage. One man, for example, simply forgot the names of his fellow condemned, though he had lived with them for years and felt himself to be a member of the death row community. The other prisoners no longer existed for him; their demise, so to speak, made it easier for him to face his own death. Relinquishing his property was a different matter. This amounted to abandoning *any* claim to a relationship with something outside himself. This radical step made oppressively real that which had been conveniently unconscious. The loss of his property hurt, since it clearly symbolized his coming loss of life. (To make a difficult situation worse for this man, some of his prized possessions, which had been stored away when he first entered the death house, turned up missing when his property was inventoried. The prisoner assumed that some prison official had stolen them because he saw the prisoner as a dead man who would have no need for material things.) At this point, with or without complications, strong feelings are apt to come to the surface, threatening unpredictable behavior. Sensing this, the officers step up security. Said one of the officers, "I really get into him; I watch him real close." The execution schedule, the officer pointed out, "is picking up momentum, and we don't want to lose control of the situation."

This momentum is not lost on the condemned prisoner. Critical milestones have been passed. The prisoner now moves in a limbo devoid of food or possessions; he has seen the last of such things, unless he receives a stay of execution and rejoins the living. At the next critical juncture, his identity is expropriated as well: His head is shaved, along with his face and right leg. Shaving facilitates a palatable electrocution. It reduces the physical resistance to electricity and minimizes singeing and burning. But the process has obvious psychological significance as well, adding greatly to the momentum of the execution.

The shaving procedure is quite public and intimidating. The condemned man is taken from his cell and seated in the middle of the tier. His hands and feet are cuffed, and he is dressed only in undershorts. The entire deathwatch team is assembled around him. They stay at a discreet distance, but it is obvious that they are there to maintain control should he resist in any way or make any untoward move. As a rule, the man is overwhelmed. As one officer told me bluntly, "Come eight o'clock, we've got a dead man. Eight o'clock is when we shave the man. We take his identity; it goes with the hair." This taking of identity is undeniably a collective process—the team makes a forceful "we," the prisoner their helpless object. The officers are confident that the prisoner's capacity to resist them is now depleted. What is left of the man erodes over the remaining three hours before the execution. In the words of another officer,

> When you get to the point of shaving the man's head, that usually will take just about all the strength a man has out of him. It's not long before he actually becomes a walking dead man. Because he knows that there is no more hope after that point. I've done six executions, and it's the same way for all of them. I have seen no change in it. Like when Delilah cut Samson's hair, that was it. It took all of his strength. There was nothing left.

After the prisoner has been shaved, he must then shower and don a fresh set of clothes for the execution. The clothes are unremarkable in themselves, though the prisoner must surely notice that buttons and zippers have been replaced by Velcro (to prevent his body from burning during the electrocution). Their real significance is symbolic, for this outfit marks the prisoner as a man ready for execution. As if to underscore this symbolism, the condemned prisoner is then weighed and photographed; his recorded image is then entered into a display case with the many others, dating back nearly to the beginning of the century, who have been executed at the prison. Physically "prepped" and with his picture and vital statistics saved for posterity, the prisoner is then stored, in effect, in an empty tomblike cell, the death cell. All that is left is the wait.

During this final period, the deathwatch area takes on a distinctively funereal ambience. The officers are quiet, moving about gingerly so as not to disturb the prisoner. One might say they behave much like attendants at a wake or funeral. They are exceedingly courteous to visitors, offering chairs, including their own, and coffee—even, in one instance, the last cup in the pot. Visitors, in turn, treat the officers cordially. The officers, ever prompt and responsive though never obsequious, give the inmate anything he is allowed, such as coffee, juice, or a light for his cigarette. (The officers are solicitous, but they remain wary; the prisoners, ever wary themselves, respond with subdued politeness.) The officers clean scrupulously to keep the area presentable to officials, who drop in and out periodically. These officials, too, are quiet and reserved, even reverent. They speak in hushed tones, as though they were visiting a grave.

Held in this increasingly lifeless milieu, the prisoner can normally count on his attorney, a chaplain, and a personal counselor for emotional support and advice. Like the team officers, these people see the prisoner's despair and deterioration. Unlike the officers, however, they try to help the prisoner cope on his own terms. A counselor who had been present at a number of executions told me that the aim of her advice, as well as that of the chaplain, depends on the status of the execution. If the prisoner has not yet exhausted his appeals, she tries to help him maintain a balance between "preparing for living and preparing for dying." Ideally, at this point, she continued, the prisoner "should be 'on hold,' ready to go either way." As execution becomes imminent, however, her objective shifts to helping the man "escape the horror" of electrocution.[5]

I know from my prior research that condemned prisoners do contemplate the horrors of execution, even years before their date with the electric chair. They shudder at the physical violence of electrocution and the indignity it visits on the body. "I already have an understanding about electricity," said one man, "it's not hard for me to imagine what an experience it would be."[6] They fear they will suffer great pain. And though many people, including the warden and the team, believe that electrocution is painless—it is thought to instantly shatter the nervous system, rendering the prisoner unconscious—nobody knows for sure. (It is little consolation to the prisoners that at least one medical authority has compared electrocution to burning at the stake.[7]) Prisoners agonize over their last walk, fearful that they will break down and leave behind a legacy of cowardice. As one man put it, "Don't nobody want to go out and the word you left behind is that you broke down." For years, the prisoners have lived with a domino theory of executions; every execution, however distant, has seemed to move their own a bit closer.[8] This theory is entirely false—each case runs its own course of appeals—but no matter. Now they are next, and they are about to fall.

There is really no way to soften these hard realities. The focus of discussion with the prisoner who stands on the threshold of execution is, in the words of the counselor, "not on what's going on around [him] in the death house, not on execution and being killed, but on dying and moving on to the next life." The prisoner is counseled to "let go, and go wherever it is you're going." Prisoners, many of whom devoutly wish for an afterlife, try to heed such counsel. Advice of this sort may be intellectually suspect (a theme developed in Chapter 9) but is as good as any in this situation. (After all, the condemned man has little hope of forgiveness from us, which is why we have sentenced him to a lonely, violent death.[9]) The execution team would no doubt concur in this advice, which encourages the prisoner to go to his death without resistance or struggle. This counsel, by promoting both denial and passive submission to the death work routine, furthers the prisoner's decline toward death.

Defeated Men

The prisoner at the point of execution is more like an object without sensation than like a flesh-and-blood person on the threshold of death. Officers had much to say about this phenomenon:

- We talked a lot among ourselves about this, and we think that when he realized that, that he's had it, is when we cut his hair off and put him in this other cell. We strip the cell [across from his old cell] and put him in this cell [the death cell]. He don't have any personal things over there or anything. Just a sheet and so forth, a mattress in it. And I think that's when he definitely thinks he's had it. . . . [He's] just calm, he just kinda accepts that this is it. I think it would be like, like almost being in a trance.

- We're cutting his hair and shaving their legs and all that stuff, and it's just more or less normal. It's just, just very quiet.. . . . Most times, he's quiet. We, you know, we tell him to move his head as we shave his head or what not. We tell him to shower and put his clothes on. He's, he's quiet. He responds to it, and he doesn't show no animosity towards you, towards any officer. . . . That's when it dawns on 'im it's gonna happen.

- When they come out of the shower, they go into a different cell; we put them in a different cell then, the death cell. Nothing but the bare essentials: the bed, the sheets, mattress, and clean clothes, that's it. Most of the time, they want a Bible, and pencil and paper to write a letter. . . . They don't say anything.

By the accounts of the deathwatch officers, these prisoners are beaten men, shells of their former selves, mentally dead or dying. Exhausted or, more properly, drained of spirit, they surrender to the execution. According to the officers,

- His mind goes first. . . . All resistance disappears, they're exhausted. I think he make it up in his mind then, you know, that he's ready to go. He blocks everything out, you know, as far as where I'm gonna be tomorrow, what I'm gonna do, you know. I know what I've got to do. There's no more pain, no more sorrow. I'm going. And that's it, gonna get it over with. I don't have to fight the lawyers and the judges and the courts no more.

- They work it out in their minds and they accept it. . . . A lot of 'em die in their minds before they go to that chair. I've never known of one or heard of one putting up a fight. . . . By the time they walk to the chair, they've completely faced it. Such a reality most people can't understand. 'Cause they don't fight it. They don't seem to have anything to say. It's just something like "Get it over with." They may be, they may be numb, sort of.

- They go through stages. And at this stage, they're real humble. Humblest bunch of people I ever seen. Most all of 'em is real, real weak. Most of the time, you'd only need one or two people to carry out an execution, as weak and as humble as they are. They're really a humble bunch of people.

These humble, beaten men seem to their keepers to be barely human and alive. But they are not dead yet, and so the officers remain vigilant. For some of these prisoners, the officers assume, a thin and precarious line may separate quiet defeat from an hysterical and perhaps violent collapse of personality. Emotions are always muted during the deathwatch; now they are taboo. Even consoling a man during the final wait might move him to tears, which in turn might precipitate an outright breakdown. An officer made this point in the following exchange with me:

> You don't want to console them, you know, 'cause then you be letting them slip back into a suicidal state. That's the most critical point.
> *Consoling them would make them suicidal?*
> I think so. I look at what they're facing—you're talking about being hit with electricity. Number one, it's much easier for them to take their own selves out than to face that. It's a real critical point. They might do anything.

In point of fact, many prisoners on death row do give serious thought to suicide as an alternative to execution (in one study, more than half).[10] Compared with execution, suicide seems to these prisoners a more dignified way to die, and one that leaves their families a more respectable legacy. Others, fewer in number, would like you to believe that they will stage a last stand, perhaps taking an officer or two with them. (One sometimes hears this brand of tough talk, which smacks of bravado, in group discussions with condemned prisoners.) Though few prisoners commit suicide at this juncture, and none, to my knowledge, has ever hurt or killed an execution team officer, the team understandably treats them with caution. From the team's perspective, the prisoners are like newly dormant volcanos—the surface calm reassures, but cataclysmic violence may not be far below.

Though by all accounts defeated and demoralized, the prisoners are not simply walking corpses the staff can direct toward the electric chair. In the warden's view, "They're numb, acting like 'I can't believe what's happening to me' or 'here I go, let's get it over with,' but I think they're very cognizant, all the way." "Very cognizant" may be an overstatement, if the officers on the team are to be believed. Still, the prisoners seem to retain a primitive sense of dignity, or at least a reflex sense of decorum, and in this respect they show some awareness of what is happening to them. From this residuum of real or feigned humanity, the condemned and his executioners forge an informal contract that goes something like this: The prisoner, obviously in distress, is admonished to walk to his death like a man, in conformity with the official script; the executioners, in control of themselves and the situation, imply that, in exchange, they will do the job cleanly and without a hitch. A fatal collusion ensues. Here's how one officer saw this delicate process:

> They get to a point where they don't know where they are. They don't really know what's happening. . . . I seen most of them right there at the end. They weaken to the point where they'll be almost crying, and I tell them, I say, "Well, you don't want to go out like that." I say, "People be here in a minute—pull yourself up." And they'll go ahead and get back on key where they were. That works every time for me. . . . They don't want to go out like that.

It is the unanimous view of the officers that the inmates want to "hold up for the row." In one officer's reckoning, "they want to go out like men."

Of the seven inmates executed by the deathwatch team, only one man broke down at the end. (Pathetically, he had to be almost carried to the chair, with his eyes closed.) The others, though they did not break down, may well have been emotionally fragile. After all, "they don't really know what is happening," as the officer on the scene said, but they must sense the gathering violence of the execution. Fear and hate and impotent rage almost certainly must stir within these men, threatening to overwhelm them, portending futile violence or demeaning tears. For this reason, all must be urged to pull themselves together and walk to the chair like men.

Whatever may be the deeper psychic life of condemned prisoners on the brink of execution, they wait meekly to be escorted to their deaths. The people who come for them, joining the two officers who stayed with the prisoner during his final hours, are the warden and the remainder of the deathwatch team, flanked by high-ranking correctional officials. The warden reads the court order, known popularly as a death warrant. This is, as one officer said, the "real deal," and nobody misses its significance. As he explained,

> They know what the real deal is, you know. When it's time to go, I more or less have drawed out a picture for the man, saying, "Hey, this is it." This is the real deal right now. And when they see people come in there and start reading the court order to 'em, they know what the real deal is.

The condemned prisoners then go to their deaths compliantly, captives of the inexorable, irresistible momentum of the situation. As one officer put it, "There's no struggle. . . . They just walk right on in there."

In the end, condemned prisoners suppress whatever residual thoughts and feelings they may have, giving themselves over to the execution process. They go to their deaths one slow and controlled and methodical step at a time, numb to the awful violence that awaits them. In this, paradoxically, they may resemble their executioners, who also seek peace from troubling feelings in mindless, mechanical conformity to the modern execution drill.

Behind-the-Scenes Preparation

While the officers in the death house prepare the prisoner for execution, the remainder of the team must get ready to carry out the act. Most of their preparations take place in the team's camp, away from the prisoner and the two officers assigned to guard him. Some of these activities are mechanical. The chair is tested and made ready. (The prisoner may hear the dull thud that accompanies the flood of electricity, and even imagine that he smells the burning of residual flesh from executions past. This upsets and embitters some prisoners, but this result is unintentional.) The cap and leg piece must be soaked (first in brine, then in cold fresh water); the electrode connections must be buffed clean. Mostly, however, the officers of the team try to ready themselves emotionally.

Psyching Up

The officers say they must "psych up" for the challenge that awaits them. "Anything can happen," one man assured me, "and we have to be ready for anything." The officers are tense, and it shows. They relate their anxieties and share ways to deal with problems; they trade jokes and insults, and tell war stories about recalcitrant inmates they subdued in times past. Their behavior is not solely a form of release. It is purposive, serving at once to calm the nerves and get the adrenaline pumping. In the words of the officers,

- We do have to get psyched up, 'cause a lot of times you never know if we're gonna have to use force to put the man in the chair or not. We never have, but we always try to get ourselves in a position that we can do it if we have to do it. And we discuss who's going in the cell, who's gonna take him out, and how we're gonna do it without gettin' ourselves hurt.

- You have to get yourself psyched up for this thing, I tell you, you got to get psyched up. And the way we do it is we play jokes, you know, act the fool, whatever. . . . Most of the time, we get to talking about things that happened back in here, you know. "I whupped that old inmate," you know, things like that. "We, we got him out of that cell and whupped him," you know, things like that. Something that we all can relate to. "Do you remember about the time that this happened?" Or something like that.

Even gross racial slurs can be exchanged with impunity, as is revealed in this exchange:

> We're always laughing and joking. We say a lot of things that come out sometimes right crude that shouldn't be said. It stays on the team, and no one ever gets mad at the other one; even when they say something wrong, we don't take that much offense in it. For instance, like there's mostly blacks on the team. We can call one a nigger (pause), and he don't get mad.
> *So you guys are pretty close then?*
> Yeah. I don't believe you would ever hear a conversation anyplace and say the names and say the things we say, anyplace. I've never heard of it before. . . . Like, one guy, I joke with him, and he outranks me. And he's black but is lighter-skinned. He looks like a Chinese fellah. Now and I told him if he just comes to be disgusted and didn't want to do this, he could always come live with me and be my laundry boy. (Laughing) He done turns

and says, "Go to hell, white man!" (Laughing) You know, we could say things and not neither one of us ever get mad.

It goes without saying that some of these activities would offend outsiders. The officers know that, but still, none of this behavior divides or weakens the team. Rather, these antics and insults reaffirm the team's primary-group bonds (see Chapter 5). One can say unspeakable things to one's "family," and doing so under stress may help affirm that reassuring bond. Psyching up in this way also promotes a collective state of mind marked by a confident and aggressive readiness for the task at hand. The "we" comes to feel very much ready to take on one of "them," in the unlikely event that force is required.

The team may also rehearse the execution during the waning hours of the evening to make certain that everything is in order. I observed one such rehearsal, which involved five separate enactments of the last walk and the strapping in of an officer serving as surrogate for the prisoner. There was considerable tension, which gave rise to nervous jokes of the gallows-humor variety and a bit of clowning around. But the rehearsal was no laughing matter. It involved real physical exertion as well as palpable emotional strain. Some officers were sweaty and short of breath when the practice session ended. Others were tense, and one was said to be "smoking" with nerves. Everyone was occupied with thoughts of the upcoming execution.

One man spoke for many of his colleagues when he observed, "I go over and over it in my mind. I play out problems and work out solutions. I want to be ready." Many such concerns are mundane but strategically critical. "What if he kicks?" this man wondered. "So I put my knee on his foot when I strap him in." But mostly the officers, like the condemned prisoner, simply wait. And again as with the condemned prisoner, a calm exterior may mask inner turmoil. In the words of one officer, "The surface is cool. Inside, we're balls of fire, we're jumping, the adrenaline is pumping." Primed for action, they must bide their time until they are signaled to proceed. "It's like the clock stops," observed one man. "But when the warden says 'It's time,' then time flies." The rest is action and reaction, following a well-rehearsed plan.

Administrative Concerns and Chronic Uncertainty

The administrative staff members who orchestrate the execution must also ready themselves. They, too, are preoccupied and tense. War stories about prior executions are trotted out. Discussion drifts to such fundamental matters as the fleeting nature of life ("here today, gone tonight" was one anxious joke), crime and punishment (especially the prisoner's past crime and impending punishment), and the so-called criminal personality (and how the criminal in question fits this reprehensible type). As among the deathwatch officers, there is much talk among administrators about the condemned man's offense, talk that implicitly justifies the upcoming execution. At the execution for which I served as an official witness, it was noted with nervous humor that the prisoner in question had even raped his mother! As if that were not enough, his sister—and only personal visitor—was said to be afraid of him. The message was clear: The world would be a better place without him!

Let me hasten to add that this is not the stuff of standard prison shoptalk. Prison staff generally don't want to know a prisoner's offense. They believe that such knowledge may lead to prejudgments that, in turn, may interfere with their handling of the offender as an inmate. It is well known, for example, that lifers, some of whom have committed heinous offenses, are terrible citizens but model prisoners. "Take the prisoner as you find him" might be the prison guard's motto. For those under the death penalty, this motto doesn't hold. Prison personnel *want* to know the condemned prisoner's offenses in all their gross and revolting details, perhaps because they *don't* want to know the inmate—at least, not any more than is necessary to control and then execute him.

Just as the inmate doesn't know until the end whether or not he will be executed, so too the staff don't know whether or not they will be asked to do their jobs. Executions are scheduled for the end of the day, at 11 P.M., to give the prisoner a full day to prepare himself and initiate any last-minute appeals.

> They're [at] eleven o'clock at night. That gives the person a full day to make peace with God, and his lawyers and his family, and [to] use every opportunity through the legal system. If [the court is] gonna give him a stay, it has time to do that. By law, when they set the date, it has to be done that day. If you can't do it before twelve o'clock midnight, then, by law you have to start all over. It has to go back to court for a new date. So, eleven o'clock is probably about the closest time you can set that'll let all the process take place, and yet still have time to carry out the order on that particular day.

Last-minute appeals to the courts, the governor, and no doubt God as well are of course quite common. Correctional officials must make sure all legal avenues of appeal have been exhausted before they proceed with an execution. A phone line is kept open, and the status of the execution is checked one last time before the execution commences at the appointed hour.

> We want to be absolutely sure that nobody makes a mistake. I mean, it's the kinda thing you can't have mistakes. No such thing as a mistake. And so it's a fail-proof system, so that when it comes time to do it . . . we know that it's proper to do it. 'Cause I don't wanna walk out there in front of the media and tell them, "Gosh, we're sorry, ya know, the governor called at 10:59 and said 'no' but we'd already done it."

Delays at the eleventh hour keep administrators on edge and raise the chilling prospect of a premature execution. These delays also complicate the job of the deathwatch team. Uncertainty about whether an execution will take place or not makes it hard for the team to remain mentally and emotionally ready.

> If everything go when it's supposed to, then it's not too bad. But you get an on-and-off thing, like the court gettin' involved, that's rough. Like with one fella, we's executin' him and, uh, that thing drug on. It be on one hour and off the next hour. And your adrenaline builds up. You have to build up, and then you get building up and then all at once they say, "Hey, it's not goin' to be tonight; it's off." Then you got to come all the way back down. And fifteen or twenty minutes later, they say, "It's back on again." And here you got to go up, pump back up, and it's really hard on ya. Courts, lawyers, and

the governor—when they get into it, it's an unsure thing, and it's, it's pretty hard on ya.

One officer even likened the experience to torture. "You crash. Your metabolism just drops. And then when it's back on, you got about a minute and thirty seconds to get up again. And you got to be professional about it and make no screwups. . . . It's emotionally painful."

Holding Up under Pressure

The team always works under great pressure, and the prospect of making a mistake looms large as the time of execution approaches. The team operates under the gaze of correctional administrators as well as of official witnesses, the latter group including representatives of the media. Any mistake, especially one that might add to the suffering of the condemned, will be noted, embarrassing the team.

> You're tense because you don't want to make a mistake, because you've got twelve witnesses watching you do that thing. All right, say you drop the headgear. You're getting ready to put the headgear on—which is not my job, but I'm just using this as an example—and you dropped it. It would be a very embarrassing thing with people watching you and this man sitting here waiting to die. (Laughs nervously) And you drop the thing and—it's just, it's a lot of tension.

The prospect of having to use force is ever on the minds of the officers, but actually doing so is almost unthinkable. That would not be a mistake so much as a disaster. The officers' collective nightmare is a botched execution, especially one involving force. "You don't want to get in a situation where you have to fight a man to the chair," stated one officer. "I think that would leave a mental scar on you worse than anything."

From the perspective of the deathwatch team, the execution is quite public. The whole world watches through the reporting of media representatives, who find newsworthy any snags that may occur in the execution drill. (A flawed execution is national news. A more typical execution is noted by the local media.) The team leader likened the situation to that of being in combat and having to scrupulously check one's machinery to make sure that it will work under fire.

> It's a whole lot like you're going in combat, you know. You don't know whether your equipment's gonna work—you got a good idea your equipment's gonna work—99 percent—but that 1 percent it might not work, you know. And you know executions are big news; people hear all over the world—England, overseas—you know, everywhere—and naturally you want everything to go as smooth as it can. So far we haven't had any problems and everything's carried out real well, normal, but I guess you always have that fear that it won't go off right.

The troops who make up the execution team have to be attended to as well, if I may pursue the team leader's combat metaphor. As is revealed in this exchange with me, the team leader finds himself measuring, and often modulating, the mood and temper of his execution team as they prepare for their battle:

> They go up, and they come down. They get to talkin'—some of 'em will get to talkin' real fast, you know. Maybe you got a better word, but I call it climbing the ladder, you know, and I have to kinda talk 'em down, you know, get 'em settled down. And then I see 'em go down the ladder— they're way down here—and then I have to bring them up, you know, to a level. Yeah, they go through, they go through changes.
>
> *So you have to keep them at a place where they can do their jobs? And they're trying to keep the inmate at the same place, right?*
>
> Yes, uh-huh. They're trying to keep the inmate cool, right. (Laughing) So it's, it's challenging. . . . You don't know how your people gonna act during or after [the execution], so I'm not only watchin' the inmate, I'm havin' to watch my team, too. And so far we haven't had nobody [on the team] crack up, but you know it could happen, and I realize that it could happen.

The execution team has held up admirably under pressure. That is an achievement, the team leader contended, that he and the warden have come to expect but cannot simply take for granted. It is, they know, a product of discipline and commitment that must be renewed, singly and collectively, at each execution the team is called upon to perform.

Notes

1. W. Berns, *For Capital Punishment: Crime and the Morality of the Death Penalty* (New York: Basic Books, 1979), 21.
2. R. Johnson, *Condemned to Die: Life under Sentence of Death* (Prospect Heights, Ill.: Waveland Press, 1989), 90.
3. R. F. Canan, "Burning at the Wire: The Execution of John Evans," in *Facing the Death Penalty: Essays on a Cruel and Unusual Punishment,* ed. M. L. Radelet (Philadelphia: Temple University Press, 1989), 74–75.
4. Johnson (n. 2), 80–88.
5. Reverend Joseph B. Ingle, who has ministered to many condemned prisoners during their final hours, takes a similar approach. See J. B. Ingle, "Ministering to the Condemned: A Case Study," in *Facing the Death Penalty: Essays on a Cruel and Unusual Punishment,* ed. M. L. Radelet (Philadelphia: Temple University Press, 1989).
6. Johnson (n. 2), 85.
7. Cited in *The Case against Capital Punishment* (pamphlet) (Washington Research Project, 1971), 36.
8. Johnson (n. 2), 87, 81.
9. Ingle (n. 5), 115.
10. Johnson (n. 2), 89.

CHAPTER 7

An Execution and Its Aftermath

As the team and administrators prepare to commence the good fight, as they might say, another group, the official witnesses, are also preparing themselves for their role in the execution. Numbering between six and twelve for any given execution, the official witnesses are meant to be disinterested citizens in good standing drawn from a cross section of the state's population. As incarnations of Every Good and Decent Person, they are called upon to represent the community and testify to the propriety of the execution.

Witnesses must ask to be present at an execution, sending a letter or filling out a form indicating their reasons. They must also submit to a criminal-records check and then be screened by the prison's public relations officer. In reviewing, as a corollary to my larger death-work study, applicants' stated reasons for volunteering to witness an execution, I found that witnesses are neither disinterested (most strongly support the death penalty) nor representative of the community at large (many work in law enforcement). They are, however, generally quite serious about the obligation they wish to shoulder. In the main, the community is well served by its witnesses.

I reviewed the applications of thirty-five official witnesses (they were all accepted, but no reasons for acceptance were given.) Of that group, eleven stated that moral considerations underlay their desire to witness an execution. Fully eight of these persons wished to reinforce or reaffirm their belief in the justice of the death penalty and the rightness of the American criminal justice system. Two of these believers hoped to educate and deter delinquent youth with whom they came in contact in their work. (Curiously, one hoped to scare himself straight as well!) The remaining three of those concerned with moral issues sought to resolve their ambivalence about the death penalty. They wanted to see in the flesh this thing with which their consciences had wrestled, often for many years.

Another nine witnesses were motivated by concerns such as service and duty, seeing the experience as a civic obligation or as an opportunity for civic education they had missed. Seven others, police officers, saw attending an execution as an extension either of their general commitment to law enforcement or of their personal involvement with the case in question. Finally, several citizens, seven in all, were simply curious about what an execution was like. (In one man's peculiar view, an execution was a case study of democracy at work!) Only one person had a purely personal interest in serving as a witness. He had known the victims but gave no specific reason why he should attend their killer's execution.

In the main, the reasons for wanting to witness an execution were serious and proper. Some reasons, though, seemed strange and even silly. One ballroom dance instructor from a small town wanted to be a witness because she had time on her hands and relations in the area whom she hasn't visited for a spell! Such frivolous, even freakish, motives debase the execution process, but, fortunately, such considerations are in the minority.

I served as an official witness at one execution, and then as a behind-the-scenes observer at another. In the latter instance, I was more or less appended to the execution team and permitted to observe and interact with them at all times during the deathwatch. I also exchanged a few words with the prisoner. Drawing on these experiences, in addition to research interviews, I am able to bear full and, I trust, authentic witness to the psychology of death work.

The experiences and reactions of the two condemned prisoners I observed did not differ in their essentials. To ease explication, and so that I may draw more fully on my personal observations, both behind the scenes and as an official witness, I have created a composite portrait of a condemned prisoner's execution. The prisoner I have named Jones. I observed his last hours firsthand; I inferred the details of his walk to the chair, as viewed by offical witnesses, from my interviews and from my prior experience as an official witness at another execution. Thus, my personal observations, supplemented by material from my research interviews, form the substance of the following account of Jones's demise. I hasten to add that though the composite character named Jones is fictitious, the dynamics of his execution are not.

Witness to an Execution

At eight in the evening, about the time the prisoner is shaved in preparation for the execution, the witnesses were assembled. Eleven in all, we included three newspaper and two television reporters, a state trooper, two police officers, a magistrate, a businessman, and myself. We were picked up in the parking lot behind the main office of the Department of Corrections. There was nothing unusual or even memorable about any of this. Gothic touches were notable by their absence. It wasn't a dark and stormy night; no one emerged from the shadows to lead us to the prison gates.

Mundane consideration prevailed. The van sent for us was missing a few rows of seats, so there wasn't enough room for the group. Obliging prison officials volunteered their cars. Our rather ordinary cavalcade reached the prison only after getting lost. Once within the prison's walls, we were sequestered for some two hours in a bare and almost shabby administrative conference room. A public information officer was assigned to accompany us and answer our questions, but when we grilled him about the prisoner and the execution procedure the prisoner would shortly undergo, he confessed ignorance regarding the most basic points. Disgruntled at this and increasingly anxious, we made small talk and drank coffee. We didn't psych up as the execution team did, but we did tense up as the execution time approached.

At 10:40, roughly two and a half hours after we assembled and only twenty minutes before the execution was scheduled to occur, we were taken to the basement of the prison's administrative building, frisked, then led down an alley that ran along the outside of the building. We entered a neighboring cell block and were admitted to a vestibule adjoining the death chamber. Each of us signed a log, and we were then led to the witness area off to our right. To our left and around a corner, some thirty feet away, sat Jones in the condemned cell. He couldn't see us, but I'm quite certain he could hear us. It occurred to me that our arrival was a fateful reminder for the prisoner. The next group would be led by the warden, and it would be coming for him.

We entered the witness area, a room within the death chamber, and were escorted to our seats. Through the picture window filling the front wall of the witness room, we had a clear view of the electric chair, which was about twelve feet away and well illuminated. A large, high-back, solid-oak structure with imposing black straps, the chair easily dominated the death chamber. The electric chair is larger than life, a paradox that no doubt derives from its sole purpose as an instrument of death. The warden had told me, "It's the biggest chair you'll ever see," and he was right. Behind the electric chair, on the back wall, was an open panel full of coils and lights; over the chair, two domed light fixtures were strung from the ceiling. Peeling paint hung from the ceiling and walls, which were stained from persistent water leaks. (The walls have since been painted, but the leaks remain.) A stark and lonely tableau, I assure you.

Two substantial officers—one a huge, hulking figure weighing some four hundred pounds, the other not much smaller—stood beside the electric chair. The deterrent message to the approaching inmate was clear. As one of these officers put it, "You got seven hundred or so pounds waiting for you at the chair, so don't go think about bucking." Each officer had his hands crossed at the lap and wore a forbidding blank expression. The witnesses gazed at them and the chair, absorbed by the scene, scribbling notes furiously. We did this, I suppose, as much to record the experience as to distract ourselves from the growing tension.

A correctional officer entered the witness room and announced a trial run of the machinery. Seconds later, lights flashed on the control panel behind the chair, as the officer had said they would, indicating that the chair was in working order. A white curtain, open for the test, separated the chair and the witness area. After the test, the curtain was drawn, allowing the officers to prepare the cap and mask that would be placed on the prisoner once he was secured in the chair. (It was thought that observing the staff preparing these paraphernalia would needlessly upset the witnesses. The impression the team wished to leave with the witnesses, at this point at least, was that executions simply happen.) The curtain was then reopened, to be left open until the execution was over. Then it would be closed to allow the officers to discreetly remove the prisoner's body.

Several high-level correctional officials were present in the death chamber, standing just outside the witness area. There were two regional administrators, the director of the Department of Corrections, and the warden. Also present were Jones's chaplain and lawyer. Other than the chaplain's black religious garb, subdued grey pinstripes and bland correctional uniforms prevailed. All parties were quite solemn.

I knew from my research that Jones was a man with a tragic past. Grossly abused at home, he went on to become grossly abusive of others. (His crime, committed while he was on drugs, was a gruesome murder of an elderly woman.) I was told he could not describe his life, from childhood on, without talking about fighting to defend his precarious sense of self—at home, in school, on the streets, in the prison yard. Belittled by life and choking with rage, he remained hungry to be noticed, even if notoriety was all he might hope for. Paradoxically, Jones the condemned prisoner had found his moment in the spotlight—though it was a dim and unflattering light cast before a small and unappreciative audience. "He'd pose for cameras in the chair—for the attention," I'd been told earlier that day by a member of the prison's psychological treatment unit. Yet the plain truth was that Jones had to endure one more losing confrontation, this time with the state. He won't be smiling, I thought, and there will be no cameras.

Virtually no one holds up well in the face of execution, and Jones was no exception. But Jones, like many other prisoners before him, did cope for a time, with the help of the outsiders the warden described as adjuncts to his team (see Chapter 6). In Jones's case, this group included two attorneys in addition to his personal counselor. Jones thought of his attorneys as allies and friends. His counselor, who had helped a number of other condemned men face their end, was known for her matter-of-fact, cut-and-dried approach. Jones called her by her last name, mixing affection and respect. He also spoke by phone with a journalist covering his story, with whom he had become close. These sources provided an inside view of Jones's efforts to hold himself together in the face of his impending execution.

The Prisoner's Decline

The View from the Cell

Jones's decline began at the very outset of the deathwatch. In the words of his journalist friend,

> He was beyond eating. His last meal was the night before, maybe some fruit. He was nervous and didn't feel like eating. . . . He was a devout exerciser, doing hundreds of calisthenics each day. He took care of his body. He needed his exercise to feel good, to feel alive. That last day, he didn't exercise. He tried, but he couldn't do more than a few push-ups. It was as though he felt his life draining out of him even then, hours before his execution.

Jones was very much affected by the countdown to death that occurs during the deathwatch period. The various procedures, especially the testing of the chair, forcefully brought home the reality of his impending execution. In the journalist's words,

> The countdown upset him. He knew the procedure, what to expect, but the experience was very hard for him. He could hear the testing of the chair, and it made him uncomfortable. He could hear it; he could smell it. It was like "they're getting ready to kill me." It made it all real. It made him depressed, saddened.

Later, Jones was horrified by the last-meal ritual, which struck him as barbaric and cruel. "He didn't even want to talk to the man who would ask him about his last meal."

Earlier that afternoon, when his last appeal had been turned down, Jones had quite simply fallen apart. In the words of his personal counselor, who was with Jones until moments before his execution, "He panicked, cried, then went through denial, talking about a hopeless last-minute appeal." Jones pulled himself together after an hour or so but remained on the verge of tears throughout the ordeal of the deathwatch. His nervousness grew as the time of execution approached, with panic never far from the surface. As his counselor put it,

> He was revving, because he just wasn't prepared. It was like turning a record up, putting a 33 [rpm record] on a 45 [rpm] speed. His pitch went up, too. And his body language was hyper. The eyes were really panicky; that's where I could really see it. He'd put real pressure on my hand now and again, and cry.

As his counselor made plain, Jones wasn't ready to die.

> My concern is that there was a lot of business that he didn't finish with himself. . . . He was trying in the end, making a hyper attempt to understand what was going to happen after he died. He was saying all the right words about an afterlife. The chaplain said, "He's got it." And my response was, "Down pat." He had it intellectually but not in his gut. Or he wouldn't have been that panicky; he would have been calmer.

Jones's belief in an afterlife, such as it was, provided him little comfort on the threshold of death.

Jones tried to distance himself from his situation by using gallows humor. "He did a mimic of himself being executed," said one of his supporters. "It was pretty graphic." What Jones thought of all this is unclear, but it proved too much for one of his attorneys, who insisted that he stop. "He wasn't doing it in bad taste," the journalist assured me. "It was his way of trying to trivialize the situation, which he really couldn't do." After he was shaved, he told his companions that he looked like a monk. Everybody kept running their hands over his head, as if physically helping him to suppress awareness of the awful significance of his bald pate. He described himself as a "lamb prepared for slaughter." To the dismay of those around him, more and more he was coming to look the part.

Physical contact, touching, was a vital part of the help Jones's supporters gave him. Jones's journalist friend remembered one scene in particular.

> There was a moment that was really moving. He was holding two people's hands, as well as a cup of coffee; someone had a hand on his knee, and another person had a hand on his shoulder. People were petting him, saying soothing things. He had the phone on his shoulder, and he said to me, "I can't even light a cigarette!" We laughed.

For a brief and fleeting moment, Jones felt protected. It was as if he felt his allies could keep him from being taken from the cell, could physically shield him from his executioners.

Yet signs of stress, of vulnerability, present at the outset of the deathwatch, became increasingly evident as the time of execution drew near. Here was a person who claimed never to be physically cold, who could sit in a chilly basement cell with nothing but a towel around his waist, proudly sporting his "pecan tan." That night, fully dressed, he shivered visibly. "The situation took the warmth and heat away from him, no matter how much we tried to help," observed one of his companions. Here, too, was a man who scrupulously cultivated the image that he was always in control. That night, the facade gave way. "What should I do?" he asked, plaintively. His supporters had no advice or comfort to give. Said one, "He was helpless, and he knew it. We knew it, too."

Jones was, however, unwilling to see himself as a pawn in a larger impersonal process; he struggled to keep the execution personal. "He felt the entire death penalty existed to get him," said his counselor. "He felt like the courts, the legislature, the law, death row, the prison guards, the execution squad—all were concentrating on getting him personally." The counselor felt, and communicated to Jones, that in an existential sense he was right.

> It's ultimately personal because he's not dead; he has a mind and a heart and a psyche that are trying to live, even at that last moment. They [condemned prisoners] are live human beings, and life itself is stretching out of them. And the only way that you can accept dying in that way is to not let it be impersonal. That's a kind of death that is more unacceptable than going to that chair and being fried.

The problem is that the execution process is both out of the prisoner's control and, for the vast majority of them, overwhelming. The counselor acknowledged these hard facts. "The other side is that they are incredibly aware of the power controlling them. They're isolated in that death cell. In the end, they collapse from within."

Jones's last hours, even his last words, reflected his sense of helplessness and his final efforts to transcend it, to exert some personal control over his situation. Listen to the journalist's account of Jones at the end:

> We talked about his life. It was almost as though he wanted to leave what was important about him with somebody; he wanted to leave bits and pieces of himself behind. He said, "I don't want to die and be a statistic. . . ." His last minutes were frantic. It was as though he was trying to articulate more things without knowing what to say. "Take care of yourself," he told me. He wanted to make sure I had somewhere to go after [the execution]. It was important for him to tell me to take care of myself and be with others. It made him feel useful, feel better, for a moment at least. His last words to me were spoken with a sense of urgency but no real emotion: "Don't forget my voice, don't forget me. . . . Celebrate the life you have."

Jones had little time left and, by all accounts, little life left in him at this juncture, but his words speak volumes about the human condition. Life is indeed personal and must be treasured as such for as long as one can.

Jones's last words bring to mind an observation by Czeslaw Milosz, from the aptly titled book *The Captive Mind:* "Probably only those things are worthwhile which can preserve their validity in the eyes of a man threatened with instant death."[1] By this hard criterion, Jones's effort, evident in his words, to preserve a sense of self in the face of its imminent annihilation was surely worthwhile. Yet, in the final analysis, his death was not personal, and he did not go to meet it as the person he was in life. Note that he did not refer in his last words to a life that *he* had had and could celebrate during its precious remaining minutes. No, for Jones, life as he had known it was over. He wished to leave a mark, to be a part of history, but only as he once was, not as he was then, a scared, shivering, emotionally numb creature on the edge of extinction.

The Executioners' Perspective

As is generally the case, the process of Jones's decay, and ultimately his collapse, was visible to the officers on the team. They saw Jones's nerves fray and his eyes redden with tears, heard his voice made hoarse by emotion. They saw—and saw through—his moments of bravado. One such moment occurred when Jones was being shaved for execution. During this solemn and intimidating procedure, he found the presence of mind to quip with the officer, telling him, "I'll meet you in heaven—if you get there." And asking, when the shaving procedure was completed, "What do I owe you for that, buddy?" The officer smiled. Jones didn't.

Each officer remarked on Jones's sadness. On a number of occasions, they agreed, he was holding back tears. He never made eye contact with anyone on the team. At one point, while he was being shaved, a clump of hair fell into his hands. Pensively, he sifted it through his fingers, then let it fall to the floor. He looked away, seemingly lost in thought, perhaps contemplating his passing mortality. In the shower after being shaved, Jones looked out at the officers and asked, "Why is everyone so sad?" No one responded. Later, the officers commented on this, claiming they weren't sad, just solemn. "That was a professional look," said one officer, "'cause no one enjoys putting a man to death." The implication, painfully obvious to the officers, was that the sadness Jones saw on their faces was really his own. As one officer put it, Jones was "falling apart from within." I learned later from Jones's companions that the officers were right. Jones was demoralized by this procedure and never really regained his composure.

Jones's sadness grew over time, sapping his strength. After the shaving procedure, he turned to putty in the officers' hands. In one officer's words,

> His expression became more subdued; his actions weren't as crisp as they had been. He was aware, but he wasn't alert. It's like when a doctor shoots you with novocaine—you just become number and number. . . . The man came to accept it, that this is gonna happen. He just let us do what we had to do to carry out the execution.

Jones's last request, for instance, made ten minutes before the execution, was turned down. Jones asked for water and a mint. The officers, their minds perhaps on the execution and not on service, told him that these things would adversely affect the body after execution. This exchange seems almost cruel in the retelling, but the officers spoke without malice, and Jones accepted their word without protest. Jones may not have been ready to die, but surely he was ready to be executed.

Minutes later, the warden arrived with the court order calling for the prisoner's execution. Jones stood erect before the warden, but the pose was strained. The warden, also showing strain, said in a kind tone, "I take no pleasure in carrying out this duty, son." Pausing, then marshaling a more official demeanor, he paraphrased the court order, which read like this:

> It is ordered and adjudged that the judgment pronounced and set forth in this order, entered herein on [a given date], sentencing the defendant to death in the manner and by the authorities as provided by statute, shall be executed at this time.

The warden asked Jones if he had a last statement to make. Jones said he had none. (He had told one of his companions that the officials of the prison, including the team, meant nothing to him and that he would have nothing to say to them.) The door to the death cell was opened, and two officers entered, each taking one of Jones's elbows. Jones went limp. In the warden's words, "He was ready—he'd made up his mind that he was gonna go on in there and get it over with. He had already partially crossed over; he was just about gone already." Jones then "fell into the arms of the team." Guided by the officers, he proceeded down a short hallway leading to the death chamber. As he turned a corner and confronted the chair, Jones faltered once more, momentarily startled by the scene before him. At this point, still out of sight of the official witnesses, Jones was again physically supported by the officers, one of whom whispered in his ear, "Go out like a man." By some lights, he did.

The Execution

At 10:58, Jones entered the death chamber. He walked quickly and silently toward the chair, his escort of officers in tow. Three officers maintained contact with Jones at all times, offering him physical support. Two were stationed at his elbows; a third brought up the rear, holding Jones's back pockets. The officers waiting at the chair described the approaching Jones as "staring off in a trance, with no meaning in his stares. It was like he didn't want to think about it." His eyes were cast downward. His expression was glazed, but worry and apprehension were apparent in the tightly creased lines that ran across his forehead. He did not shake with nerves, nor did he crack under pressure. One could say, as did a fellow witness, "Anybody who writes anything will have to say he took it like a man." But a scared and defeated man, surely. His shaven head and haggard face added to the impression of vulnerability, even frailty.

Like some before him, Jones had threatened to stage a last stand. But that was lifetimes ago, on death row, with his fellow condemned to lean on. In the death house, alone, Jones joined the humble bunch and kept to the executioner's schedule. At the end, resistance of any kind seemed unthinkable. Like so many of those before him, Jones appeared to have given up on life before he died in the chair. His execution, like those of the men who preceded him, was largely a matter of procedure.

That procedure, set up to take life, had a life of its own. En route to the chair

Jones stumbled slightly, as if the momentum of the event had overtaken him, causing him to lose control. Were he not held secure by the three officers, he might have fallen. Were the routine to be broken in this or, indeed, any other way, the officers believe, the prisoner might faint or panic or become violent, and have to be forcibly restrained. Perhaps as a precaution, when Jones reached the chair, he did not turn on his own but rather was turned, firmly but without malice, by the officers in his escort. Once Jones was seated, again with help, the officers strapped him in.

The execution team worked with machine precision. Like a disciplined swarm, they enveloped Jones, strapping and then buckling down his forearms, elbows, ankles, waist, and chest in a matter of seconds. Once his body was secured, with the electrode connected to Jones's exposed right leg, the two officers stationed behind the chair went to work. One of them attached the cap to the man's head, then connected the cap to an electrode located above the chair. The other secured the face mask. This was buckled behind the chair, so that Jones's head, like the rest of his body, was rendered immobile.

Only one officer on the team made eye contact with Jones (as he was affixing the face mask), and he came to regret it. The others attended to their tasks with a most narrow focus. Before the mask was secured, Jones asked if the electrocution would hurt. Several of the officers mumbled "no" or simply shook their heads, neither pausing nor looking up. Each officer left the death chamber after he finished his task. One officer, by assignment, stayed behind for a moment to check the straps. He mopped Jones's brow, then touched his hand in a gesture of farewell. This personal touch in the midst of an impersonal procedure was, in the warden's opinion, an attempt to help the officer himself live with the death penalty. The warden noted that it also by implication helped the team of which he was a part. "It's out of our hands," the gesture seemed to imply. "We're only doing our job."

During the brief procession to the electric chair, Jones was attended by a chaplain from a local church, not the prison. The chaplain, upset, leaned over Jones as he was being strapped in the chair. As the execution team worked feverishly to secure Jones's body, the chaplain put his forehead against Jones's, whispering urgently. The priest might have been praying, but I had the impression he was consoling Jones, perhaps assuring him that a forgiving God awaited him in the next life. If Jones heard the chaplain, I doubt that he comprehended his message. At least, he didn't seem comforted. Rather, he looked stricken and appeared to be in shock. Perhaps the priest's urgent ministrations betrayed his doubts that Jones could hold himself together. The chaplain then withdrew at the warden's request, allowing the officers to affix the mask.

The strapped and masked figure sat before us, utterly alone, waiting to be killed. The cap and mask dominated his face. The cap was nothing more than a sponge encased in a leather shell, topped with a metal receptacle for an electrode. Fashioned in 1979 in replica of a cap dating back to the turn of the century, it appeared decrepit, presumably from sitting in brine for a number of years. It resembled a cheap, ill-fitting toupee. "It don't fit like a normal hat," said the officer responsible for securing this piece of hardware to the prisoner, in a matter-of-fact tone, "it's for a person with no hair." The mask, also created in 1979 and modeled on a turn-of-the-century original, was made entirely of leather. Somehow it, too, looked well-worn, perhaps because it was burned in places—from saliva that had spilled from the mouths of some of the executed prisoners, then been brought to a boil by the heat of the electricity coursing through the chair and its appurtenances. The mask had two parts. The bottom part covered the chin and mouth; the top, the eyes and lower forehead. Only the nose was exposed. The effect of the rigidly restrained body, together with the bizarre cap and the protruding nose, was nothing short of grotesque.

A faceless man breathed before us in a tragicomic trance, waiting for a blast of electricity that would extinguish his life. The internal dynamics of an electrocution are quite profound. As the electrician affiliated with the team made clear to anyone who would listen, in one swift and violent instant twenty-five hundred volts of electricity, at five to seven amps, shoot through the body, starting at the head, passing through the brain, then on to the heart and other internal organs, some of which explode, before the current comes to ground through the ankle. Jones presumably did not know the details, but the general picture is vividly impressed in the minds of all condemned prisoners facing death by electrocution.[2]

Endless, agonizing seconds passed. Jones's last act was to swallow, nervously, pathetically, his Adam's apple bobbing. I was struck by that simple movement then and can't forget it even now. It told me, as nothing else did, that in Jones's restrained body, behind that mask, lurked a fellow human being who, at some level, however primitive, knew or sensed himself to be moments from death.

Jones sat perfectly still for what seemed an eternity but was in fact no more than thirty seconds. Finally, the electricity hit him. His body stiffened spasmodically, though only briefly. A thin swirl of smoke trailed away from his head, then dissipated quickly. (People outside the witness room could hear crackling and burning; a faint smell of burned flesh lingered in the air, mildly nauseating some people.) The body remained taut, with the right foot raised slightly at the heel, seemingly frozen there. A brief pause, then another minute of shock. When it was over, the body was inert.

Three minutes passed while the officials let the body cool. (Immediately after the execution, I'm told, the body would be too hot to touch and would blister anyone who did.) All eyes were riveted to the chair; I felt trapped in my witness seat, at once transfixed and yet eager for release. I can't recall any clear thoughts from this time. One of the officers later volunteered that he shared this experience of staring blankly at the execution scene. Laughing nervously, he said,

> It's a long three minutes. It hits him and then you wait. The [current] goes on a couple of times. And you wait three minutes after the machine goes off; the doctor comes in and checks him. You just, you just, you just watch the whole thing. There's nothing really (pause) going through your mind.

Had Jones's mind been mercifully blank at the end? I hoped so.[3]

An officer walked up to the body, opened the shirt at chest level, then went to get the physician from an adjoining room. The physician listened for a heartbeat. Hearing none, he turned to the warden and said, "This man has expired." The warden, speaking to the director of corrections, solemnly intoned, "Mr. Director, the court order has been fulfilled." The curtain was then drawn, and the witnesses filed out.

The deathwatch team commenced its final duties. Approaching the chair, they found Jones's body frozen in an arched position, his right leg bent and rigid from the force of the electricity. The leg had received second-degree burns where the electrode touched the skin. Jones's head was facing upward, his eyes puffy and closed. This all looked quite grotesque to me, but the warden was of the opinion that Jones had died with a look of peace on his face. (The warden could speak comparatively on this matter. The inmate before Jones evidently had fared much worse. In the warden's words, "It looked like something terrible had reached in and snatched his soul right out through the mouth on his face, like his soul had been yanked from him.") Jones's inert body was lifted from the chair. This took several men, each now wearing protective rubber gloves to shield them from disease. (The officers feared AIDS, though there was no evidence Jones had had the dread disease. They speculated that germs would proliferate wildly in reaction to the heat generated by the electrocution.) The body was then placed on a gurney and wheeled into a nearby room to cool. Aptly, the room is known as the cooling room.

The team milled around the cooling room, congregating near the body. No one had specific duties at this point, and the mood was subdued. No congratulations were exchanged here, though the feeling seemed to be one of a job done well. The officers were clearly relieved to be finished. For the doctor and his assistants, however, work was just beginning. They used sandbags to flatten Jones's right leg and otherwise prepared the corpse for the morgue. Their labors took some six or seven minutes. By the time they were finished, everyone was ready to go home.

The Morning After

As the body was prepared for the morgue, the witnesses were led to the front door of the prison. On the way, we passed a number of cell blocks. We could hear the normal sounds of prison life, including the occasional catcall and lewd comment hurled at passersby. But no disturbance of any kind followed the execution. Small protests were going on outside the walls, we were told, but we could not hear them. Soon the media would be gone, and the protesters would disperse. Like the executioners, they would simply go home.

The prisoners, already home, had been indifferent to the proceedings, as they always are unless the condemned prisoner is a figure of some consequence in the convict community. Then there might be tension and maybe even a modest disturbance on a prison tier or two. But few convict luminaries are executed, and Jones was not one of them. Our escort officer offered a sad tribute to Jones: "The inmates, they didn't care about this guy."

I couldn't help thinking they weren't alone in this. The executioners went home and went about their lives. Having taken life, they savored a bit of life themselves. They showered, ate, drank, made love, slept, then took a day or two off. For some, Jones's image lingered through the night. The man who met Jones's gaze kept picturing his eyes, haunted for a time by their vacant look. The men who strapped Jones in remembered what it was like to touch him at the end. They showered as soon as they got home, to wash off the feel and smell of death. (The smell, I learned, was faint but would persist for a few days, teasing the nostrils, causing a mild, lingering feeling of nausea.)

The warden sat up into the early morning hours, mulling over the events of the evening. It was his second night of troubled sleep.

> I didn't sleep well that night. I didn't sleep well the night before either. I'd sleep a bit, then wake up. When I think about this, it washes over you, it comes in a jumbled up mess of things: The job's over, it's been accomplished, nothing went wrong. And I think we're all under this little spyglass: If something goes wrong, your ass is gonna swing. And in so many words, we've been told that. Mess up an execution, or you don't get the man dead like you should get him dead, there'll be hell to pay. So there's a lot of pressure. Then there's the nightmare of having to fight the man into the chair. This has never happened, and it probably never will, but you worry. How would I explain all that? You want everything to go along fine, but here you're taking a man's life. How deep should you get into that, to ask that everything go along fine? Like I say, it comes in a jumbled up mess of things.

The warden, like his team, felt the pressure of getting the procedure right. Like them, he worried over likely and unlikely contingencies (see Chapter 6). The team was on display, to be sure, but the warden was the responsible party. He knew it, and the strain showed. The warden also felt some ambivalence about the death penalty, which he supports intellectually but about which he has emotional reservations. That is why he cannot wholeheartedly want "everything to go along fine." Executions can, indeed, evoke "a jumbled up mess of things."

It is the warden's impression that none of the men on the team were hurt by the experience of carrying out this or any other execution. In his words,

> It affects them, even if they don't let on, but they handle it. They're a strong bunch of men. They've come to terms with their conscience; they've been able to not get lost in the right or wrong of the situation here. And the cohesion of the team is good. They're not gonna be hurt; it's not gonna leave any scars.

Several of the officers on the team seconded this view. Said one, in no uncertain terms, "Nobody has any problems from this." For the most part, these sanguine assessments are right. As dutiful agents of the law and loyal team members, the men understand and accept their roles as executioners. They "double," to borrow Robert Lifton's notion, developing a dehumanized work identity but retaining a humanized personal identity.[4] Quite simply, they carry out their jobs impersonally and go on with their personal lives as though nothing out of the ordinary had happened. They do not dwell on the right or wrong of executions, but instead concern themselves only with what is demanded of them as professionals with a job to do.

But problems would surface for some of the officers, I learned from my research, with the passage of time. One of the men had a recurring fear of being attacked by disgruntled cons seeking vengeance. When I spoke with him, there had been only rumors, but this officer remained alert and on guard: "You learn not to pay rumors no mind. You go in there and do your job and you try to have a contingency plan for what can happen out of the ordinary. You try to stick basically to what's happening now—keep control of that." Two other officers, perhaps sobered by the execution, spoke of limiting a person's tenure on the team, though the range bandied about, from five to twenty years, seemed pretty generous. One of these men estimated that he could count on putting somewhere in the neighborhood of twenty men to death over a twenty-year period, then he would step down. "Enough is enough," he said, without a trace of irony. The other man, in his fifth year on the team, felt ready to step down right then. He was the one who put the tenure cap at five years. "I think it's time for me to come off," he said somberly, though, as it turned out, he elected to stay on the team anyway.

Two officers worried about possible emotional problems in the wake of executions. One man, who assured me that he felt fine now, nevertheless harbored fears that a delayed guilt reaction might dog him in his declining years.

> Sometime I might wonder whether some day, after I retire, this here might come back and hit me in the face. Religious, like. When I'm an old man, ready to die, maybe this here will haunt me. I don't think it will, but it could. . . . I don't know how it will affect me in the future. Right now, I don't really think about it one way or the other.

As it happens, some executioners do in fact suffer delayed reactions, which may feature morbid dreams of men they have put to death.[5] I saw no value in pointing this out to the officer, however, though I did encourage him and his colleagues to seek help if they experienced difficulties.

The other officer, less fortunate, labored under the weight of substantial emotional problems. He traced his susceptibility to his role in the execcutution process: He was one of the two men who sat with the condemned at the end and then strapped him in the chair.

> What I do, people don't wanna do that—physically have to touch this man after sitting with him. We all be with him [on our shifts], but most of the team don't actually have that much contact with him. But you be the one to sit with him his last few hours of his life and you have to walk him in and you strap him in—it takes a lot. And it's only a few others on the team that actually got to do that. So they really don't get that touch, get all their senses involved; they can more or less just cut theirselves off from what's happenin'. Like they don't have a great part in it.

Interestingly, his colleague on the deathwatch, who also sits with the prisoner until the end and then must strap the prisoner in the chair, reported no problems at all. None! Never a moment's afterthought! Even in the retelling, which loses some of the force of the original, this man's words suggest a profound level of denial:

> I don't think about it, you know. The man is executed, the body is gone, and I clean the place up and close the books out, and, hey, I go home and eat me a hearty meal. I just block it out, that's it. It all blocks out until the next

time. . . . I say, "Hey, we got a job to do. We did the job. Let's go about our business, you know, go home." So that's the way I look at it, you know.

This same man could, when expedient, laugh and joke with a condemned prisoner during his last meal (see Chapter 6).

Our troubled officer was less resilient. He suffered an emotional numbness that, over time, came to affect his entire life. The cause of the problem, he explained in an extended exchange with me, was not being around death; it was taking part in a killing.

> I just cannot feel anything. And that was what bothered me. I thought that I would feel something, but I didn't feel anything. . . . When I was small, I guess about seven or eight, I used to spend time with my uncle and aunt. They ran a funeral home service, so death to me was nothing new, being around death. But the actual participation of killing a person—I hadn't experienced that. And I didn't feel anything. That was the thing that bothered me.
>
> *You know you should feel more but you don't, and that's what troubles you?*
>
> Yeah, 'cause you're supposed to feel something.
>
> *So somewhere along the line, you've shut down some faculties to get through this?*
>
> You better believe it.
>
> *Do you find this in other parts of your life? Less feeling than you would normally expect? Or is it just in this one area?*
>
> It's laying over my whole life.
>
> *So it seems to have started here and spread elsewhere?*
>
> Ever since I joined the team. Very seldom do I get upset or get upset to a point where I would feel my voice rise. I just shut everything down.

The officer fears that this emotional numbness, disquieting in itself, may portend deeper problems.

> I don't want to wake up tomorrow and recognize that my mind is gone, because I figure the stress will come later. . . . There's nothing to protect you from that. If it do come, like it's something that I'll have to deal with for the rest of my life. You never know when you might wake in the middle of the night in a cold sweat and you lost your mind.
>
> *Do you have any hints that something is going on inside you that would get worse if you kept going?*
>
> The hint is that I haven't felt anything.

This man harbors a grievance against the prison for the inadequate psychological counseling available to him. His first bone of contention is that counseling was forced on him, whether he liked it or not. He didn't, and neither did his colleagues on the team.

> When I first began, we had one administrator who tried to make us go to a counseling session afterwards, far as debriefing, psychological support.

> You'll find a lot of resentment anytime it's not voluntary; it's not going to be that much of a help. First you gotta want help and accept help before you get it. If you just gonna like force it on him, you know, it's no good; you're defeating your own purpose.

He also resents the fact that help was offered after the fact, when it was too late for him to make an informed decision about the wisdom of his involvement in executions.

> It's almost degrading for anyone to tell us to go see a psychologist after the fact. After the fact! If you want me to see one, I think you should let me see one before I do it. 'Cause if anything was gonna happen, it was gonna happen while I'm in the process of doing this. I need to be prepared to do this. I need to know if I'm able to do this. After the fact, what's done is done, and if I need help, I can ask for help or I can go get help. And if you can see that I do need help, then come ask me and then give me the opportunity to volunteer for it. But don't put it to me that, you know, "I must do this," 'cause I may feel that I'm all right. Maybe I don't want to think about it; I don't wanna even bother with it; I don't wanna think about this. I wanna go ahead on livin', you know.

Competent, voluntary mental health care offered prior to his joining the execution team might or might not have predicted or prevented this man's deadening of feelings. In any event, emotional numbness is now, for this man, a legacy of executions. That this reaction bears a striking resemblance, at least on the surface, to that of condemned prisoners during their final hours is perhaps paradoxical. For the condemned, who face a violent death, the muting of feelings, and perhaps of thoughts as well, appears to be a kind of anesthetic. To the extent that this officer's colleagues experience emotional numbness as a situation-specific corollary of their role as executioners, it may be a useful anesthetic for them as well. But for him, the result is a deep, abiding, and potentially disabling anxiety. He is, then, an unintended psychological casualty of the death penalty.

Whatever may be their personal reactions to carrying out executions, these undertakings have a way of making people contemplate the larger meaning of life and savor the privilege of living. Even our emotionally impaired officer can point to lessons about life he has learned from executions that offer hope for a better future.

> I know death is my destiny. I find that now I can accept death. I won't look for it. But if it, you know, if it happens, I'd rather die than suffer. I try to enjoy life more. I try to get the full meaning out of life. I try to learn more, as far as, not so much as just about living, but just being a person.

Other executioners, less hurt by their experience than this man, concur in these existential lessons. "Learned something about life? Yeah. Get ready. Prepare yourself." The officers laugh nervously when they say such things, but they speak with conviction.

Though people react differently to executions, some with blunted feelings, others with heightened anxiety, they have one thing in common: No one on the team was haunted by Jones's memory, nor did anyone grieve for him. "When I go home after one of these things," said one man, "I sleep like a rock." His may or may not be the sleep of the just, but one can only marvel at such a thing, and perhaps envy such a man.

A Personal Postscript

My son Patrick was born only a few days before Jones's execution. I thought a lot about both of them that night, and the tragic circles life can take as we progress from birth to death. The connection between innocent Patrick and guilty Jones, no doubt strange to some people, was an easy one for me to forge, because I see condemned prisoners as good and innocent babies grown bad, spawning tragedy in life and coming to a tragic end in death. So I, like the officers of the team, did not grieve for Jones that night. I simply did not know him well enough to be personally moved by his death. Yet I knew him as a terribly flawed human being and, through that knowledge, cared for him, and felt I could mourn the fate of all condemned prisoners before and after him. That's a sentimental view, I know, but for me, at least, it endures.

Notes

1. C. Milosz, *The Captive Mind* (New York: Random House, 1981), quoted in R. Klein, "Molding a Cry and a Song," *Commonweal,* 15 January 1988.
2. See R. Johnson, *Condemned to Die: Life under Sentence of Death* (Prospect Heights, Ill.: Waveland Press, 1989), esp. Chap. 5.
3. Some people who have had near-death experiences or who have been clinically dead for a short while have memories of their encounters with death. Their minds are not blank but instead are alive with activity.

   > There is no pain or despair, grief, or overwhelming anxiety . . . [M]ental activity at first became enhanced and accelerated, rising to a hundred-fold velocity and intensity. Then the individuals experienced feelings of calm and profound acceptance. . . . This was followed in many cases by a sudden review of the victim's entire past. Finally the person facing the threat of death often heard heavenly music and had an experience of transcendental beauty.

   See S. Grof and J. Halifax, *The Human Encounter with Death* (New York: E. P. Dutton, 1977), 132. It would seem to be just such a transcendent experience that Jones's counselor sought for him. The progressive deterioration of condemned prisoners like Jones does not suggest transcendence, however, but rather capitulation in the face of a uniquely arranged death. In this context, a blank mind, which allows the person to deny the impending violence of the execution, is perhaps the best one can hope for.
4. See R. J. Lifton, *The Nazi Doctors: Medical Killing and the Psychology of Genocide* (New York: Basic Books, 1986), esp. Part 3, and R. Johnson, "Institutions and the Promotion of Violence," in *Violent Transactions: The*

Limits of Personality, ed. A. Campbell and J. J. Gibbs (London: Basil Blackwell, 1986).

5. One retired Canadian executioner, John Robert Radclive, reported the following delayed reaction to carrying out executions:

> I used to say to condemned persons as I beckoned with my hand, "Come with me." Now at night when I lie down, I start up with a roar as victim after victim comes up before me. I can see them on the trap, waiting a second before they face their Maker. They haunt me and taunt me until I am nearly crazy with an unearthly fear. I am two hundred times a murderer, but I won't kill another man.

See *Illinois Death Penalty Coalition Newsletter,* 16 June 1986, 3. Others associated with executions, such as attending physicians, have reported traumatic after-effects as well. See A. H. Hussain and S. Tozman, "Psychiatry on Death Row," *Journal of Clinical Psychiatry* 39(3):183–88 (March 1978).

PART IV

Moral Considerations

The barbaric punishments condemned by history, "punishments which inflict torture, such as the rack, the thumbscrew, the iron boot, the stretching of limbs and the like," are, of course, "attended with acute pain and suffering." When we consider why they have been condemned, however, we realize that the pain involved is not the only reason. The true significance of these punishments is that they treat members of the human race as nonhumans, as objects to be toyed with and discarded. They are thus inconsistent with the fundamental premise of the [Eighth Amendment] Clause that even the vilest criminal remains a human being possessed of common human dignity.

Supreme Court Justice William J. Brennan

Until we stop determining that some human beings are not worthy of life itself, we will continue to warehouse those we think unworthy of really living.

Life sentence prisoner

CHAPTER 8

A Modern Instance
of Torture

Thus far I have placed the death penalty in historical perspective (Part I), then examined in detail the nature and impact of death row confinement (Part II) and the modern execution process (Part III). With regard to modern executions, I have, on the one hand, examined the pivotal function served by confinement under sentence of death in preparing prisoners to play their part in the execution drill (Part II, especially Chapter 4). On the other, I have considered the parallel socialization process through which the staff, notably the deathwatch or execution team, are prepared to play their roles in confining and executing condemned prisoners (Part III). I now return to my claim, asserted at the beginning of the book, that death row confinement and the executions that are the fruits of such confinement are a form of torture. In this chapter, I defend that claim and examine its implications for the justice of the death penalty.

Death row confinement today is a two-stage process. There is death row proper, where prisoners may spend years of close confinement, and there is the deathwatch, a period of total confinement usually ending in execution. As recently as the 1950s, all death rows were run like deathwatches. This is not the case today, since death rows have been liberalized. However, the social climate on death row remains essentially unchanged. Condemned prisoners today are still isolated, whether singly or as a group, and feel powerless and alone; they still feel vulnerable, sometimes starkly so, though executions remain for many prisoners a distant and perhaps even unlikely possibility.[1]

Once a prisoner reaches the deathwatch stage, the likelihood that he will be executed is high. At this juncture, the prisoner is warehoused for death by the very people who will be his executioners. He has experienced a long, lonely, and often debilitating wait on death row. Now, on death row or in another setting, usually designated the death house, he must endure the total and ultimately dehumanizing confinement that is the deathwatch. This is the condemned man who, in Camus's reckoning, suffers torturous confinement and dies twice under sentence of death. It is his confinement, culminating in the deathwatch and ending with his execution, that epitomizes death row confinement. This confinement-unto-death, I will argue, is a clear and complete case of torture.

Defining Torture

The term *torture* is sometimes used casually, and this has led some observers to see the word as devoid of meaning. Edward Peters was correct when he asserted that the word *torture* is often used in a purely figurative sense to describe "generalized emotion and suffering of any particularly extreme kind, from whatever cause." Professors periodically hear students refer to their exams as a form of torture; Peters gave an example of a social activist who decried poverty and its attendant frustrations as forms of torture. Given such loose usage, one might suppose that "everyone may now be accused of torturing everyone else, and therefore no one tortures anyone."[2] In a sense, then, the term has been gutted of meaning. But people readily distinguish between figurative and literal usage of words. When students (and others) are asked to give examples of torture, they do not cite final exams or general sources of unhappiness but instead describe gross acts of physical violence used to extract information simply to inspire terror. Thus, torture is typically seen as raw physical violence deployed in service of ignoble goals. This is an imperfect definition, to be sure, but not a meaningless one.

Death row confinement is surely an awful experience, but it is hard to think of it as true torture. Even during the admittedly bleak deathwatch phase, there is no violence or brutality of any kind. Yet the notion that torture must involve overt physical violence, though simple and even compellingly clear, is needlessly narrow. Drawing on its first worldwide survey of torture, published in 1973, Amnesty International offered a broader definition: "Torture is the systematic and deliberate infliction of acute pain *in any form* by one person on another, or on a third person, in order to accomplish the purpose of the former against the will of the latter"[3] (emphasis added). By this definition, the pain of torture may take any form, be it physical, psychological, or both, and may serve any purpose, including an unconscious or unrecognized purpose.

The spirit of the Amnesty definition was echoed in the United Nations Declaration against Torture, adopted unanimously in 1975. In this declaration, torture

> means any act by which severe pain or suffering, whether physical or mental, is intentionally inflicted by or at the instigation of a public official on a person for such purposes as obtaining from him or a third person information or confession, punishing him for an act he has committed, or intimidating him or other persons.[4]

The specifying of public officials is an improvement over the Amnesty definition. As Peters's historical study made clear, torture "has always had as its essence its public character"; torture has always been the prerogative, legitimate or illegitimate, of public officials or their agents.[5] The UN definition of torture falls short, however, in excluding "pain or suffering arising only from, inherent in, or incidental to lawful sanctions."[6] This is a logical fallacy. Any punishment that requires torturous conditions for its administration, or in which such conditions occur incidental to its administration, is no longer a lawful punishment. Torture must be defined independently of law. To hold otherwise is to contend that anything can be done under color of law.

The same logical fallacy, in this instance in regard to restrictive conditions of confinement, underlies the Supreme Court decision in *Bell* v. *Wolfish*. This case reads, in pertinent part, as follows:

> A court must decide whether the disability is imposed for the purpose of punishment or whether it is but an incident of some other legitimate governmental purpose. . . . Absent a showing of an expressed intent to punish on the part of [correctional] officials, that determination generally will turn on "whether an alternative purpose to which [the restriction] may rationally be connected is assignable for it, and whether it appears excessive in relation to the alternative purpose assigned [to it]" [citations omitted]. . . . Ensuring security and order at the institution is a permissible nonpunitive objective, whether the facility houses pretrial detainees, convicted inmates, or both.[7]

The holding in *Wolfish* would seem to indicate that death row confinement, whether or not it meets independent criteria defining torture, may nevertheless be considered a reasonable restriction if it is imposed without expressly punitive intent.

Yet inmates do in fact experience the objectively harsh conditions of death row confinement as punishment, as the following observations by death row prisoners indicate:

- You know, they are hurting me over here waiting on death. That's the hurting part. Waiting on death. The real cruel and mean things what they done in here is keep you locked up waiting on death. Waiting on death. Every day go around, it come in your mind: "When all of this going to be over with?" That's how they really punish you. They know how they punishing you, they know how they hurting you. But just by putting that needle in or putting you in the electric chair or whatever, they not hurting you that way. If they do come, I'll probably be glad they fixing me up because I won't have to suffer days in that cell.[8]

- If they were to come to my cell and tell me I was going to be executed tomorrow, I would feel relieved, in a way. The waiting would be over. I would know what to expect. To me, the dying part is easy; it's the waiting and not knowing that's hard. . . . I have reached the point where I no longer really care. . . . They're killing me a little bit each day.[9]

In a perverse way, some condemned prisoners come to hunger for execution as an escape from the death-in-life they suffer on death row. When told of his last-minute commutation of sentence, Isodore Zimmerman responded with disbelief and then with despair.

> I didn't believe it. What was more, I didn't care. For nine long months I'd been rehearsing my death, dying a little every day, dying a little more every night, while just up the hall from my cell they were killing men, thirteen of them. I knew my role as victim too well, knew it by heart, couldn't back down now. "I don't want clemency," I heard myself saying.[10]

Others "volunteer" for execution, dropping their appeals. Escape from death row is often a salient motive.[11]

That death row confinement is not in itself punishment, as implied in the *Wolfish* holding, is psychologically inconceivable, even if one can distinguish legalistically between intended and unintended suffering. (It is also legally suspect, at least according to holdings of the state supreme courts of California and Massachusetts.[12]) Even if the restrictions of *Wolfish* are accepted, death row confinement can be shown to be "excessive in relation to the alternative purpose assigned [to it]," because condemned prisoners can be confined more humanely than is now the case. That such reforms would make executions more difficult to carry out is existentially significant but legally irrelevant. No one ever promised that lawful executions would be easy.

If we put aside the question of whether or not torture can serve legal ends, the Amnesty and UN definitions of torture are useful as a starting point. They are unsatisfactory by themselves, however, because both hinge on the ambiguous notion of severity of pain and suffering. Punishment is, by definition, the intentional infliction of pain and suffering, and a serious crime, not to mention a heinous one, would seem as a matter of simple justice to warrant a severe punishment. Does this mean that we torture all serious offenders in the name of justice? More to the point, does this mean that we may inflict any pain we want on serious offenders and never cross the threshold of torture?

Distinguishing Torture from Punishment

We must distinguish torture from legitimate punishments that involve severe pain and suffering as well as from illegitimate punishments of great severity that do not constitute torture. Examples of the latter include isolated instances of guard brutality. A guard who beats up a prisoner inflicts severe pain and suffering, but this illegitimate violence is not, by itself, an instance of torture. For torture to have occurred, there must be a *pattern* of severely abusive treatment that is *deliberate* in that it is formally or informally sanctioned by persons in authority. In the words of the UN Declaration against Torture, there must be a series of encounters marked by "an aggravated and deliberate form of cruel, inhuman or degrading treatment or punishment."[13] Thus, regular, sanctioned campaigns of guard violence might well constitute torture.

Distinguishing torture from severe but lawful punishments is more difficult, since such punishments are systematically and deliberately administered and are meant to inflict severe pain. To make this distinction, a more refined definition of torture is needed. I will arrive at this definition inductively, analyzing acts presently thought to constitute torture that can be *intuitively* excluded from the category of severe but legitimate punishments (like lengthy prison sentences, which have never been classified by Amnesty or the UN as a form of torture) and *logically* distinguished from severe and illegitimate punishments short of torture (like sporadic guard violence, as mentioned above). My goal is to determine the underlying commonalities of the various forms of torture, and hence to identify the nature or essence of torture per se. I will then attempt to show that death row confinement, unlike regular confinement, is indeed an instance of torture.

What practices, then, qualify as torture, and what do they have in common? The Amnesty and UN definitions of torture encompass the ferocious physical violence of beatings and mutilations used systematically to inspire terror, as well as the suffering administered using thumbscrews and racks to facilitate interrogations. The catalog of gross physical abuses reported by Amnesty in its various reports on torture is chilling, both because of the cruelty of the methods and because of the routine and even cold-blooded way in which they are employed.

The Amnesty and UN definitions also encompass more subtle psychological forms of torture. Included, for instance, is the insidious psychological violence of brainwashing, a widely recognized form of torture in which various forms of psychological deprivation are used to inflict pain and suffering. Also included is ritual degradation, a less well-known form of psychological torture. Used on women by Spanish interrogators, ritual degradation has been described as pure psychological torture. Victims interviewed by an Amnesty International mission "told of sexual threats, including sterilization, of being made to walk naked in the police station, of being manhandled in front of male friends . . . and of insults that are (above all within the mores of Spanish society) so degrading as to be a form of psychological torture."[14] In this context, overt physical violence is superfluous. The psychological assault on the person is devastating, producing pain and suffering on an order normally associated with physical torture and never countenanced in law.

Cases of purely physical torture, moreover, are rare. In practice, physical and psychological abuse are often combined. Brainwashing, perhaps the twentieth-century version of the rack, is in many ways the paradigm of modern torture. I shall therefore use it as a case in point.

Brainwashing occurs in the context of a psychologically torturous regime of confinement, often accompanied by physical violence. Yet physical violence is not integral to brainwashing or to torture in general. Instead, as we have learned from Amnesty International, "gross acts of torture (such as electric shock, rape or tearing out fingernails) are situated within a coercive context of which such methods are *merely an extension*"[15] (emphasis added). The *method* of torture is often physical, in other words, but the *process* and the ultimate *goal* of torture are psychological. This is apparent from an analysis of the confinement conditions associated with brainwashing and, in less organized form, virtually all types of torture.[16]

The dominant features of the confinement regime associated with brainwashing are as follows:

1. *Total control:* "The prisoner's entire existence, down to the most intimate needs, is governed by strictly enforced rules that cover both waking and sleeping hours. The objectives are to keep the subject under constant psychological harassment and to drive home the lesson that his jailers are omnipotent and he is powerless." Where physical torture is used, it is an extreme and painful exercise of total control of the prisoner by his keepers.

2. *Isolation:* The person is "completely cut off from the outside world and receives only such information about his family and friends as his custodians see fit to give him." Persons may be isolated as a group, rather than singly, with individuals allowed varying degrees of interaction within their isolated world.

3. *Personal humiliation:* The prisoner is "deprived . . . of any previous claim to personal dignity or status."

4. *Uncertainty:* The prisoner's fate is uncertain. What abuses await him? Will he live or die? The prisoner is made to feel anxious and afraid.

5. *Physical debilitation and exhaustion:* The confinement regime is spartan, resulting in "loss of weight, strength, and stamina. Eventually the subject is so weakened that prolonged mental effort becomes increasingly difficult, if not impossible."[17]

Exposure to such conditions produces a syndrome marked by "dependency, debility, and dread," which culminates in dehumanization.[18] The goal of this confinement regime, and indeed of all forms of torture, whether explicit or not, is to "destroy the victim's personality, to break him down."[19] To "break" a person means, quite simply, "to destroy his humanity"[20]—that is, to literally dehumanize him, often completely. Once reduced to the status of something subhuman—an animal writhing in pain or an insensate object—the victim of torture is then used to further the torturer's ends. Under no lawful punishment can offenders be treated in this way, a point I shall return to later. Hence it is the literal dehumanization of individuals that distinguishes torture from punishment.

Death Row as Torturous Confinement

The death row regime, particularly during the crucial deathwatch period, incorporates many of the standard elements of torturous confinement. It features total control of basic life activities, isolation of condemned prisoners either singly or as a group, uncertainty about one's fate, and indifference and sometimes abuse at the hands of the guards—all in the context of impoverished physical conditions. To be sure, the overall conditions of confinement on death row are less oppressive than the standard regime of confinement associated with brainwashing. In particular, though the control on death row is total, especially during the deathwatch, it is less intrusive than in brainwashing. Thus, harassment is standard fare during brainwashing, but is never a matter of policy on death row. Still, the psychological impact of death row confinement parallels that of brainwashing and other forms of psychological torture. Both death row prisoners and brainwashing victims are powerless, vulnerable, and alone. Both groups, moreover, share a common psychological fate: literal and often extensive dehumanization.

There is a basic difference between confinement during brainwashing and confinement on death row, and this difference accounts for a difference in emphasis in the two regimes and in the psychological reactions they produce. In brainwashing, psychological suffering is *systematically* inflicted and exploited to produce a result (such as a political confession). On death row, the suffering stems primarily from abandonment and neglect, and is not inflicted *expressly* because its effects are useful. Nevertheless, this suffering is known to exist, and is exploited because its effects are useful. The execution team recognizes the dehumanization process, watches it unfold, and knowingly benefits from it (see Chapters 6 and 7). For example, though condemned prisoners are not shaved prior to execution to take their identities, loss of identity is the known result of that procedure, and nothing is done to counteract that useful effect. Likewise, prisoners are not placed in a barren death cell to further erode their capacity to resist, but this is the known effect of that procedure, and the procedure continues to be followed.

The execution team has inherited much of the routine by which it operates. The various procedures, distantly rooted in security or convenience, are perpetuated for the same reasons—security or convenience. The warden noted, for instance, that "it's not necessary to completely shave that head; all you need is a bald spot on the top." But it is easier to shave the entire head, in the manner of earlier executions. The warden similarly sees no purpose in moving the prisoner to the barren death cell after he has been shaved and showered.

> Why do we do that? You're taking him out of the cell that has been his home. You're putting him through two stages. And you're putting him in a stark, cold, tomblike cell. And every time you go for him, to read him the court order, he's standing at the bars in this desolate, ungodly place. That how it appears to me. Why not let him out of his [regular] cell and let him have a seat? You've got the team all around him. Then I can go in and pull my chair up and say, "I got to read this here to you. . . ." There's not even a decent place to sit down in the death cell.

This procedure is maintained because it works. As one officer made clear, the death cell, being empty of any possessions, is perfectly secure. It is also a "straight shot" from there to the execution chamber, which further simplifies matters. Change, in any case, is seen as risky. "I don't dare change anything," observed the warden. "It works the way it is. I don't want to do anything that would upset things." If people's identities go with their hair, or if their will is suffocated in a conveniently accessible storage cell that is also a tomb, those are unintended but accepted corollaries of conducting the business of death work as it has always been done.[21]

We have seen that brainwashing, in contrast, involves active, intentional, systematic abuse of subjects to establish control. Abuse is often artfully mixed with leniency, which cultivates dependency and hence enhances control of the prisoner. This process is a calculated invasion, and ultimately a usurpation, of the victim's personality. As Robert Lifton has noted, "penetration by the psychological forces of the environment into the inner emotions of the individual person is perhaps the outstanding psychiatric fact of thought reform," or brainwashing. The hallmark of this procedure is manipulation marked, on the one hand, by "the fluctuation between assault and leniency," and, on the other, by "the requirements of confession and reeducation." It is Lifton's view that "the physical and emotional assaults" characteristic of this manipulation "bring about the symbolic death; leniency and the developing confession are the bridge between death and rebirth; the reeducation process, along with the final confession, create the rebirth experience." The person subjected to brainwashing feels helpless, vulnerable, and alone; he "dies to the world," in Lifton's fine phrase, and then is reborn in his captor's image.[22]

In brainwashing, control of even the smallest details of life is sought. Such control produces a profound dependency. This dependency, in conjunction with debility and fear, makes the person easier to manipulate in a systematic and sometimes elaborate way. In contrast, control and dependency on this order are avoided on death row. They would foster unwanted and, indeed, counterproductive relationships, relationships that would complicate rather than facilitate executions, which require nothing more from the prisoner than simple, passive compliance with the execution drill. But aside from this difference in the degree of control exercised by their agents, brainwashing and death row share essentially the same basic confinement conditions, with essentially the same impact. Both dehumanize and both qualify as instances of torture.

Dehumanization

Since this argument hinges on the notion of dehumanization, let me detour briefly to define this term. Like *torture*, the term *dehumanization* has been used loosely, but I have something quite specific in mind when I invoke the concept.

Dehumanization as I use the term is not solely or even primarily a symbolic experience, as when one feels "dehumanized" because one has been treated in an impersonal or insulting or even demeaning manner. Rather, dehumanization entails the loss—in whole or in part, situationally or generally—of one's humanity. A dehumanized individual is in some sense dead as a person, either with respect to a segment of his behavior (such as his job) or more generally, such that his existence is more that of an object or automaton than that of a rational, sentient human being. Executioners and the condemned each suffer dehumanization, though of different types.

Human Nature Defined

To explore the ways in which humanity can be lost, one must specify what it means to be a person or human being. My claim, building on the work of my colleague Jeffrey Reiman, is that the essence of personhood or humanity is a sense of self that conveys the capacity and moral right to make choices and hence be self-determining.[23] Self-determination, in turn, both finds expression in and presupposes—that is, requires—some degree of (1) autonomy, defined as the capacity to influence one's environment and hence shape one's fate: (2) security, defined as the capacity to find or create stability in one's world and hence shelter oneself from harm; and (3) relatedness to others, defined as the capacity to feel for oneself and others and hence to have caring and constructive relationships. I shall examine each of these dimensions of self-determination to show how a sense of self both shapes and in turn is shaped by all three.

Scholars have variously seen each of the three dimensions of self-determination—autonomy, security, and relatedness to others—as the cornerstone of personhood. Autonomy, rooted in the use of reason, has been said to mark us as responsible moral beings rather than merely advanced or precocious animals. Accordingly, such classical philosophers as Socrates, as well as, more recently, Ernst Cassirer and Herbert Morris, have identified the capacity to reason and hence to be responsible for ourselves as the *sine qua non* of personhood.[24] In contrast, Abraham Maslow and others have seen security as the essential psychological precondition to the unfolding of human nature, observing that without stability and safety in one's world, self-determination would give way to determination by external forces.[25] Finally, John Dewey and others have seen relatedness to others—

to things outside ourselves and, more specifically, to other people—as basic to our nature as social animals that exercise self-determination through self-defining trans-actions with the world.[26] In addition, anthropologists and sociologists have demon-strated that each of these dimensions is central to human nature.[27] My point is not merely that each attribute is relevant to an understanding of human nature. Rather, I wish to argue that, *taken together,* they represent that which is distinctively human in the social and moral sense of the term.

To be self-determining, individuals must influence their environment, both the inner—their personal thoughts and feelings—and the outer—their interactions with others. This both presupposes and produces stability and hence safety, and es-tablishes relationships with others in the social world. Autonomy, security, and relatedness to others thus develop in interaction with one another as individuals become persons. In Lewis Mumford's words,

> Each individual makes over the life-course of the species and achieves a character and becomes a person. The more fully he organizes his environ-ment [autonomy], the more skillfully he associates in groups [security], the more constantly he draws on his social heritage [relatedness], the more does the person emerge from society as its fulfillment and perfection.

The process of becoming a person is never fully finished, Mumford asserted, as "man's nature is a self-surpassing and a self-transcending one."[28] We are emergent persons, in Mumford's reckoning, and this dynamism is central to our nature.

The distinctive dynamism of human nature derives from the ongoing interaction among the three dimensions of self-determination. Autonomy, security, and relatedness are interconnected at birth: Helpless human infants can only gain control over their world, and be secure in it, through their relationships with their parents.[29] The continuing interrelatedness of these dimensions has been inversely confirmed by Hans Toch. Toch studied human breakdowns in confinement, looking at the experiences of hundreds of inmates in more than a dozen jails and prisons. He found that the absence of these dimensions—that is, impotence instead of autonomy, fear instead of security, and isolation instead of relatedness—interacted with one another so as to provoke "existential questions" that influenced "crises of every kind in every setting" and ultimately represented "universal motives" associated with hu-man despair.[30] My own work with cotton mill workers suffering from terminal cases of brown lung extended Toch's analysis, uncovering the interplay of the same existential concerns among persons undergoing life-threatening crises.[31] Con-demned prisoners, as well as victims of recognized forms of torture, also share these concerns. If no man is an island unto himself, neither is he merely autonomous or secure.

Persons of every known culture develop, in one form or another, a sense of self and self-determination. And though the potential is present at birth, these attributes are not birthrights. A sense of self and self-determination do not emerge auto-matically from the simple fact of our existence. Instead, as Reiman makes clear, the development of a sense of self and self-determination require the social institution of privacy.[32]

Privacy is honored in all cultures—is, indeed, a social and psychological universal.[33] As Barry Schwartz has noted, "some provision for removing oneself from interaction and observation must be built into every establishment." More-over, each stage of personal development "has its own mode of privacy, which may be defined in terms of the ego's relationship to those from whom privacy is sought and the manner in which withdrawal is accomplished." It was first noted by Simmel that "human associations require a definite ratio of secrecy which merely changes its objects."[34]

Privacy confers and confirms selfhood and permits individual selves to become persons—that is, to negotiate their lives with some degree of autonomy, security, and relatedness to others. In effect, privacy constitutes a "social skin" that at once preserves the integrity of the individual as distinct from the external world and allows the individual to modulate his inner thoughts and feelings as well as his contacts with the outer world. An existential dialectic is at work here, featuring the interplay of privacy and society, self and person.[35]

Human Nature Defiled

As we have seen, to be a person is to have a sense of self and self-determination that set one apart from the rest of the world and relate one to that world at least partly on one's own terms. One develops and maintains these attributes through the social institution of privacy. Under this definition of personhood, dehumanization occurs in the absence of privacy and involves the loss of one's sense of self; one's capacity to make choices affecting either one's fate, one's security, or one's relationships with others; or all of these attributes. Partially dehumanized persons have lost some aspect of their personhood; for example, the capacity to make decisions that affect their (internal or external) environment or their relationships to other people. Fully dehumanized persons have lost all aspects of their personhood, becoming, for all intents and purposes, physical objects or automatons.

Just as dehumanization varies in degree, it varies also in scope, in its nature, and in the role played by individual choice or volition. Dehumanization may be situational in scope, affecting only a limited segment of one's life, or general, affecting all or most facets of one's life. It may be symbolic in nature, limited to perceptual distortions of one's humanity, or literal, involving the actual suspension or loss of one's personhood. Finally, dehumanization may also involve an element of collusion under pressure, a conscious or unconscious relinquishing of one's humanity "to get by" or "to get the job done."

Now it is immediately obvious that punishment infringes on the personhood of the punished. Conviction and imprisonment, for example, necessarily reduce the prisoner's privacy. In the setting of prison, most of one's life falls under the ambit, if not the control, of a formal authority. Furthermore, the right to violate someone else's privacy and yet to remain inviolate oneself is integral to authority. But even prison authorities may violate a prisoner's privacy only with valid reason (primarily to maintain security) and with discretion (to minimize suffering)[36]. Prisoners, though they have only a very limited legal right to privacy, are protected against "maliciously motivated searches"; moreover, intrusions of privacy that constitute "intentional harassment" are not to be "tolerated by a civilized society".[37] Still, imprisonment and the violations of privacy inherent in confinement threaten each prisoner's familiar sense of self and limit his capacity to make meaningful choices. (Guards, too, are imprisoned, as Lucien Lombardo has recently made clear,[38] insofar as they perform public roles that are narrowly defined by the prison organization and further limited by the conditions of imprisonment.)

The limitations on privacy in prison are quite real and substantial, but they lend themselves to overstatement. For example, it is simply untrue that

> the prison is, almost by definition, a place where the resident has lost his privacy, and his identity, and has become a number. . . . Every day in every way, the prison reinforces the inmate's image of himself as that of something less than a human.[39]

In point of fact, neither inmates nor guards typically lose or relinquish their humanity in the context of regular confinement; they do not normally become faceless, stereotypical "cons" and "hacks." Regular prisoners generally have sufficient mobility, resources, and companionship to develop a familiar round of life and, in effect, carve out a niche for themselves within the prison.

It has long been known, for example, that prisons and mental hospitals, the typical total institutions discussed by Erving Goffman and other social scientists, offer sanctuaries to their inhabitants, places where the inmate may "be his own man."[40] From an existential perspective, these niches provide privacy; they shield individuals from the particular pressures of prison life they find most noxious and allow them to live in ways that at least partially satisfy their personal preferences and needs.[41] By the same token, guards attempt to establish what might be termed "work niches" in which they can interact with inmates, exercise authority, and define goals in a way that is distinctively their own.[42] Prisons' inhabitants do periodically think and act collectively, the collective violence of riots being a tragic, though comparatively rare, case in point.[43] But the norm is for inmates and guards to live and work as individuals, not as role types—which is to say, as persons, not as dehumanized entities.

All this changes on death row, in particular during the deathwatch. Roles are sharply circumscribed. The daily work of death row guards makes them susceptible to situation-specific, symbolic dehumanization. They are cast in the anonymous role of agents of violence, for violence is inherent in their job. They are by definition agents not only of custody, which implies forceful restraint, but also of execution, which entails killing.

The role that death row guards play is necessarily marked by a substantial loss of individuality and choice. Their private feelings and sentiments—their very identities as individual officers, let alone as individual persons—are largely irrelevant. Others respond to them primarily, if not exclusively, in terms of their public roles. Autonomous, trusting relationships with prisoners are virtually precluded. Even superficially amicable relations with inmates are hard to establish. Still, even though prisoners complain about uncaring officers, some officers clearly do construe their role to include caring (see Chapter 4). The prisoners, however, usually cannot see beyond the guards' public role.

Role boundaries are pronounced during the deathwatch. The psychology of working the deathwatch is such that guards will actively embrace their role as agents of violence—will merge with and become what the job calls for—because this role is the one most readily offered them. During the execution process itself, of course, this is literally the only role available to them (see Part III).

Condemned prisoners, like their guards, are offered a dehumanized role, that of a subhuman creature, a thing that is an appropriate object of violence. This dehumanized identity is, at first, situation-specific and symbolic, involving prisoners' perceptions of their identity relative to the context of death row. As is true for the guards, such critical events on death row as execution rehearsals and, of course, actual executions of other prisoners, presumably intensify the prisoners' perception's of their dehumanization. Gradually, each prisoner's identity becomes more generally and literally dehumanized. The prisoners come in reality to resemble the dehumanized creatures they are thought to be by their keepers and the larger society that has consigned them to the death chamber. On death row, Charles Cooley's famous dictum that "the imaginations which people have of one another are the solid facts of society" is given full play.[44]

Death row confinement features all the standard "mortifications, debasements, and profanations of self" identified by Goffman as potential sources of situation-specific and symbolic dehumanization among inmates of such total institutions as mental hospitals and prisons.[45] It entails, moreover, a profound loss of privacy. On death row proper, privacy is greatly reduced; during the deathwatch, surveillance is constant. The result is a daily round of life that negates any sense of self separate and apart from the environment. Prisoners become, in effect, mere extensions of the environment, items in the schedule, objects of custody. Those controlling the environment thus have achieved the distinctive psychological "penetration" that is at the heart of brainwashing and other forms of psychological torture.

Now, some events in the lives of the condemned, like visits with loved ones, do take place away from death row proper. Within these contexts, the condemned prisoners can resume a normal identity, such as that of husband, father, son, or friend. The difficulty in maintaining a normal individual identity, however, is that the inmate's "situation" on death row is quite pervasive, affecting nearly all aspects of his existence. As relationships with loved ones and others in the free world wane, and they typically do, the prisoner's entire world shrinks to fit the world of death row. This world, as we have noted, has a markedly barren underlife (see Part II). Existence there is public and exposed, and hence one's identity as a condemned man necessarily dominates.

As time passes and the prisoners' execution dates approach, the death row world and their identity as condemned prisoners naturally take on increasing weight. Supportive relations with counselors and other "outsiders" during the deathwatch may blunt this process, as we saw in Chapter 6, but ultimately, when he takes his last walk, the prisoner is alone, in a psychological void. At this juncture, it is essentially if not solely in terms of his dehumanized prisoner role that he is defined by others and, it would seem from the accounts of those on the scene, by himself as well. If he knows anything at this juncture, he knows in his gut that "the death sentence is the ultimate rejection a society can impose," that there is "no other status . . . so demeaning and damaging as that of being formally condemned as unfit to live."[46]

The objective conditions of death row confinement reinforce the subjective identity of the condemned as a dehumanized entity. The condemned prisoners' actions are constrained by their dehumanized role. They spend virtually all their time in an environment that is, in fact, arranged to store them like objects and that limits their behavior accordingly. As a result, their very capacity to maintain an independent sense of self and to exercise self-determination is undermined. The prisoners' subjective identity, treated as the reality in the death row setting, is thus apt to become the objective reality over time. Persons perceived and treated as objects become, in part if not in whole, exactly that.

Condemned prisoners thus typically suffer a more extensive and insidious form of dehumanization than their guards, literally losing their human attributes. The prisoners' dehumanization is a direct result of the guards'. For, whether intentionally or not, guards adopt a dehumanized view of themselves and the prisoners as an ego defense. This, in turn, enables them to participate in a confinement regime that defines and treats inmates as objects and eventually reduces them to objects. Object–object relations prevail during the deathwatch, and culminate in bureaucratically administered executions.

The link between the guards' dehumanization and the death work they perform is fairly straightforward. One can see how normal persons would adopt a dehumanized and dehumanizing view of the prisoners and of themselves, within the death row setting, given the social forces at work on the row, especially during the deathwatch and execution procedure. To do so would not seem to require any special sort of personal background or disposition; to do otherwise would be to expose oneself to great emotional pain and suffering. Organizations engaged in the business of violence must recruit and socialize their personnel to be dutiful agents of violence. In extreme cases, institutional arrangements foster in the staff the development of personality types that allow guilt-free violence on the job. Almost any person can be trained to kill following a socialization process that emphasizes dehumanization of self and others. There is, sad to say, nothing inherently remarkable about this process or the people that are affected by it.[47]

The claim that prisoners suffer literal dehumanization as a direct result of their confinement under sentence of death is subject to question. Were not the prisoners dehumanized to begin with, as a result of their impoverished lives? To be sure, prisoners, particularly condemned prisoners, do not arrive at the penitentiary gates in the full bloom of their personhood. Condemned prisoners typically have prior records, and virtually all of them are products of bleak, brutal lives.[48] (There is evidence, in addition, that neurological and psychiatric impairments may be quite prevalent among this group.)[49] Yet, though many condemned prisoners are impaired or damaged human beings prior to their death row confinement, they are persons nonetheless. They generally have a fragile but sharply defined sense of self. Manipulation and violence, regrettably, are avenues to autonomy and security; both activities, and particularly violence, keep a dangerous and rejecting world at bay and allay doubts about one's potency and worth. These men hunger for relatedness to others, even as their abusive behavior precludes the stable ties on which loving and rewarding relationships are built.

Chronically violent men cope with life in immature and ultimately destructive ways, but they remain human beings, not dehumanized animals or monsters.[50] Sentenced to prison, they adapt to stress much as they did on the outside—by violence, bluster, and bluff; by strategic retreat and calculated relationships; above all, perhaps, by manipulation and deception. Under a death sentence, and particularly during the deathwatch, these tactics break down. Confined, vulnerable, alone, they are unable to muster the behavior that preserved self and self-determination in the free world and in the prison. As a result, dehumanization, the literal dying of the person that is the hallmark of torture, is a fact of life on death row.

The Benefits of Torture

Most familiar forms of torture are intentional, a fact recognized in the definitions of torture set forth earlier in this chapter, but torture need not be restricted to conscious, systematic, and purposeful brutality. That the brainwashing regime is carefully and elaborately calculated to make the victim do the bidding of his keepers while the death row regime serves no such explicitly understood purpose is irrelevant to whether or not the subjects of either regime experience torture. Standard instances of torture and death row confinement have in common an assault on defenseless persons that (1) causes them intense suffering through the imposition of a regimen of total control, whether this control is achieved through physical force, psychological coercion, or both; (2) violates their integrity as human beings by treating them as if they were mere animals or objects, and thus (3) damages or destroys the victims' humanity. Moreover, as with other forms of torture, death row confinement serves the ends of the torturer, even if unconsciously or unintentionally. For it cannot be denied that the dehumanized prisoner who goes passively to his death is easier to execute than the prisoner who, alive to his own feelings and hurts, struggles for freedom or, worse, protests his innocence or pleads for mercy.

If one is tempted to doubt the proposition that dehumanized and hence passive prisoners are comparatively easy to execute, one need only envision executions in which the prisoner behaves like a full human being—most likely, one in the throes of fear and despair. Surely such a prisoner would resist, maybe even panic and become violent. The execution team members I studied were alert to such a possibility. Indeed, their worst fear, one shared by the warden, was having to use force to get a man into the chair (see Chapter 7). That fear is well founded. Executions marred by such violence, though rare, are nightmares.

A case in point was the execution of one Leanderess Riley. Described as a "33-year-old, one-eyed, nearly deaf man" who weighed in for his execution at just over eighty pounds, he went kicking and screaming to his death in San Quentin's gas chamber.

> The next morning, a Friday, I went into the Holding Cell area about eight-thirty. The guard said Leanderess had slept for only fifteen minutes, around six o'clock. I offered to read from the Bible; he appeared to listen. I read from the Psalms, and parts of two hymns: "Rock of Ages" and "Abide

with Me." Leanderess held up his hands, palms out, in a gesture for me to stop. He had not paid any noticeable attention at any time and had continued pacing around his tiny cell.

He still had about an hour to live. I sat down outside his cell door. The guards talked about retirement, and whether the golf course would be too wet the next morning. At nine-fifty, Associate Warden Rigg and the doctors came in. I told Leanderess to say a prayer to himself, if he did not care to have me pray, and to relax in God's care. He did not seem to hear me. When the doctors started to approach his cell, he made a throaty, guttural growling sound. Frantically, at random, he picked up some of the old legal papers on his table and began passing them through the bars to the associate warden, as if they were appeals or writs. A guard unlocked his cell. He gripped the bars with both hands and began a long, shrieking cry. It was a bone-chilling wordless cry. The guards grabbed him, wrestled him violently away from the bars. The old shirt and trousers were stripped off. His flailing arms and legs were forced into the new white shirt and fresh blue denims. The guards needed all their strength to hold him while the doctor taped the end of the stethoscope in place.

The deep-throated cry, alternately moaning and shrieking, continued. Leanderess had to be carried to the gas chamber, fighting, writhing all the way. As the witnesses watched in horror, the guards stuffed him into the chair. One guard threw his weight against the struggling little Negro while the other jerked the straps tight. They backed out, slammed the door on him.

Leanderess didn't stop screaming or struggling. Associate Warden Rigg was about to signal for the dropping of the gas pellets when we all saw Riley's small hands break free from the straps. He pulled at the other buckles, was about to free himself. The Associate Warden withheld his signal. San Quentin had never executed a man ranging wildly around the gas chamber. He ordered the guards to go in again and restrap the frenzied man. One of the guards said later he had to pinch the straps down so tightly the second time that he "was ashamed of himself."

Again the door was closed. Again Leanderess managed to free his small, thin-wristed right hand from the straps. Rigg gave the order to drop the pellets. Working furiously, Leanderess freed his left hand. The chest strap came off next. Still shrieking and moaning, he was working on the waist strap when the gas hit him. He put both hands over his face to hold it away. Then his hands fell, his head arched back. His eyes remained open. His heartbeat continued to register for two minutes, but his shrieking stopped and his head slowly drooped.[51]

The anxiety and guilt that that spectacle must have aroused in the executioners is not hard to imagine. A deathwatch officer termed Riley's demise "the nastiest execution we ever had." The warden, noted for his tough, pro–death penalty stance, elaborated. "The fact that the fellow is crying and baying like a dog . . . you just can't deal with it at that point. You've got to carry out the job at hand. . . . You feel sympathy for him, but you have to put those feelings aside."[52]

Executions of prisoners who meet their fate with resignation are, in comparison, almost easy. It is the dehumanized and hence compliant prisoner of whom observers like Camus and others speak when they state that "the rule is for the condemned to walk toward death passively, in a sort of dreary despondency," so that his death—and our execution—conforms to the etiquette of a dignified official killing.[53] Significantly, the same etiquette applies in other situations of torturous confinement and execution. Discussing the systematic dehumanization of concentration camp inmates, Terrence Des Pres observed:

> This made it easier for the SS to do their job. It made mass murder less terrible to the murderers. . . . Inhibited by pity and guilt, the act of murder becomes harder to perform and results in greater psychic damage to the killer himself. If, on the other hand, the victim exhibits self-disgust; if he cannot lift his eyes for humiliation, or if lifted they show only emptiness— then his death may be administered with ease or even with the conviction that so much rotten tissue has been removed from life's body.[54]

On death rows, as in the death camps, killing is made easier by the dehumanization of the victims.[55]

Killing is also made easier by the dehumanization of the killers. Graeme Newman was correct when he maintained that "perfect authoritarian conditions," such as exist on death row, "provide the best possible situations for the ordinary man to turn into a torturer"—and, we might add, a killer.[56] Perfect authoritarian conditions, for Newman, comprise a clear-cut situation of dominance and submission combined with a neutralization of personal responsibility for authorized agents of violence. Under these conditions, the agents *want* to punish others and, as a result, embrace their role. They are "psyched up," as we saw in Chapter 6, and may even be disappointed should the execution be delayed or postponed. (Ironically, interruptions of the execution procedure are painful—one man said torturous—for the staff.) To act without guilt, the agents simply need support from their peers and permission from their superiors. As we have seen, however, dehumanization is fundamental to "perfect authoritarian conditions" and to the resulting desire to punish. Dehumanization of what I would term a situational and symbolic nature is necessary for those serving on the execution team, who are parties to both torture and killing. To the extent that the guards are dehumanized, their job is easier. Numb to their feelings and those of the ostensibly subhuman creatures in their custody, they are able to execute prisoners without moral qualms.[57]

The underlying function of death row confinement, then, is to facilitate executions by dehumanizing both the prisoners and, to a lesser degree, their executioners, making it easier for both to play their roles in the execution process. The confinement that produces these results is a form of torture. Indeed, the essence of torture is the death of the person—that is, his conversion into a subhuman object, a nonperson. Persons whose consciences have been muted by the official authorizations and routines that shape their work as well as by the dehumanization they too have sustained can then, without guilt, commit violence against that nonperson. Stated differently, the death penalty is simply a form of bureaucratically administered violence, a bureaucratization of death in which death row is an integral component. The executions that culminate this confinement are the work of "*in-*

struments of authority acting within stipulated *routines* on condemned prisoners rendered as *objects* to be stored and ultimately dispatched in the execution chamber"[58] (emphasis added).

The Limits of Reform

Though death row confinement serves a function that is essential to the death penalty as it is presently administered, it would seem to be a form of torture that can, in principle, be abolished. One can readily envision a humane death row. It would operate as a kind of high-security hospice with the objective of preparing "full-blooded human beings for a dignified death," whether death takes the form of "the physical death of execution" or "the civil death of extended death row confinement followed by life imprisonment." Such a setting would be staffed by mature, service-oriented correctional officers able to relate to condemned prisoners as persons in the process of dying at the hands of the state, a class of individuals analogous to and as deserving of humane care as terminally ill patients. A humane death row would be "characterized by custody that is not an end in itself, to be maximized at all costs, but by custody that is instead a means to maintain an ordered and secure milieu within which emotional support and personal relationships can develop." Visits would be encouraged, as would recreational activities and "programs of work or study that can take place in cells or in small groups." Also encouraged would be "self-help programs, preferably developed by and for the prisoners," which would be promoted as "collective adaptations to the stresses of death row confinement" and impending execution. The deathwatch, as the culmination of this process, might feature counseling aimed at helping the prisoner put his life in order and accept his demise. One might even find in all of this "a poetic justice in requiring the pariahs of death row to rehabilitate themselves" and prepare themselves for a fully human death.[59]

The members of the National Medical Association Section on Psychiatry and Behavioral Sciences recently adopted a position statement that supports the claim that condemned prisoners have a right to care comparable to that afforded terminally ill patients. After calling for psychiatric interventions with death row prisoners that are designed to provide "the same type of psychotherapy that a terminally ill patient deserves, i.e., psychotherapy designed to work through the psychological issues everyone grapples with when knowingly facing death," they go on to state that "it is truly unfortunate that the same efforts and technology that ensure a swift, painless death [have] not been applied to the psychological being in an effort to make the execution emotionally painless."[60] Yet, in an execution, unlike with a terminal illness, death results from an intentional killing of an unwilling victim. At issue here, then, is not so much a humane death as a humane killing, which may well be a contradiction in terms, at least as humaneness and killing are understood in the modern world.

Be this as it may, the presumption underlying the concept of a humane death row is that even the worst offender retains some humanity that must be respected even as he is put to death. If a person deserves to die—if that is his just desert—then he should die as a human being, not as a dehumanized entity. This means, quite simply, that the condemned person has "a right to be treated as a human being until the moment of his death" so that he may have "the opportunity to prepare for and meet his death with the decency and dignity our laws demand for all human beings."[61] This has recently been asserted as a constitutional right. Pertinent here is the *Autry* case, which raised the issue of "the dignity due any person" facing imminent execution.[62] Also relevant is the *Harries* case, in which the court held that "a death-row inmate has an Eighth Amendment right to die with dignity." In *Harries,* that right was violated by "demeaning" and "degrading" conditions of confinement amounting to "wanton infliction of physical and psychological pain, which is anathema to the standards of decency that our society demands."[63]

The condemned prisoner thus has a right to humane confinement on death row, particularly during the deathwatch. No such death row exists in the real world, however, and one can readily understand why. A humane death row would preserve and indeed highlight the humanity of the condemned, and hence would complicate enormously the already difficult business of death work. Officials would be unable to ignore the hurt and loss they, as persons, would inflict on their prisoners, whom they would know to be full human beings. The prisoners, too, no longer dulled to their own feelings, might well suffer greatly. Executions would be traumatic events, the virtual antithesis of their current bureaucratic reality.

Rather than attempting to make death rows less dehumanizing, another avenue of reform would be simply to close them and confine condemned prisoners with regular maximum security prisoners. Except for their sentences, condemned prisoners are not very different from typical prisoners. The vast majority of the condemned have criminal records that are no worse than those of other chronic felons, and a sizeable minority, in fact, have no prior record of felony convictions or imprisonments.[64] Moreover, condemned prisoners can expect to live behind bars for years awaiting execution, and this can be arranged more cheaply and more humanely in a regular prison than on death row. Thus, condemned prisoners are, at least for those years when their executions are not imminent, no more dangerous or desperate than other prisoners and, accordingly, could be managed in regular prisons.

This reform would free the condemned from the excessive restrictions and pressures of death row confinement. They would have greater opportunity to live in prison on their own terms and hence to prepare themselves for their deaths in a manner of their own choosing. Like virtually all other prisoners, they would no doubt be stressed by their confinement, but they need not be dehumanized. They would have a chance to live in prison—and, if need be, die in an execution chamber—as human beings.

But how different would life in prison be from life on death row? The prisoners would still be condemned men, not regular convicts. Would this not set them apart from others in the prison community? Might they not live as pariahs, suffering a social isolation comparable to life on death row?

At present, we know little about the experience of living with a death sentence under conditions other than those of death row confinement. Currently, only Maryland's condemned, numbering roughly twenty, are housed in a regular prison population.[65] An interview with one of them suggested that even within the relative freedoms of standard prison life, the condemned show a pattern of adjustment similar to that of death row prisoners. This prisoner spoke of a loneliness born of self-segregation, a heightened sense of helplessness and vulnerability, and a blunting of his feelings for himself and others. The researcher who conducted the interview summarized her impressions as follows:

> Life under sentence of death was a painful and solitary one for this condemned prisoner. He felt that none of the other prisoners could possibly understand his situation. He was not interested in people anyway, unless they had something to say that was relevant to his situation. He felt the need to protect himself and tried to live one day at a time, taking things as they came. Yet his life was marred by trauma, the trauma of living with the thought that he was marked for death by the very prison system that today housed and fed him but tomorrow might turn around and kill him.[66]

Another Maryland prisoner told me in no uncertain terms that he sees his keepers as executioners: "They could come and get me out of my cell and kill me any time." Though he knows intellectually that such a fate is technically impossible, he nevertheless feels vulnerable and alone. And if he ever is slated for execution, he will be taken from a deathwatch cell, not a regular prison cell. For the policy in Maryland is to establish a deathwatch once executions become imminent, under the presumption that condemned prisoners will be desperate, and hence will require close custody for their secure containment.[67]

Here again, we see that torturous death row confinement conditions serve an essential function in the implementation of the death penalty. This function, moreover, cannot be served by other, ostensibly more humane regimes of confinement, because the dehumanization that is at the heart of torturous confinement is essential to the bureaucratic administration of the death penalty. This reflects a paradox of bureaucratically administered violence; namely, that men must be dehumanized, dead as persons—that is, as moral beings—to play their roles as killers and victims. Death row produces the moral deaths necessary to carry out the physical killing of condemned prisoners.

This has been long known, though perhaps only vaguely appreciated, at least as it applies to the prisoners. Prisoners on death row are sometimes explicitly referred to as "dead men." The announcement "Dead man coming. Make way. Dead man coming" was a common warning to the living when a condemned man left the confines of death row and traveled, under heavy guard, through the prison. This macabre practice has ceased in most prisons.[68] But nothing has changed on any death row to alter the reality that the condemned are dead men whose bodies are being held for their executions—executions that will be carried out by men who, in the context of their roles as executioners, are perhaps as much marked by death as the prisoners themselves.

Implications

The death penalty, when preceded by long confinement and administered bureaucratically, dehumanizes both the agents and the recipients of this punishment and amounts to a form of torture. This raises two related moral arguments against the death penalty, one focusing on dehumanization, the other on torture.

By dehumanizing both the executioners and the victims, the death penalty violates a basic tenet of just punishment: that punishment be administered by and on persons in the name of the persons who make up the larger moral community. As Herbert Morris has made clear, a person, unlike an animal or object, has the capacity to choose and, moreover, has "a right to institutions that respect his choices." Furthermore, institutions have an obligation to cultivate the capacity for rational choice where it has not yet developed (for example, among children) or where it has been lost (for example, among the mentally ill). Since the capacity for choice cannot be abrogated or waived, the right to be treated as a person is a "natural, inalienable, and absolute right," violation of which "implies the denial of all moral rights and duties."[69] This analysis can be extended to other aspects of personhood. Thus, individuals have a right to institutions that respect their need for security and relatedness to others, denial of which would also "imply the denial of all moral rights and duties." It follows that even the worst offender must be treated within the justice system in a way that will either preserve or restore his personhood. Since only persons can choose to respect the actual or potential personhood of others, the justice system and the society it represents must also be composed of persons.

A justice system that engages in dehumanization hurts us all, making us accomplices to the devaluation of human life. It is perhaps with this thought in mind that Camus enjoined us to be "neither victims nor executioners."[70] As members of a society that inflicts the death penalty, we ignore his sage advice. We consent to executions and are made victims of the brutalization of the human spirit necessary to carry them out. We are a part of what Colin Turnbull eloquently termed "an ever widening circle of tragedy" that includes victims, criminals, those who authorize and implement death sentences, and ultimately the "society throughout, threatening our very understanding of the word humanity."[71] Our only genuinely humane alternative is to abolish the death penalty and devise less brutal punishments for our worst offenders, a topic I address in the next and final chapter of this book.

The second moral objection to the death penalty is simply that torture is inherently wrong. That the agents of torture are dehumanized along with the victims is irrelevant to this point. Even if executioners could torture and kill condemned prisoners while remaining autonomous and caring moral beings, torture would still be unjust. The goal of torture is never justice; torture seeks the destruction of the person, not his punishment. Camus's observation that the death penalty inflicts a "double death" and hence is an inherently excessive punishment is, in this context, not so much right or wrong as irrelevant. Some offenders, such as mass murderers, may well deserve a double death and more—and should receive it, presuming that pain commensurate with this notion of just desert could be administered equitably and without violating the personhood of the criminal. But condemned criminals are not tortured because this is what they deserve. They are tortured because the destruction of their person is useful to their torturers. It is the goal of destruction of the person that distinguishes torture from punishment and renders it gratuitous and hence immoral.

Fundamental reforms of death row conditions are unlikely to occur, or to endure, under a policy of regular execution of criminals. Thus today, and for the foreseeable future, the administration of the death penalty involves torture. Any justification of the death penalty must therefore also justify torturing condemned prisoners, not simply killing them. It is hard to envision such a justification. None can be found in the United States Constitution, for example, which expressly bans torture under the Eighth Amendment prohibition of "cruel and unusual punishments." Torturous confinement, which involves conditions at odds with the requirements of personhood, is by definition a flagrant violation of the legal standard of "minimal civilized measures of life's necessities,"[72] which, when met, is presumed to produce an "environment which does not result in [the prisoner's] degeneration or . . . threaten . . . his mental or physical well being."[73]

This is true, moreover, even though some offenders transcend their environment and, by virtue of strength of character, resist the threat of dehumanization inherent in the conditions of their confinement. It would be true even if many, perhaps even if most, offenders escaped dehumanization on death row. There are survivors of forced labor camps, prisoner-of-war camps, and even Nazi death camps who somehow emerged complete human beings. The Italian writer Primo Levi, for example, is a much heralded death camp survivor credited with having

> preserve[d] an extraordinary humanity. In the three books he has written about his time in Auschwitz and his return to Turin, Levi never gives way to bitterness or to easy feelings of victimization. His books are more than documentations of the atrocities man is capable of inventing; they are a study of the limits of being human.[74]

Levi and others like him are moving testimony to Fyodor Dostoyevski's dictum that "man is a creature that can get accustomed to anything" without changing his essential nature.[75] But these persons do not, by their survival, exonerate the prisons that confined them. Their confinement was inherently inhumane. It violated their personhood because it objectively denied prisoners a sense of self and self-determination. Their transcendent adjustment evokes awe, but to expect such accomplishments from the rest of us is unreasonable.

In making this claim, I am aware that the current procedure is to assess the humanity (or inhumanity) of confinement conditions primarily, if not exclusively, in terms of their impact on offenders. As Justice Brennan has stated, "In determining when prison conditions pass beyond legitimate punishment and become cruel and unusual, the 'touchstone is the effect upon the imprisoned.' "[76] This emphasis is mistaken, however, for two reasons. First, social scientists cannot provide impact or effect data of the kind the court presupposes. As Toch has cogently observed, effect, as understood by the Court, "assumes average impact (or impact on the average) that rarely occurs. . . . Few 'effects' are cross-sectional, immediate, and 'purely out there,' because personal susceptibilities that intersect with environments are built up through personal histories."[77] Hence, the effects of prison conditions are almost always differential, varying with individual susceptibilities. Effects almost always vary, too, in the course of a given person's experience with punishment, which may promote adaptation, maladaptation, or simple stagnation.[78]

This raises a second point, alluded to above. One upshot of the natural diversity of the effects of punishment is that some people can adapt to any harm we might inflict in the name of justice, including even the worst forms of torture. And some situations—notably life-threatening ones—elicit a distinctively human transcendence, sometimes of heroic proportions, from at least a stalwart minority of individuals. Yet it is patently absurd to declare a punishment such as death row confinement to be humane simply because some or even many persons can endure it without losing their humanity in the process.

Moreover, those inmates who in fact preserve their personhood while confined awaiting execution do so, with rare exceptions, by protecting or sheltering it much as one would a helpless infant; they do not live in confinement as persons, but rather allow their selves to become dormant. On death row, even those who escape dehumanization tend merely to simulate personhood rather than to live fully as persons. Only after the confinement ordeal do those who physically survive confinement experience a reawakening of the self and a reassertion of self-determination.[79]

The point, then, is that condemned prisoners and others exposed to torturous confinement are dehumanized in the context of confinement and for the purposes of their keepers. Their confinement violates any notion of humaneness or respect for persons one can adduce, and hence violates the Eighth Amendment to the U.S. Constitution, which bans "all punishments which do not comport with 'broad and idealistic concepts of dignity, civilized standards, humanity and decency.' "[80] As such, death row confinement "makes no measurable contribution to acceptable goals of punishment and hence is nothing more than the purposeless and needless infliction of pain and suffering."[81]

Nor, finally, is there any legal system in the modern world that countenances torture.[82] Even the philosopher Immanuel Kant, who maintained that "only execution would satisfy the requirements of legal justice" for murder, acknowledged that, to be just, "the death of the criminal must be kept entirely free of any maltreatment that would make an abomination of the humanity residing in the person suffering it."[83] The Supreme Court, in effect, endorsed this standard in *In re Kemmler,* a case that may be the Court's most fundamental holding on the constitutionality of the modern death penalty. The Court in *Kemmler,* decided in 1890, required that the death penalty, to comport with the Eighth Amendment, must result in "the mere extinguishment of life" and nothing more.[84] Torture or "a lingering death" were explicitly prohibited. Yet today, death row confinement followed by execution results in both torture and a protracted death, claiming first the person and then the body of the condemned. Our most basic legal standard for lawful executions, then, is widely and regularly violated in the United States today in the form of a punishment that involves the torture and eventual killing of condemned prisoners.

Notes

1. Recent experience suggests that nearly half of today's death row inmates may in fact win appeals, gain clemency, or otherwise have their sentences changed. See J. Berger, "Living on Death Row in the 1980s," *Augustus* 10(1):11–14 (January 1987).

2. E. Peters, *Torture* (Oxford: Basil Blackwell, 1985), 152, 154–55, 152.

3. *Amnesty International Report on Torture* (New York: Farrar, Straus & Giroux, 1975), 35.

4. *Torture in the Eighties: An Amnesty International Report* (London: Amnesty International, 1984), 13.

5. Peters (n. 2), 4.

6. *Torture in the Eighties* (n. 4).

7. Bell v. Wolfish, 441 U.S. 520, 60 L. Ed. 2d 447, 99 S. Ct. 1861, 483.

8. B. Jackson and D. Christian, *Death Row* (Boston: Beacon Press, 1980), 267.

9. Quoted in V. L. Streib, "Juveniles' Attitudes towards Their Impending Executions," in *Facing the Death Penalty: Essays on a Cruel and Unusual Punishment*, ed. M. L. Radelet (Philadelphia: Temple University Press, 1989), 45.

10. I. Zimmerman with F. Bond, *Punishment without Crime* (New York: Clarkson N. Potter, 1964), 97.

11. G. R. Strafer, "Volunteering for Execution: Competency, Voluntariness and the Propriety of Third-Party Intervention," *Journal of Criminal Law and Criminology* 74(3):889 (1983).

12. See People v. Anderson, 6 Cal. 3d 628, 494 P.2d 880, 100 Cal. Rptr. 152, *cert. denied,* 406 U.S. 958 (1972), and Commonwealth v. O'Neal, 369 Mass. 242, 339 N.E.2d 676 (1975). These decisions examined the "total impact of capital punishment," with emphasis on the "dehumanizing effects" of death row confinement (see, for example, *Anderson,* 892). These cases also endorsed the view, expressed as an intuitive assertion rather than a formal argument, that the overall process of execution amounts to "psychological torture" (see, for example, *Anderson,* 894). To date, neither the public nor the U.S. Supreme Court has shown sympathy to this line of analysis.

13. *Torture in the Eighties* (n. 4), 13.

14. *Report of the Amnesty International Mission to Spain* (London: Amnesty International, 1975), 9.

15. *Amnesty International Report on Torture* (n. 3), 52.

16. Note, for example, that Biderman's generic "Chart of Coercion" parallels closely the conditions of brainwashing. (See *Amnesty International Report on Torture* [n. 3], 53.) For a similar conceptualization of the elements of coercion, see also P. Watson, *War on the Mind: The Military Uses and Abuses of Psychology* (New York: Basic Books, 1978), esp. Table 25, pp. 292–293.

17. A. Somit, "Brainwashing," *International Encyclopedia of the Social Sciences,* 18 vols. (New York: Macmillan and Free Press, 1968), 2:138–143.

18. A. D. Biderman, "Social–Psychological Needs and 'Involuntary' Behavior as Illustrated by Compliance in Interrogation," *Sociometry* 23(2):120–147 (June 1960). Quoted in *Amnesty International Report on Torture* (n. 3), 53.

19. I. K. Genefke, Medical Director of the International Rehabilitation and Research Center for Torture Victims, University Hospital, Copenhagen. Quoted in the *Washington Post,* 16 May 1983, A13.

20. *Amnesty International Report on Torture* (n. 3), 34.

21. In some states, only the crown of the condemned man's head is shaved. The psychological effect of this modified procedure has not been examined. It is

likely that having a sizeable patch of hair shorn from one's head is as psychologically disfiguring as having the entire head shaved. After all, one's identity has to do not only with the presence of one's hair (for people who have hair) but also with the person's capacity to preserve its distinctive and presumptively flattering arrangement.

22. See R. J. Lifton, "Thought Reform: Psychological Steps in Death and Rebirth," in *Readings in Social Psychology,* ed. A. R. Lindesmith, A. L. Strauss, and N. K. Denzin, 2nd ed. (New York: Dryden Press, 1975), 275.

23. See J. H. Reiman, "Privacy, Intimacy, and Personhood," *Philosophy and Public Affairs* 6(1):26–44 (1976).

24. For an illuminating general discussion, see E. Cassirer, *An Essay on Man* (New York: Bantam Books, 1970).

25. See A. Maslow, *Eupsychian Management* (Homewood, Ill.: Irwin, 1966), and M. Rokeach, *The Open and Closed Mind: Investigations into the Nature of Belief Systems and Personality Systems* (New York: Basic Books, 1960).

26. See J. Dewey, *Human Nature and Conduct* (New York: Holt, 1922).

27. For a review of the pertinent literature, see B. Moore, Jr., *Injustice: The Social Bases of Obedience and Revolt* (New York: Sharpe, 1978).

28. L. Mumford, *The Condition of Man* (New York: Harcourt, Brace, 1944), 7.

29. W. Gaylin, "In the Beginning: Helpless and Dependent," in W. Gaylin et al., *Doing Good: The Limits of Benevolence* (New York: Pantheon, 1978).

30. H. Toch, *Men in Crisis: Human Breakdowns in Prison* (Chicago: Aldine, 1975), 24.

31. See R. Johnson, "Labored Breathing: Living with Brown Lung" (Paper presented at the Annual Meeting of the American Society of Criminology, Fall 1982).

32. Reiman (n. 23).

33. E. A. Hoebbels, *The Law of Primitive Man* (Cambridge, Mass.: Harvard University Press, 1954), 286–287.

34. See B. Schwartz, "The Social Psychology of Privacy," *American Journal of Sociology* 73 (1968):741, 749.

35. E. Goffman, *Asylums* (New York: Doubleday, 1960), 319–320.

36. Schwartz (n. 34), 748.

37. See Hudson v. Palmer, 82 L. Ed. 2d 393 (1984), 404. The holding in *Hudson* read as follows:

> A right of privacy in traditional Fourth Amendment terms [prohibiting unreasonable searches and seizures] is fundamentally incompatible with the close and continual surveillance of inmates and their cells required to ensure institutional security and internal order. We believe that it is accepted by our society that '[l]oss of freedom of choice and privacy are inherent incidents of confinement.' (Bell v. Wolfish, 441 U.S., 537)

Nevertheless, prisoners cannot be indiscriminately and gratuitously searched; searches that are not justified as security measures or that are otherwise malicious or intended to harass are impermissible. There is, in other words, some residual concern for privacy, even if it is not expressed in "Fourth

Amendment terms." Moreover, Stevens, in dissent, quotes Burger (the author of the majority holding), to the effect that prisoners do have limited rights to privacy in contexts other than searches.

> Inmates in jails, prisons, or mental institutions retain certain fundamental rights of privacy; they are not like animals in a zoo to be filmed and photographed at will by public or by media reporters, however "educational" the process may be for others. (*Hudson,* 413)

Thus, to claim that the *Hudson* holding amounts to a "declar[ation] that the prisoners are entitled to no measure of human dignity or individuality" and that prisoners are "to be little more than chattels" (421) is something of an exaggeration.

Nevertheless, flagrant violations of privacy such as occur in strip-searches and body-cavity searches, even when justified by security considerations, are poor correctional management practices. Respect for inmates' privacy may be incompatible with some notions of imprisonment, but we maintain such intrusive regimes in defiance of human needs and at great cost in terms of tension and conflict. The Court in *Hudson* would have been wiser to echo Schwartz's insightful observations about balancing the institutional need for security and order with respect for the privacy and dignity of convicts:

> If highly efficient regimentation through mass processing and storage is inimical to the value of privacy, a measure of cost-efficiency may be candidly renounced in its favor. . . . While lessened surveillance places a great burden on trust, it may also build trust and obviate the tension and hostility that its absence entails. And while respect for an inmate's rights concerning his own body and his own past may impede custody and security, it may also promote the dignity that would make them less necessary. . . . [Hence] expansion of the right to privacy may be in the interests of the prison as well as its prisoners.

See B. Schwartz, "Deprivation of Privacy as a 'Functional Prerequisite': The Case of the Prison," *Journal of Criminal Law and Criminology* 63(1972):230.
38. L. X. Lombardo, *Guards Imprisoned: Correctional Officers at Work* (New York: Elsevier, 1981).
39. R. Singer, "Privacy, Autonomy, and Dignity in the Prison: A Preliminary Inquiry Concerning Constitutional Aspects of the Degradation Process in Our Prisons," *Buffalo Law Review* 21(1972):669–670.
40. See Goffman (n. 35) and Schwartz (n. 34).
41. H. Toch, *Living in Prison: The Ecology of Survival* (New York: Free Press, 1977), and J. Hegel-Seymour, "Environmental Sanctuaries for Susceptible Prisoners," in *The Pains of Imprisonment,* ed. R. Johnson and H. Toch (Prospect Heights, Ill.: Waveland Press, 1988).
42. Lombardo (n. 38).
43. For an analysis of prison riots that examines how individual inmates and guards come to think of themselves as members of stereotypical collectivities and then turn to violence, see L. X. Lombardo, "Stress, Change and Collective

Violence in Prison," in *The Pains of Imprisonment,* ed. R. Johnson and H. Toch (Prospect Heights, Ill.: Waveland Press, 1988).

44. C. H. Cooley, *Social Organization* (New York: Scribner's, 1909), 10.

45. Goffman (n. 35), esp. Chap. 1.

46. M. L. Radelet, M. Vandiver, and F. Berardo, "Families, Prisons, and Men with Death Sentences: The Human Impact of Structured Uncertainty," *Journal of Family Issues* 4(4):597 (December 1983).

47. See R. Johnson, "Institutions and the Promotion of Violence," in *Violent Transactions: The Limits of Personality,* ed. A. Campbell and J. J. Gibbs (London: Basil Blackwell, 1986).

48. See R. Johnson, *Condemned to Die: Life under Sentence of Death* (Prospect Heights, Ill.: Waveland Press, 1989), esp. Chap. 2; H. Wisnie, *The Impulsive Personality* (New York: Plenum, 1977); and H. Toch, *Violent Men* (Cambridge, Mass.: Schenkman, 1980) and "The Management of Hostile Aggression: Seneca as Applied Social Psychologist," *American Psychologist* 38:1022–1026 (September 1983).

49. See D. O. Lewis et al., "Psychiatric, Neurological, and Psychoeducational Characteristics of Fifteen Death Row Inmates in the United States," *American Journal of Psychiatry* 143(7):838–845 (July 1986). The fifteen death row inmates were "chosen for examination because of the imminence of their executions and not for evidence of neuropsychopathology." The examinations produced some rather startling findings:

> All had histories of severe head injury, five had major neurological impairment, and seven others had other, less serious neurological problems. . . . Psychoeducational testing provided further evidence of CNS [central nervous system] dysfunction. Six subjects had schizophreniform psychoses antedating incarceration and two others were manic-depressive. (838)

Interestingly, none of these prisoners was "flamboyantly" psychotic; indeed, they consciously tried to mask their symptoms, evidently preferring to appear "bad" rather than "mad" (841). The researchers concluded that "many condemned individuals in this country probably suffer a multiplicity of hitherto unrecognized psychiatric and neurological disorders that are relevant to considerations of mitigation" (841–842) and may be unable to obtain, or to assist in, competent legal representation at trial (844).

50. Hugo Bedau has made a similar observation:

> However dangerous, irrational, self-centered, stupid, or beyond improvement such a person may in fact be, these deficiencies do not overwhelm all capacity for moral agency. . . . No plausible empirical argument can support an alleged loss of moral agency in a convicted murderer as a result of the act of murder. . . . [T]he doctrine that certain persons, who had basic human rights prior to any criminal acts, forfeit or relinquish all those rights by such acts and thereby cease to be moral persons, receives no support from experience.

See H. A. Bedau, "Thinking of the Death Penalty as a Cruel and Unusual

Punishment," *University of California, Davis, Law Review* 18(4):921 (Summer 1985).

51. Chaplain Byron Eschelman, in *Death Row Chaplain,* quoted in W. J. Bowers, *Executions in America* (Lexington: Lexington Books, 1974), 196–197.

52. M. A. Kroll, "Fraternity of Death," *I.E.* 7(11):20 (1984).

53. A. Camus, "Reflections on the Guillotine," in *Resistance, Rebellion, and Death* (New York: Knopf, 1969), 205. A number of wardens who oversaw executions in their time support Camus's observation. See C. T. Duffy with A. Hirshberg, *Eighty-Eight Men and Two Women* (New York: Doubleday, 1962); J. Sweat, "Anatomy of an Execution," *Nashville,* September 1979; and Kroll (n. 52).

54. T. Des Pres, *The Survivor: An Anatomy of Life in the Death Camps* (New York: Pocket Books, 1977).

55. A dehumanized perception of one's victim may be all that is needed to kill at a distance. The fighter pilot drops bombs on victims who amount to faceless statistics and consequently suffers little or no remorse. Killing at close range, particularly after extended contact, requires the actual dehumanization of the victims so that the illusion of their subhuman status is preserved and the killer does not have to confront the human consequences of his violence. See Johnson, "Institutions" (n. 47).

56. G. Newman, *The Punishment Response* (Philadelphia: Lippincott, 1978), 258.

57. H. Kelman, "Violence without Moral Restraint: Reflections on the Dehumanization of Victims and Victimizers," *Journal of Social Issues* 29(4):25–61 (1973).

58. Johnson, *Condemned to Die* (n. 48), 131.

59. See R. Johnson, "Life under Sentence of Death," in *The Pains of Imprisonment,* ed. R. Johnson and H. Toch (Prospect Heights, Ill.: Waveland Press, 1988), 142–44.

60. C. C. Bell, "Position Statement on the Role of the Psychiatrist in Evaluating and Treating 'Death Row' Inmates," 1985.

61. C. Turnbull, "Death by Decree: An Anthropological Approach to Capital Punishment," *Natural History* 87(1978):56.

62. See Autry v. McKaskle, 727 F.2d. 358 (5th Cir.), 363.

63. See Groseclose *ex rel.* Harries v. Dutton, 594 F. Supp. 949 (1984), 962.

64. Johnson, *Condemned to Die* (n. 48); Jackson and Christian (n. 8).

65. Arkansas's condemned were allowed to mingle freely with regular prisoners at one juncture in the late sixties, during the moratorium on executions. They behaved well, though no research was done on their emotional or psychological reactions to the threat of execution, which was quite remote at that time. See T. Murton, "Treatment of Condemned Prisoners," *Crime and Delinquency* 15 (1969):94–111.

66. J. Hoyle, personal communication following an interview with a condemned prisoner in Maryland State Penitentiary, 1984. I interviewed a Maryland Penitentiary inmate as recently as 1988 who described his life in the same terms.

67. Beverly Marabel, public relations officer, Maryland Department of Public Safety, personal communication, 1984 and 1989.

68. Condemned prisoners are still referred to as dead men in the Texas system and perhaps elsewhere as well. See J. R. Sorensen and J. W. Marquart, "Working the Dead," in *Facing the Death Penalty: Essays on a Cruel and Unusual Punishment,* ed. M. L. Radelet (Philadelphia: Temple University Press, 1989), 174.

69. H. Morris, "Persons and Punishment," in *Punishment and Rehabilitation,* ed. J. Murphy (Pacific Grove, Calif.: Wadsworth, 1973), 48, 50, 41.

70. A. Camus, "Neither Victims nor Executioners," *Liberation,* February 1960.

71. Turnbull (n. 61).

72. Ruiz v. Estelle, 679 F.2d 1115 (5th Cir. 1982), *modified,* 688 F.2d 266 (5th Cir.).

73. Battle v. Anderson, 564 F.2d 388, 393 (10th Cir. 1977). See also Newman v. Alabama, 559 F.2d 283, 291 (5th Cir. 1975). Dehumanization as I have defined the term is essentially an existential concept, but it nevertheless encompasses the notion of degeneration as it has been defined by the courts.

74. V. Crapanzano, "Primo Levi: The Limits of Being Human," *Washington Post Book World,* 16 March 1986, 1. See P. Levi, *Survival in Auschwitz and The Reawakening: Two Memoirs* (New York: Summit, 1986) and *Moments of Reprieve* (New York: Summit, 1986). For a superb study of the phenomenon of preserving one's humanity in the death camps, see Des Pres (n. 54).

75. F. Dostoyevski, *House of the Dead* (New York: Dell, 1959), 34.

76. Rhodes v. Chapman, 452 U.S. 337, 69 L. Ed. 2d 59, 101 S. Ct. 2392, 80.

77. H. Toch, "The Role of the Expert on Prison Conditions: The Battle of the Footnotes in Rhodes v. Chapman," *Criminal Law Bulletin* 18(1):44 (January–February 1982).

78. See H. Toch and K. Adams, *Coping: Maladaptation in Prisons* (New Brunswick: Transaction Books, 1988).

79. See P. Levi, *The Reawakening* (n. 74).

80. Strafer (n. 11), 889.

81. Coker v. Georgia, 433 U.S. 584, 592 (1977).

82. J. H. Reiman, "Civilization and the Death Penalty: Answering van den Haag," *Philosophy and Public Affairs* 14(2):115–148 (Spring 1985).

83. I. Kant, "The Right to Punish," in *Punishment and Rehabilitation,* ed. J. Murphy (Pacific Grove, Calif.: Wadsworth, 1973), 36.

84. *In re* Kemmler, 136 U.S. at 447, 34 L. Ed. 519, 10 S. Ct. 930. Though *Kemmler* is, in important constitutional respects, an "antiquated authority" (see Justice Brennan's dissent in Glass v. Louisiana, 85 L. Ed. 2d, 517), this principle has endured.

CHAPTER 9

Punishing Murderers

Choosing Life Over Death

Retribution and the Death Penalty

Most Americans support the death penalty for the crime of murder. The threat of execution, they contend, scares potential killers straight and hence saves the innocent lives they would have taken. At a deeper, more visceral level, however, most people simply want murderers to be paid back for their crimes. When pressed, the average person will concede that deterrence, if it actually occurs, is gravy.[1] The main course is retributive justice, seasoned with revenge: a life for a life. Justice can sometimes be a grisly, even torturous business, but justice must be done.

In general, opinions on the death penalty, for or against, reveal more about one's ideological self-image than about one's thoughtfulness.[2] A pro–death penalty stance often indicates a self-image of tough-minded pragmatism, someone who sees himself (or herself) as having the fortitude, nerve, and will to punish the guilty. (According to this line of analysis, the minority who oppose the death penalty wish to advertise their compassionate, forgiving natures.) Most death penalty supporters emphasize not the fine points of the law, sociological findings on deterrence, or treatises on justice, but an essentially gut-level "belief that murderers deserve to die."[3] That condemned murderers should suffer in the process, even suffer greatly, is self-evident to many of those who support the death penalty.

The popular view of justice as just deserts, though in some respects ill informed and even smugly self-righteous, has merit. Retribution means giving criminals the punishment they deserve, and this is a sensible and just notion. The virtues of retribution can easily be lost sight of, however, because retribution is generally tinged with revenge, and vengeance is considered a base motive that in turn debases any punishment with which it is associated. Yet vengeance means more than a desire for retaliation; it also means "a reassertion of human dignity or worth after injury or damage." Vengeance may be primitive, but it is nevertheless a "form of moral outrage."[4] As a moral act and not simply an eruption of passion, vengeance should not be dismissed out of hand as barbaric or uncivilized. Indeed, one might say that retribution is, at bottom, vengeance constrained by some notion of just deserts.

Retribution understood as constrained vengeance is not only just, it is also humane. Unlike pure revenge, in which the criminal is devalued and thereby made open game for any harm the victim or his representatives wish to inflict on him, retribution, because it presupposes "the equality of persons,"[5] limits punishment. Retribution thus treats criminal and victim alike as fellow human beings of equal worth who have a score that must be settled fairly.

The just and humane aspects of retribution are lost, however, when we resort to the death penalty. The process by which we try, convict, sentence, confine, and ultimately execute condemned criminals has, when seen from the condemned's vantage point, distinctly Kafkaesque qualities. These proceedings—some of which we examined closely in this book—are nothing short of harrowing for those who must undergo them. Anthony Amsterdam's observations on this matter are, in my view, quite compelling.

> First we bring men or women into court and put them through a trial for their lives. They are expected to sit back quietly and observe decent courtroom decorum throughout a proceeding whose purpose is systematically and deliberately to decide whether they should be killed. The jury hears the evidence and votes; and you can always tell when a jury has voted for death because they come back into court and they will not look the defendant or defense counsel in the eyes. The judge pronounces sentence and the defendant is taken away to be held in a cell for two to six [or more] years, hoping that his appeals will succeed, not knowing what they are all about, but knowing that if they fail, he will be taken out and cinched down and put to death . . . [He knows that] the people in prison . . . are holding him there helpless for the approaching slaughter; and that once the final order is given, they will truss him up and kill him, and that nobody in that vast surrounding machinery of public officials and servants of the law will raise a finger to save him.[6]

There is nothing just or humane about executions, if we understand these concepts to mean, at bottom, showing respect for the humanity of the person being punished. Rather, in executing a criminal, we treat him, in the words of Justice Brennan, "like an object to be toyed with and discarded."[7] One is led to hope, with Amsterdam, that the death penalty is indeed a dying institution, and that it shall pass quickly and quietly from the current scene.

Opposition to punishments that treat a person like an object—and that thus harm us by assaulting our humanity—has a long and venerable lineage in philosophy. Plato once observed, for example, that, ideally, "judgment by sentence of law is never inflicted for harm's sake. Its normal effect is one of two; it makes him that suffers it a better man, or failing that, less of a wretch."[8] Perhaps even more to the point, he also stated, "We ought not to repay injustice with injustice or to do harm to any man, no matter what we may have suffered from him."[9] The pain of punishment, as distinct from gratuitous suffering, must engage the offender as a person and offer a moral lesson in the process.[10] Thus, to be humane, punishment must be not only civilized, conforming to some notion of a fair measure of pain or loss, but also civilizing, offering at least the possibility of personal reform.[11]

Some methods of execution are more civilized than others, and there have been progressive efforts to limit and even eliminate the physical pain caused by execution (see Part I). The assumption, widely shared among legal authorities though less popular with the average citizen, is that the penalty is solely the loss of life, and hence any pain attendant on the taking of life should be minimized or avoided altogether. The use of a lethal injection, complete with a battery of anesthetics, represents the most recent effort to civilize executions. Were this method shown to be painless (some anesthesiologists contest this), and further, were its administration combined with a humane confinement regime, one might argue that the death penalty extinguished life and nothing more, in accord with the demands of the Supreme Court. Such executions would exact a heavy psychological toll on executioners, however, and perhaps on the prisoners as well, because killing and dying do not come easily to full human beings. Still, one might maintain that such executions were civilized.

But not civilizing. Given our current understanding of human nature and the finality of death, the death penalty, however it is administered, can never be civilizing. If, as science seems to indicate, death is the termination of all experience, then execution cannot offer the criminal the experience of his just deserts,[12] and it is the experience of one's just deserts that alone holds out the prospect of reform and marks a sanction as humane. (Even the proper *anticipation* of one's just deserts is eliminated by the dehumanization inherent in modern executions.) Hence, there can be no such thing as a humane execution in the modern world—only executions that are more or less smoothly and painlessly orchestrated by the state.

The Finality of Death

In taking this stand, I am mindful of the fact that Plato envisioned executions in his republic. He saw crime as a kind of disease that contaminated and tortured its host. Execution would release serious and incurable criminals from their earthly bondage; the oblivion of death was presumed to be humane because it made the offender "less of a wretch."[13] The French historian Phillippe Aries has noted that other notions of death prevalent before the twentieth century, particularly those associated with a personal God and a congenial afterlife, made a foreseen death desirable. Here, too, execution might be conceived as a blessing of sorts, allowing criminals to reform themselves by coming to terms with their Maker and experiencing an exemplary afterlife in His care. The views of Robert Bellarmine, a seventeenth-century Jesuit, are instructive. For him, Aries reported,

> the condemned man was actually rehabilitated by his suffering and his repentance. His piety transformed his execution into an expiation, and his death became a good death, better than many others. "When they have begun to depart from mortal life," Bellarmine wrote almost admiringly of condemned criminals, "they begin to live in immortal bliss."[14]

On some occasions, offenders were permitted to confess and receive absolution on the scaffold, virtually ensuring their salvation.[15]

One can readily see how executions in this context could partake of a public and even celebratory nature, with religious and other officials prominently involved (see Chapter 1). The tortures of the condemned, often serving as the centerpiece of the execution, provided the time and the motivation for the prisoner's repentance. "The more the condemned was tortured on his way to release from this life," Samuel Edgerton observed, "the more penance he was privileged to offer up for possible redemption." The ceremony would be brought to a satisfying close when the "brave but penitent" criminal renounced his evil ways and died "like a stoic Christian martyr."[16] In this fashion, offenders would at once secure forgiveness for their sins and clear the community they had compromised in God's eyes. Finally, everyone would take comfort in the fact that God was the ultimate authority. He would take responsibility for the proceedings, which after all occurred in His name, and could be expected to ameliorate any earthly injustices in the next life.[17]

To be sure, the masses did not attend executions to watch criminals ascend blissfully into heaven. Instead, most common folk saw the condemned as bound for an eternity of punishment and were happy to see them go. "For a large part of the Middle Ages," Aries noted, "it was commonly believed that the criminal about to be executed was a diabolical creature who had already gone to hell. Under the circumstances, all spiritual consolation was seen as useless and forbidden, if not sacrilegious."[18] But the actual fate of the condemned was always ambiguous. Was the church or the populace right? And how would one know?

The meaning of the condemned's suffering on the scaffold was unclear. Their final agonies could be considered a form of penance. Certainly this was implied by the presence of a confessor, who would offer spiritual comfort to the condemned.[19] Or the criminals' suffering could be considered a harbinger of what awaited them in the hereafter, as many citizens believed. In any event, a symbolic struggle was waged on the scaffold between the devil (personified by the executioner) and God (variously represented by a visible confessor and invisible angels). The executioner, "frequently recruited from the swarthy races" because this would make "his appearance on the scaffold all the more devilish," was supposed to look like an agent of Satan; his victim, though generally reviled in life, was at this time of utter vulnerability "a pitiable soul struggling for salvation."[20] No one could know in advance how this struggle would end. Furthermore, there was often room for doubt about the accuracy of the verdict. (Criminal procedure was still comparatively crude and self-serving, with evidence often obtained through ordeals or torture.) The prisoners' suffering might shed light on their guilt or innocence as well. For all these reasons, people watched executions closely, with a curiosity that was both morbid (literally) and almost insatiable.

The scaffold, then, was nothing less than a grand stage on which was prominently displayed for all to see a

> spectacle of sufferings truly endured; there one could decipher crime and innocence, the past and the future, the here below and the eternal. It was a moment of truth that all the spectators questioned: each word, each cry, the duration of the agony, the resisting body, the life that clung desperately to it, all this constituted a sign.[21]

The communal nature of life in premodern times, together with the typical citizen's deep religious beliefs about an afterlife, meant that death was never "a solitary venture," to quote Aries, but rather had worldly and otherwordly implications for the community.[22] The arranged death of an execution, in particular, involved the community as a whole as well as the separate souls of its members—hence the preoccupation with signs. Church bells tolling the advent of an execution tolled for everyone.

Things are, of course, profoundly different today. In the West, at least, we live in a secular, individualistic age. A preoccupation with signs from God is likely to be regarded now as a symptom of mental illness. Today, condemned criminals are neither believed to be possessed by demons nor considered the confident recipients of a guaranteed afterlife. (Some major religions still promise an afterlife, but many Christian theologians now view "the idea of an afterlife [as] clearly an embarrassment to modern thinking.") Death no longer has any accepted communal or transcendental meaning; it is regarded simply as the end of individual life as we know it. Some religious leaders acknowledge this quite bluntly: "Dead is dead," Rabbi Terry Bard, director of pastoral services at Boston's Beth Israel Hospital, has stated.[23] It is increasingly hard to sustain the belief that death is not an end to this life but instead the beginning of a life hereafter in the arms of a personal God. "In recent times," as Barrington Moore has noted, "a fairly large number of educated people [has] come to realize that there is not and cannot be any source of moral authority except human beings themselves."[24] Like Camus's stranger, some of us have concluded that we would be wise to lay our "heart[s] open to the benign indifference of the universe," acknowledging that we are ultimately alone in this world and that life ends with death.[25] Others, we learn from Norman Podhoretz, choose to serve and praise the concept of God—the spiritual ideal of goodness—"by cherishing life on this Earth to the very end and by refusing to curse it" even as death encroaches.[26] Still others see God embodied, or at least presaged, in the workings of nature and the maturing of human reason; death, ever final for the individual, punctuates the gradual but inexorable perfection of the species.[27] For many thoughtful people, at least, today's God, if they believe one to exist at all, has been shorn of personal attributes and evicted from a personal hereafter. These ideas have been slow in coming to human consciousness and even slower in gaining popular acceptance. But accepted they are becoming, and they alter drastically the nature of death as a punishment. As a result, neither the spiritual significance nor the justice of a life in the hereafter can be invoked to defend the death penalty. Gone are executions that are genuine rituals. Gone are spiritual defenses of the death penalty.

Punishments should respect the criminal's personhood.[28] Earlier in this book, I took the liberty of defining a person as an individual with a sense of self and a capacity for self-determination based on and expressed as autonomy, security, and relatedness to others (see Chapter 8). An afterlife negates the finality of death; hence, a person's self and capacity for self-determination can be regarded as continuing after death. Death as a punishment, therefore, does not inherently violate a criminal's personhood. One enters the hereafter as a soul (self) separate and distinct from other souls (selves). One's fate there is a product of prior autonomous choices, including any choice to repent, even if made as one mounts the scaffold. In the hereafter, one can find security in one's relatedness to God as well as to God's other creatures. One can knowingly forfeit these benefits—for example, by refusing to repent—but this is something one chooses, and hence one suffers the consequences as a person. Once the notion of an afterlife is relinquished, however, the penalty of death can no longer be seen as a punishment that respects the criminal's personhood. Instead of offering a moral lesson to the offender, the death penalty then simply terminates all moral discourse with him.

To be sure, popular belief in an afterlife persists in the modern world. Most of us *want* to believe in a personal God and be comforted by the prospect of some type of morally satisfying life after death, and some of us do and are. Public opinion polls indicate that such beliefs are alive and well among the laity if not among their religious leaders.[29] This is perhaps to be expected. We yearn to be immortal, as Ernest Becker reminds us, and for the common man this desire is "the basic motive for . . . religion."[30] Unfortunately, the wish to live ever after in the presence of a kind and forgiving God is, as Sigmund Freud made clear, profoundly self-serving and hence deeply suspect as a basis for religion:

> We say to ourselves: it would be very nice if there were a God, who was both creator of the world and a benevolent providence, if there were a moral order and a future life, but at the same time it is very odd that this is all just as we should wish it ourselves. And it would be still odder if our poor ignorant enslaved ancestors had succeeded in solving all these difficult riddles of the universe.[31]

Such wishes, however devoutly they may be embraced, are no substitute for a solid bedrock of religious faith. Death is the acid test of faith, and our response to death reveals the poverty of our faith. For, sad to say, belief and comfort come hard nowadays, and it is difficult indeed "to die with the peaceful resignation of a true believer."[32] Knowing death to be final—at the very least, sensing and fearing, even dreading, its finality—we hide from death. We prefer the sudden death, a death that strikes without warning and is over so swiftly that it seems not even to happen to the person at all. (By contrast, during the Middle Ages, a sudden death was considered to rob persons of the chance to die with dignity and prepare themselves for a peaceful afterlife. As Aries has observed, "In this world that was so familiar with death, a sudden death was a vile and ugly death; it was frightening; it seemed a strange and monstrous thing that nobody dared talk about."[33]) When death threatens to linger in the modern world, we relegate the dying to hospitals and nursing homes, far from the ebb and flow of contemporary life.[34] Our heroes no longer die nobly for a good cause, then go on to receive their just deserts from their Maker in a pleasing hereafter. They merely survive adversity—often to bear witness to evil, always to celebrate life.[35]

Faced with the ugly prospect of the finality of death, we have become a death-denying culture, perhaps even inaugurating a death-denying era. Hence, according to our own cultural values, capital punishment today is both cruel (because it forces the offender to confront his mortality) and unusual (because it radically departs from our normal denial of the reality of death). It is also perversely arrogant. For it is unconscionable to take the lives of individuals who might have been able, even if only in some small way, to make up for the wrongs they have caused. In a world without an afterlife, Camus maintained, "a right to live, which allows a chance to make amends, is the natural right of every man, even the worst man."[36] In taking the lives of criminals, we reduce them to pieces of meat—inert bodies, so much decaying matter—when the *persons* could have been punished in life and, potentially at least, reclaimed by society. Whether or not criminals can be reclaimed through punishment, however, our evolving standards of decency, as seen in how we as a society understand and deal with death, can be said to have changed sufficiently to render the death penalty no longer permissible under the Eighth Amendment prohibition of cruel and unusual punishments.[37]

Then why so much current enthusiasm for the death penalty? Desperate, last-ditch crime control measures like the death penalty may have a special appeal today. More than at any other time in recent memory, we fear crime and distrust our justice system, which we view as ineffectual and lax.[38] Feeling helplessly at the mercy of criminals, many of us want to punish at least some of them as forcefully as we can. If nothing else, we want a potent and hence reassuring symbol of a tough-minded approach to crime. The death penalty fills the bill quite handily.[39]

On a deeper level, popular support for the death penalty is, in part, a product of the modern denial of death. We talk tough on the subject of death, I fear, because we do not know what we are talking about. Executions are nothing more than an abstraction for us, insofar as we have, through our denial, reduced death itself to an abstraction that is, in Aries's words, "invisible and unreal."[40] Our current bureaucratic execution procedure in itself denies the reality of death inherent in executions revealing the moral bankruptcy of the modern death penalty, a sanction we use but cannot look squarely in the face and call our own.[41] Instead, perversely, we try to make the dehumanization of the condemned prisoner seem decent and humane: "He felt nothing; he was dead to the world before we took his life." Executions masquerade as morally neutral events—as tactical moves in a war on crime, not as face-to-face killings of other human beings. All of this is, at bottom, a tragic charade that masks the inhumanity of the death penalty.

A Civil Death Penalty

If we reject death as a legitimate sanction, what punishment do we use instead? More to the point, how do we decide what punishment fits the crime of murder, particularly the premeditated and often heinous murders that people think of when they call for the death penalty? What do we do with the "monsters" who commit monstrous crimes?

Murderers treat their victims "like objects to be toyed with and discarded," if I may transpose Justice Brennan's fine phrase, but murderers are reprehensible people and we as a society must not fashion our punishments after their acts. Murderers must be paid back for what they have done to their victims, but this must be done justly and properly, showing due regard for their inherent human dignity.[42] (At the heart of the Eighth Amendment ban on cruel and unusual punishments is the prohibition of punishments that deny the inherent dignity of human beings.[43]) Like other criminals, murderers must be punished as persons in a way that is commensurate with the harm they have caused. Thus, their punishment must approximate death and yet treat them as full human beings.

This means lengthy prison terms for murderers, including, for our worst murderers, true life sentences without possibility of parole. When we sentence criminals to prison we suspend their civil lives, rendering them civilly dead until•

they are deemed worthy of return to the society of the living.[44] A civil death entails the loss of one's freedom and of the attendant benefits of civil life in the free world. Civil death should not be confused with moral death, the dehumanization suffered by the condemned. During their confinement, regular prisoners do not suffer a moral death. They remain persons, even if their circumstances are impoverished and they suffer great privations: They are still individuals (of admittedly low status), and they are afforded a degree of autonomy (by officials and within their society of captives), security (usually by virtue of the staff's policing and human-service roles), and relatedness to others (selected fellow prisoners and staff, as well as loved ones who write or visit). Prison life may not be much of a life, but it is a life nonetheless.

How much time behind bars, how much of a civil death, is enough punishment for the crime of murder? At what point does a prison term inflict suffering commensurate with a murderer's crime? The answer varies. The context in which the crime occurred, for example, is a critical factor in assessing punishment. In sentencing, judges currently take into account some specific contextual factors such as duress or the presence or absence of explicit prior intent. But rarely considered are more general, often crucial social factors, such as those relating to poverty and brutality. Psychiatrist Willard Gaylin has reminded us that the impoverished lives of violent men typically give rise to a host of mitigating factors that should be, but presently are not, taken into account in assessing their just punishment.[45]

Individual sensibilities also come into play. Pain is a subjective experience. It would be futile, in my view, to attempt to precisely and systematically calibrate the pains of punishment, at least in part because of the substantial variations in sensitivity to suffering one can expect to find, first among victims, whose degree of suffering would determine the punishment, and second, among offenders, who are to suffer commensurately. Nevertheless, what constitutes even a gross notion of sufficient pain for any given crime will depend on the capacity of the person inflicting or authorizing punishment to empathize with the criminal and hence to have at least a primitive sense of when the criminal has or will have suffered his just deserts.

This presents a serious problem in the case of murder. Though murderers are people, too, many of us have no empathy for them. Some of us, for instance, see murderers as so many anonymous crime statistics. For others, murderers are monsters, animals, or psychopaths. These jaundiced views, moreover, are not restricted to an uninformed and vindictive segment of the populace. Walter Berns, a scholar and advocate of the death penalty, openly mocked Supreme Court Justice Brennan for contending that "even the vilest criminal remains a human being possessed of human dignity." It was only a few years back that the chief justice of Georgia's Supreme Court likened murderers to mad dogs. That must still unsettle the one hundred or so condemned prisoners housed (kenneled?) on Georgia's death row and subject to his rulings on their appeals. Similarly, an editorialist in Alabama described execution as "an act approaching judicial euthanasia," a merciful gesture putting brutish criminals out of their (our?) misery. William Raspberry, a syndicated columnist, summed up this point of view when he observed that "it is possible for a criminal to commit acts so heinous as to place himself outside the category of human, to render him subject to extermination as one might exterminate a mad dog, without consideration of how the animal came to contract rabies in the first place."[46] Never mind that the "rabies" may have originated in an abusive home, during the criminal's impressionable years.[47] Or that it may have been the predictable result of harsh and inequitable social conditions (like poverty) that we as a society permit to exist because of the benefits we reap from them (such as cheap labor to do menial tasks for our convenience).[48] Or that it may have reflected neurological impairments produced by genetic anomalies, physical abuse, or inadequate diet (especially during the prenatal period).[49]

If we are unable to empathize with murderers, unable to feel for them, we cannot develop a sense of their lives and their suffering and hence cannot determine when they have suffered enough. In fact, in the absence of empathy, there is no limit to the pain one can inflict, since by definition the pain affects individuals for whom one feels nothing and who one naturally assumes feel nothing themselves. Thus, we imagine we are dealing with cold-blooded felons who are impervious to normal hurts and hence must be punished according to a scale of suffering far in excess of what we would apply to ourselves or others like us. We may even believe that no punishment is really adequate. This may explain how we can bandy about prison terms of five, ten, twenty, forty, or (in states like Texas) literally hundreds or thousands of years as though they were civilized, even soft, penalties.

Perhaps a way out of this dilemma is to relate prison sentences to our own life experiences. Four years in prison, for instance, sounds like a snap, a travesty of justice in the case of murder. But imagine spending the whole of your high school years, including summers, separated from your loved ones and confined for the greater part of each day to a cage. Ten years behind bars would equal your entire twenties. A thirty- or forty-year sentence would equal the entire life of the average American, who is middle aged. A natural-life sentence or true life sentence comes close to obliterating any life at all. Though a true life sentence falls short of execution, surely no criminal deserves a harsher fate than this.

The vast majority of murderers can point to a host of mitigating circumstances in their lives (though, as noted above, only some are currently recognized in law). For them, serving sentences of roughly ten years would probably be sufficient punishment. (This is approximately the average sentence murderers serve today, and their recidivism rates after release from prison are reassuringly low.) Some are more culpable and would no doubt deserve longer sentences; a few might marshall such an impressive array of mitigating circumstances that they would warrant shorter terms of confinement. Our worst murderers, those seeming monsters we presently consign to the death chamber because their actions are thought to place them beyond the bounds of human decency, would of course be subject to lengthy prison terms, including a natural or true life sentence without possibility of parole.

Under a true life sentence, the offender is slated to spend the remaining years of his life in prison. Though our courts do mete out true life sentences, this sentence is not recognized as being, in fact, a kind of death penalty. To be sure, true life prisoners remain physically alive and in the company of other convicts and guards; they are treated as human beings and remain members, however marginal, of the human community. They can forge a life of sorts behind bars, but a limited life steeped in suffering, for at a profoundly human level they experience a permanent civil death, the death of freedom. The prison is their cemetery, a six-by-nine-foot cell their tomb. Interred in the name of justice, they are consigned to mark the passage of their lives in the prison's peculiar dead time, which serves no larger human purpose and yields few rewards. In effect, they give their civil lives in return for the natural lives they have taken. Yet they can, through their suffering, atone for their crimes. And they can make amends, in small but meaningful ways, by living decently in the prison community. They might, for example, establish a modest career of service to others built around the work and remedial opportunities available within the prison's walls. A true life sentence, then, can and should serve as an alternative to the death penalty. It is a civilized—and potentially civilizing— application of retributive justice in the extreme case of premeditated murder in the absence of mitigating circumstances.

Obstacles to Reform

Economic Objections

One objection to this proposal is the price tag. We've all heard about the cost of new prison construction, which can run in the neighborhood of sixty thousand to one hundred thousand dollars per cell, and about per capita confinement costs of anywhere from fifteen thousand to fifty thousand dollars a year.[50] True life sentences would presumably cost a fortune in new cell construction and in the cumulative cost of confining individuals for forty or more years each, depending on how long the prisoners live, on average. With factors such as inflation and unexpected costs figured in, the tab could reach a million or more dollars per life-term prisoner. If nothing else, taxpayers are apt to see executions as humane.

But the actual cost of true life sentences would fall considerably short of these estimates and may be less than the cost of executions. We will not have to build new cells expressly for true life prisoners. (Or at least not many new cells. At present we execute about twenty prisoners a year out of a total prison population of more than half a million. Even if the execution rate were to double over the coming years, executions would free few cells for other prisoners.) Today's condemned prisoners would be confined under any sentencing scheme, whether on death rows or in standard maximum security prisons. Where crowding is a problem, less serious offenders can be released to make room for murderers, a policy that seems eminently sensible. (It has been long known that a sizeable minority of prisoners, such as nonviolent property and public-order offenders, could be safely sentenced to community-based sanctions. These include such restrictive programs as intensive probation, electronic monitoring, and house arrest.[51]) Moreover, according to John Conrad, the true or actual out-of-pocket cost of confining any given prisoner in an existing prison is somewhere between five thousand and ten thousand dollars a year.[52] In states like Texas, where confinement costs tend to be low, it may be cheaper still.[53] Higher estimates of per prisoner costs incorrectly attribute to individuals the prisons' overhead expenses—that is, the fixed costs of running prisons, independent of who and how many people are in them. Such estimates also overlook one unique economic aspect, noted by Conrad, of the confinement of life-sentence prisoners: "Most lifers tend to be employed, sooner or later, on productive jobs, which may eliminate the cost of keeping them altogether."[54]

A true life term, then, calculated as a forty-year sentence of imprisonment, would directly cost taxpayers some two hundred thousand to four hundred thousand dollars per prisoner in states like New York and California (less in other states). These estimates are necessarily imperfect: Inflation would, of course, push the cost up, and cost-defraying labor by the prisoners would lower it. Though high, and perhaps getting considerably higher over time, these figures compare favorably with the estimated cost of death sentences. Death sentences, appearances to the contrary, are elaborate enterprises. They require complicated trials, lengthy appeals, years of special custodial housing for the condemned, and carefully arranged executions. It is unclear how much of these costs represent specific out-of-pocket expenses, but what is clear is that a single execution costs millions of dollars.[55] There are, in other words, no bargain punishments for murder. Neither life sentences nor death sentences come cheaply.

Beyond the matter of cost, some people will balk at the idea of a true life sentence because they don't believe prison is punishment. They refuse to subsidize the lives of luxury that country club prisons are presumed to afford their inmates. This cynical but widely held view is seriously misleading. A prison joke has it that the country club prison is much like the Loch Ness monster: There have been sporadic citizen sightings but no scientific confirmations. On closer examination, one cannot fail to note that our "country club" prisons permit no heterosexual contact, issue nondescript clothing or sharply limit prisoners' choice of civilian attire, and serve meager portions of poor food in noisy mess halls (well named) filled with dangerous guests. The accommodations feature iron bars or steel doors, bare furniture, dim lighting, and poor ventilation. Guards control the inmates' daily movements. Like country clubs, prisons are costly to operate, but unlike country clubs, little of the money is spent on convict sustenance, let alone on amenities. For instance, in New York, a state noted for its progressive penal system, a prisoner's meal bill comes to under two dollars a day.[56] Some country club! In point of fact, prisons are impoverished environments. A lifetime in prison is a lifetime of suffering and privation.

Public Safety Questions

Other objections to this proposal relate to public safety. After all, dead prisoners pose no threats, whereas life-term prisoners are at least potential dangers to the community. For all intents and purposes, however, prisoners serving true life sentences are punished and incapacitated for life. Maximum security prison walls, in contrast to the notoriously permeable fences that enclose medium and minimum security prisons, virtually assure that society has nothing more to fear from these prisoners. To be sure, convicts sometimes escape from maximum security prisons (and have from at least one death row). The rate of such escapes, however, is quite low. Even less common are escapes from prison that are accompanied by violent crimes against the public. As Ernst van den Haag has reminded us, prisons are costly, in the main, "because they are too secure."[57]

Nor are life prisoners a special threat to other prisoners or to guards. Thorsten Sellin long ago established, and the relevant statistics bear him out, that "prison homicides are not usually committed by prisoners serving [life] sentences for capital murder and that such persons . . . pose no special threat to the safety of their fellow men."[58] When paroled, these prisoners, again, pose no special threat to others. The same holds true for formerly condemned prisoners. Indeed, when the sentences of condemned prisoners are reduced to life terms (usually following court decisions) and these prisoners are paroled, they have "recidivism rates as low as or lower than those of other offenders."[59]

Most lifers are good prisoners. Those who are troublesome can be segregated from the main prison population. (Secure systems of custodial segregation can be mobilized in the rare instances when long-termers are persistently violent.[60]) The notion that lifers typically are unmanageable prisoners—that they have nothing to lose and hence disobey prison rules, harming and even killing others in the prison world with seeming impunity—would appear to be a practical stumbling block to my proposal, were it not completely without foundation.

As a group, lifers simply do not rebel, nor do they make life miserable or dangerous for their keepers or fellow prisoners. Paradoxically, lifers are usually compliant prisoners. Why? Quite simply, because prison becomes their home. To make the most of a bad situation, they try to get through each day in prison with as little trouble as possible. More than other prisoners, who from the lifers' point of view are essentially impetuous tourists, lifers have a vested interest in the stability and integrity of the prison. Lifers and other long-termers "are not necessarily more *accepting* of their situation than short-term prisoners, [but] they appear to more fully realize the need to *co-exist* with correctional authorities within the confines of the institution." One might say that they have " 'wised up' to the exigencies of the situation."[61] In my experience, many American prison wardens privately concur with these observations, though I am aware of no systematic research on their perceptions of lifers. The findings of a recent survey of Australian prison wardens support my position: "The replies of 64 wardens showed overwhelmingly that, as a group, long-term inmates are not a management problem. On the contrary, they are a stabilizing influence in the institution."[62]

Perhaps more to the point, a number of empirical studies support the claim that lifers are less likely to break prison rules than the average inmate. (Sometimes the differences in infraction rates are statistically insignificant, but I am aware of no instance in which long-termers were found to break rules more often than other prisoners.) In a recent rigorous study conducted in several maximum security prisons in New York, Timothy Flanagan concluded that "the infraction rates of long-term inmates are significantly lower than the rates for short-term prisoners." This was true, moreover, "even in the early years of confinement," when the long-term prisoners could be expected to be angry and resentful about their sentences. Furthermore, "the types of infractions committed by long-term and short-term prisoners tend to be similar," though the data did indicate "that the infractions committed by long-term inmates may be somewhat more serious in nature" than those committed by short-termers.[63]

Lifers are defined in this body of research as including (1) prisoners serving long sentences that are technically not life terms (a person sentenced to fifty-six years, for instance, might not be officially termed a lifer), (2) prisoners sentenced to life terms who are eligible for parole, and (3) prisoners serving true life sentences who are ineligible for parole. Long-termers and lifers eligible for parole are usually released after ten to fifteen years of imprisonment, though in some states (notably Minnesota) the average lifer serves twenty years or more.[64] This raises a pertinent question. Are true lifers, whose sentences are counted in decades rather than in years and who presumably expect to die behind bars, more desperate and hence more disruptive than others serving lengthy terms? Only one study of this question has been conducted to date. The conclusion: True life sentence prisoners do in fact commit more rule infractions that other long-termers, but they *still* are less troublesome than the typical prisoner.[65]

That lifers are decent prisoners would count for little if life sentences were to deter fewer potential murderers than does the death penalty. If would-be murderers are less afraid of life sentences than of death sentences and hence are less likely to be deterred from violence, we might wish to execute at least some murderers for the greater good of deterring others and hence preserving the innocent lives of their prospective victims. Yet here we have another paradox. Life sentences may well be a better deterrent than death sentences.

There are no data bearing directly on this point, because deterrence studies compare death sentences with all other sentences for murder, not specifically with life sentences. But the logic is compelling. Criminals tend to be present-centered; they live for today and let tomorrow take care of itself.[66] Executions may be notable when they occur, but they take place long after the crime, are over quickly, and may fade from memory after but a brief period or time. Life sentences are less dramatic than death sentences, to be sure, but they are experienced in the present and last well into the future. Life sentences envelop the prisoner. By virtue of their pervasiveness, they also impinge on the other convicts, who observe at close range— and often with great apprehension—the melancholy fate of lifers.[67] Unlike executed prisoners, who are dead, gone, and soon forgotten by their fellows, lifers stand as tangible, enduring, flesh-and-blood testaments to the wages of violent crime.

Moral Objections

A final objection to this proposal is that it does not really represent an improvement at all, but rather will do more harm than good. This objection takes two forms, the first being that life in prison is worse than death. This claim was originally advanced by the nineteenth-century philosopher John Stuart Mill, who saw the lifer as immured "in a living tomb," which Mill took to be a uniquely degrading punishment that was worse than "the short pang of a rapid death."[68] A modern advocate of this position is Jacques Barzun. Those who would abolish the death penalty, Barzun has observed, speak of the sanctity of life, but have no concern for its quality. . . . They read without a qualm, indeed they read with rejoicing, the hideous irony of "Killer Gets Life"; they sigh with relief instead of horror. They do not see and suffer the cell, the drill, the clothes, the stench, the food; they do not feel the sexual racking of young and old bodies, the hateful promiscuity, the insane monotony, the mass degradation, the impotent hatred. . . . Quite of another mind, the abolitionists point with pride to the "model prisoners" that murderers often turn out to be. As if a model prisoner were not, first, a contradiction in terms, and second, an exemplar of what a free society should not want.[69]

Yet it is precisely because prison offers more than either an empty tomb or a life of polluted human community that model prisoners can and do emerge from their midst. (Whether this was true or not in Mill's time is unclear. On the other hand, not all executions in Mill's day produced a rapid death.) Barzun might well "choose death without hesitation" rather than suffer a life in prison,[70] but the vast majority of prisoners he would have us kill surely would not. Like Barzun, some of them talk about being better off dead, but unlike him, they discover that a hallmark of a free society is its willingness to spare their lives and allow them a place in the prison community. Some of these prisoners also come to delight in the simple esthetic pleasures of living. As one lifer housed near death row reluctantly admitted, "Living above the electric chair has a way of giving new meaning to cliches about the joy of beholding the natural beauty of a sunrise."[71]

Some penologists, particularly those working during the late nineteenth and early twentieth centuries, thought of the prison as an inherently destructive environment. They presumed that lifers deteriorated as a matter of course amid the monotony and degradation that surrounded them. Accordingly, respected men like William Tallack thought of "absolute life imprisonment . . . not so much as a substitute for capital punishment, as a slower and more disadvantageous method of inflicting it."[72] Such conclusions are clearly wrong. Research does not support claims about the deterioration of lifers.[73] (Interestingly, lifers tend to be a healthy lot; they have a slightly greater life expectancy than comparable persons in the free world.[74]) Dying in prison, moreover, is not the same as being executed there. We all die, but few of us are killed in *any* way, let alone being executed by the state.

Some early wardens also reinforced the image of the deteriorating lifer. Warden Lawes of Sing Sing, for example, noted that some 10 percent of lifers were declared insane during their tenure in prison.[75] Lawes failed to note that, at that time, commitment to a mental asylum required little more than a history of self-injury and that such confinement meant doing easier time than was possible in the prison. One must also remember that the condemned prisoners in Lawes's time were confined in what he termed "wire-caged traps" on a death row known as "the slaughter house." There, Lawes believed, no prisoner was assured of his sanity (see Chapter 3).

A second form of moral objection to the proposed reform consists of concern about potential abuses of the true life sentence. Is it not possible that true life sentences will be used in addition to, and not instead of, the death penalty? The result would be a growing population of lifers even while executions continue. There is also the possibility that true life sentences will be used for less extreme crimes than murder; indeed, recent evidence from Alabama indicates that most offenders sentenced to life without parole in that state had committed unspecified "crimes against property" rather than homicide.[76] In addition, because due-process protections are less substantial when the penalty is life rather than death, some true life sentences will be handed down arbitrarily.[77] It is hard to prevent such mis-adventures; they are the product of political and legal factors rather than moral analysis. But it is worth emphasizing that the essence of this proposal is that a true life sentence should be the most severe punishment a civilized society can inflict upon its criminals, and that it should be used with great caution and care. Accordingly, this sanction should be limited to cases of premeditated, aggravated murder, and those cases should be adjudicated using high standards of due process. To do less would be to mete out sentences that are both arbitrary and excessive, serving no valid penological objective.[78]

Conclusion

A true life sentence is an awesome sanction but, unlike a death sentence, it need not destroy the prisoner or result in an irreversible miscarriage of justice. (Innocent people have been executed in the past, including the recent past; there is no reason to suppose that such tragedies will not recur as long as the death penalty remains in force.[79]) Though painful, a life sentence can be borne with dignity. It can also be changed, if and when authorities deem it appropriate. New evidence may alter a verdict or indicate a lesser sentence; substantial and enduring changes of character may, in extraordinary cases, permit a few prisoners to be resurrected—for example, through special pardons. New evidence is only rarely discovered, of course, and pardons are even harder to come by. But at least with true life sentences, avenues of mercy and redress remain open to us in our search for justice.

Now some will claim that all of this is well and good but that the loss of a civil life is never commensurate with the loss of an actual life. They will contend that murderers, at least the worst ones, deserve to die in payment for the lives they have taken. I am willing to concede that point, but not its corollary: that we must execute some murderers. As things stand today and for the foreseeable future, we cannot execute prisoners without also torturing them, which is always unjust. And even if reforms were to enable us to execute people justly, pitting fully human executioners against fully human prisoners, I would urge that we refrain from such an undertaking. The suffering that would attend such executions would be awful and, in a very real sense, gratuitous. For the loss of one's civil life is punishment enough for any murderer, even though some or even many murderers may deserve to die. Partial justice is justice enough here. Once again, I must fall back on the wisdom of Albert Camus. Like Camus, I find it better to be wrong without killing fellow human beings than to be right in the cold stillness of the death house.

Notes

1. Deterrence is the main reason most people cite in support of the death penalty. When presented with evidence that the death penalty does not deter, or may not deter, opinions are largely unchanged. This implies that retribution or revenge

were all along the main reason for advocating the death penalty. See P. Ellsworth and L. Ross, "Public Opinion and Capital Punishment: A Close Examination of the Views of Abolitionists and Retentionists," *Crime and Delinquency* 29(1):116–169 (1983), and P. Harris "Oversimplification and Error in Public Opinion Surveys on Capital Punishment," *Justice Quarterly* 3 (4):429–455 (December 1986). For an interesting discussion on the import of public opinion regarding the death penalty, see J. O. Finckenauer, "Public Support for the Death Penalty: Retribution as Just Deserts or Retribution as Revenge?" *Justice Quarterly* 5(1):81–100 (March 1988).

2. Ellsworth and Ross (n. 1), 116.

3. Ibid., 168.

4. B. Moore, Jr., *Injustice: The Social Bases of Obedience and Revolt* (New York: Sharpe, 1978), 17. "All acts of vengeance," claim Pietro Marongiu and Graeme Newman, "arise from an elementary sense of injustice" that vengeance is meant to ameliorate. See P. Marongiu and G. Newman, *Vengeance: The Fight against Injustice* (Totowa, N.J.: Rowman & Littlefield, 1987), 9. Marongiu and Newman have provided an interesting and insightful analysis of the evolution of revenge, from an almost unfettered, instinctual act of individual violence against one's enemies to a social and morally restrained act of punishment or retribution orchestrated by the state. Finckenauer (n. 1) has taken a different view of this matter from that of Moore or Marongiu and Newman, arguing that offenders should pay back society (retribution as just deserts), rather than society's demanding the chance to pay back the offender (retribution as revenge). For Finckenauer, retribution as revenge is not a proper basis for punishment. However, as long as society demands a retributive punishment that accords with the principle of proportionality (an eye for an eye) rather than simply giving vent to indiscriminate rage, it is hard to see how this is bloodthirsty, excessive, or otherwise illegitimate.

5. J. H. Reiman, "Civilization and the Death Penalty: Answering van den Haag," *Philosophy and Public Affairs* 14(2):121 (Spring 1985).

6. A. G. Amsterdam, "Capital Punishment," in *The Death Penalty in America,* ed. H. A. Bedau (Oxford: Oxford University Press, 1982), 347.

7. Furman v. Georgia, 92 S. Ct. 2726, 368.

8. Plato, *Laws,* 854.

9. Plato, *Crito,* 10.49.

10. See H. Morris, "Persons and Punishment," in *Punishment and Rehabilitation,* ed. J. Murphy (Pacific Grove, Calif.: Wadsworth, 1973), and "A Paternalistic Theory of Punishment," *American Philosophical Quarterly* 18(4):263–271 (October 1981); and J. Hampton, "The Moral Education Theory of Punishment," *Philosophy and Public Affairs* 13(3):208–238 (1984).

11. The notion that punishments should be both civilized and civilizing was first developed by Reiman (n. 5). His point of reference, particularly for determining what constitutes a civilizing punishment, is the society administering the punishment. My point of reference is the offender, the person being punished.

12. See M. E. Gale, "Retribution, Punishment and Death," *University of California, Davis, Law Review* 18(4):973–1035 (1985). Retribution, according to Gale,

Gale, keeps the individual offender at the center of the institution of punishment. The consequences that make punishment legitimate must occur in the life of the individual offender. There is no other way in which the offender can experience "just deserts." . . . Yet, if at the instant of the infliction of the punishment the offender is rendered forever unable to appreciate the justness of her punishment, much if not all of its moral force is lost. (1028)

Elsewhere Gale stated,

Retribution itself has a moral content inconsistent with final punishments. . . . Retribution appeals to nothing more than the stark right to continue to exist, to experience the pain, duration, and consequence of punishment. These characteristics describe all punishments except those that extinguish consciousness and life itself. (1030)

Note that an afterlife would make death acceptable as a punishment on retributive grounds, because offenders would experience their just deserts after death.

13. See Plato, *Laws,* esp. Books 5 and 9.
14. P. Aries, *The Hour of Our Death* (New York: Vintage, 1982), 308.
15. S. Y. Edgerton, Jr., *Pictures and Punishment: Art and Criminal Prosecution during the Florentine Renaissance* (Ithaca, NY: Cornell University Press, 1985), 181.
16. Ibid., 15, 198.
17. The unjustly executed were virtually guaranteed salvation: "Such a case of mistaken execution, which so horrifies us today, would, in the pure Christian logic of the Middle Ages, have been considered the highest form of justice" (Ibid., 16).
18. Aries (n. 14), 308.
19. The aim of the confessor, like that of the counselor and, presumably, the priest associated with Jones's execution, was to help the prisoner transcend the grim realities of the scaffold and dwell instead on the promise of life after death (see Chapter 7).

Confessors might also have helpers, usually brothers from religious orders. Noteworthy are the scaffold labors of the brothers of Santa Maria della Croce al Tempio, a confraternity formed in 1343 out of concern "about the lack of interest on the part of public officials in the spiritual needs of prisoners of death" (Edgerton (n. 15), 179). These brothers developed the tavoletta, a religious painting, or "devotional image," that was held before the gaze of the condemned as he made his way to the scaffold and awaited his demise. Equipped with a handle and featuring the image of Christ crucified on one side and a secular execution scene on the other, the tavoletta reinforced the link between pain on earth as penance and redemption in heaven as one's reward for renouncing sin.

The brothers produced a manual on the proper ways to use the tavoletta to comfort the condemned. In Edgerton's words,

The brothers were instructed to hold the tavoletta directly before the face of the victim, blocking as much as possible his field of vision. This was especially important as the afflitto [afflicted one, a euphemism for condemned prisoner] approached the scaffold and the instruments of his imminent death. Sometimes the frame at the sides of the picture was considerably widened in order to ensure that the afflitto would not inadvertently see the executioner and suddenly lose his nerve. (180)

The brothers were also admonished "to stand a little back" from the executioner, yet keep the devotional image within easy view of the condemned (180).

The purpose of the tavoletta was to provide "a kind of visual narcotic to numb the fear and pain of the condemned criminal during his terrible journey to the scaffold" (172). By many accounts, the condemned were indeed comforted. "The devotional image succeeds best," we are told, "when it manages to lift the viewer from consciousness of the sensate world to a transcendental feeling of spiritual ecstasy" (173). The use of the tavoletta "represents one of the earliest acts of recognition that the condemned criminal remains a fellow human being deserving of charity no matter how heinous his crime" (219).

20. Edgerton (n. 15), 135.
21. M. Foucault, *Discipline and Punish: The Birth of the Prison* (New York: Pantheon, 1977), 46.
22. Aries (n. 14), 604. This was particularly true in the Middle Ages, when people "lived collectively in infinite numbers of groups, orders, associations, brotherhoods. . . . If a man was condemned to be executed, fellow members accompanied him to the scaffold." See B. W. Tuchman, *A Distant Mirror: The Calamitous 14th Century* (New York: Knopf, 1978), 39–40. The presence of one's fellows must have been immensely supportive to the condemned, since, as we have seen, those outside the criminal's immediate world would normally reject him as a damned soul en route to perdition who had had the temerity to jeopardize the spiritual well-being of the larger community. See Aries (n. 14).
23. K. L. Woodward, "Heaven," *Newsweek,* 27 March 1989, 55, 54.
24. Moore (n. 4), 434.
25. A. Camus, "Reflections on the Guillotine," in *Resistance, Rebellion, and Death* (New York: Knopf, 1969).
26. N. Podhoretz, "Do Not Go Gentle into the Night," *Washington Post,* Op Ed Section, 18 March 1986, A19.
27. Phillip Scribner has advanced a fascinating "naturalistic argument for the existence of God." He has shown, to my satisfaction at least, that "given a world of objects in space like our own, the existence of a perfect being is necessary." This perfect being is not a personal God, however, nor can this God be said to be the creator of this world or, for that matter, a world hereafter. See P. Scribner, "A New Proof for the Existence of God" (Paper delivered at a Philosophy Department Symposium at The American University, 25 February 1986).
28. Morris, "Persons and Punishment" (n. 10).

29. Ibid., 53.

30. E. Becker, *Escape from Evil* (New York: Free Press, 1975), 4.

31. S. Freud, *The Future of an Illusion* (New York: Doubleday, 1957), 57–58.

32. Podhoretz (n. 26). The near-dead and the once-dead (who have revived after being clinically dead for a brief period) sometimes report transcendent experiences, which they take to be incontrovertible evidence of a life after death. They no longer hide from death because they no longer fear its finality. Unfortunately, what is at work here is almost certainly a profound form of denial that is fed by both biological and psychological processes. A more plausible view of this phenomenon, in Pfister's words, is that it is "a brilliant victory of wishful thought over dreadful fact and illusion over reality." Quoted in S. Grof and J. Halifax, *The Human Encounter with Death* (New York: Dutton, 1977), esp. 144.

33. Aries (n. 14), 11.

34. See E. Kübler-Ross, *On Death and Dying* (New York: Macmillan, 1969), and E. Kübler-Ross, *Death: The Final Stage of Growth* (Englewood Cliffs, N.J.: Prentice-Hall, 1975).

35. See T. Des Pres, *The Survivor: An Anatomy of Life in the Death Camps* (New York: Pocket Books, 1977), and C. Lasch, *The Minimal Self: Psychic Survival in Troubled Times* (New York: Norton, 1984).

36. Camus (n. 25), 221.

37. The Eighth Amendment prohibition of cruel and unusual punishments "must draw its meaning from the evolving standards of decency that mark the progress of a maturing society." See Trop v. Dulles, 78 S. Ct. 590 (1958) (Plurality opinion).

38. J. Gorecki, *Capital Punishment: Criminal Law and Social Evolution* (New York: Columbia University Press, 1983).

39. Given the comparatively rare use of the death penalty today, the message this sanction sends is mainly a symbolic one. See F. E. Zimring and G. Hawkins, *Capital Punishment and the American Agenda* (New York: Cambridge University Press, 1986). At least one pair of anthropologists finds a magical component to this symbolization. See E. D. Purdum and J. A. Paredes, "Rituals of Death," in *Facing the Death Penalty: Essays on a Cruel and Unusual Punishment,* ed. M. L. Radelet (Philadelphia: Temple University Press, 1989).

40. Aries (n. 14), 599.

41. As Lofland has noted, modern execution procedures have a "concealment dramaturgics" that give them "a definite death-denying quality." See H. Bleackley and J. Lofland, *State Executions Viewed Historically and Sociologically* (Montclair, N.J.: Patterson Smith, 1977), 321.

42. As mentioned earlier, beliefs about the nature of crime and the existence of an afterlife may at other times have made executions proper punishments that were commensurate with some crimes. Those times have passed. Today, killing criminals, even our worst criminals, does most certainly treat them "like objects to be toyed with and discarded."

43. As Strafer has cogently noted, the Eighth Amendment ban "applies to all punishments which do not comport with 'broad and idealistic concepts of

dignity, civilized standards, humanity and decency' " (citations omitted). See G. R. Strafer, "Volunteering for Execution: Competency, Voluntariness and the Propriety of Third-Party Intervention," *Journal of Criminal Law and Criminology* 74(3):889 (1983).

44. Interestingly, prisoners, until fairly recently, were viewed as the legal equivalent of dead men. They were *civilites mortuus,* and their estates, if they had any, were managed like those of dead men.

45. W. Gaylin, "In the Beginning," in W. Gaylin et al., *Doing Good: The Limits of Benevolence* (New York: Pantheon, 1978), 33–34. It is true, as an anonymous reviewer has reminded me, that Lockett v. Ohio, 438 U.S. 586 (1978) and related cases require that all "relevant" mitigating factors must be considered at a capital sentencing. The difficult is in establishing the relevance of broad social forces in the minds of jurors. Being raised in a poor and brutal home is a case in point. People from such environments are hurt and hostile because of their maltreatment. Some express their hostility in criminal violence; others develop mental health problems; still others react in a mix of ways. A few transcend the brutality in their lives and go on to be healthy, decent citizens. Yet the fact remains that most violent offenders have been maimed by the neglect and abuse that have pervaded their lives, and this should be counted as a mitigating factor even though some, perhaps even many, other people treated in this way do not turn to criminal violence. Convincing a jury of this, however, is another matter altogether.

46. See R. Johnson, *Condemned to Die: Life under Sentence of Death* (Prospect Heights, Ill.: Waveland Press, 1989), 25.

47. The link between abuse during the formative years and impulsive violence later in life is widely supported. See, for example, H. Wisnie, *The Impulsive Personality* (New York: Plenum, 1977).

48. See J. H. Reiman, *The Rich Get Richer and the Poor Get Prison,* 2nd ed. (New York: Wiley, 1984), and J. H. Reiman and S. Headlee, "Marxism and Criminal Justice Policy," *Crime and Delinquency* 27 (1): 24–47 (1981).

49. See, for example, D. O. Lewis et al., "Psychiatric, Neurological, and Psychoeducational Characteristics of Fifteen Death Row Inmates in the United States," *American Journal of Psychiatry* 143(7):838–845 (July 1986).

50. See, for example, D. McDonald and B. J. Berstein, *The Price of Punishment: Public Spending for Corrections in New York* (Boulder: Westview Press, 1980), and R. J. Lauen, *Community-Managed Corrections* (Laurel, Md.: American Correctional Association, 1988), esp. Chap. 4.

51. See B. R. McCarthy, *Intermediate Punishments: Home Supervision, Home Confinement and Electronic Surveillance* (Monsey, N.Y.: Criminal Justice Press, 1987), and R. A. Ball, C. R. Huff, and J. R. Lilly, *House Arrest and Correctional Policy: Doing Time at Home* (Beverly Hills, Calif.: Sage, 1988).

52. J. P. Conrad, personal communication during Conrad's tenure as a Research Fellow at the National Institute of Justice, when he had access to the relevant figures, 1986. (I have adjusted these figures for inflation.)

53. See K. Krajick, "Profile Texas," *Corrections Magazine* 4(1):4–25 (1978).

54. J. P. Conrad, personal communication, 1986.

55. See Comment, "The Cost of Taking a Life: Dollars and Sense of the Death

Penalty," *University of California, Davis, Law Review* 18(4):1221–1273 (1985). The New York State Defenders Association has estimated a staggering $2-million tab for each offender who is convicted, sentenced, and executed in New York State. Their report draws attention to the unusually high costs of capital appeals, which involve a *minimum* of ten state and federal appeals and may take ten or more years to complete. See New York State Defenders Association, *"Capital Losses: The Price of the Death Penalty for New York State"* (pamphlet), 1 April 1982. Reviewing the most recent literature on the subject, Radelet summarized the situation as follows:

> Homicide trials are more expensive if the death penalty is being sought, as are the costs in the executive and especially the judicial branches of government as the case is being appealed. Some, of course, will argue that costs would drop if we further restricted the appellate process in capital cases, although the Constitution presents strong barriers to such restrictions. Thus, for now and the foreseeable future, it is clear: each execution costs millions, several times more than the cost of incarcerating an offender for his or her natural life.

See M. Radelet, "Introduction and Overview," in *Facing the Death Penalty: Essays on a Cruel and Unusual Punishment,* ed. M. L. Radelet (Philadelphia: Temple University Press, 1989), 9. Nathanson reminds us that costly appeals are the price we must pay if we wish to administer the legal proceedings attendant to the death penalty in a way that shows due respect for the value of life. See E. Nathanson, *An Eye for an Eye* (Totowa, N.J.: Rowman & Littlefield, 1977), 37–40.

56. In New York, approximately 80 percent of the spending for state prisons goes for staff salaries and fringe benefits, with $1.83 per day allocated for inmate meals. See McDonald and Berstein (n. 50).

57. E. van den Haag, "Prisons Cost Too Much Because They Are Too Secure," *Corrections Magazine* 6(2):39–42 (1980).

58. Sellin's observations hold for regular life-term prisoners (as distinct from true life-term prisoners) who have been released on parole. See T. Sellin, *The Penalty of Death* (Beverly Hills, Calif.: Sage, 1982), 120. This finding has been confirmed for English lifers released on parole. See J. B. Coker and J. P. Martin, *Licensed to Live* (London: Basil Blackwell, 1985).

59. A number of studies support this claim. The pertinent literature is discussed in J. R. Sorensen and J. W. Marquart, "Working the Dead," in *Facing the Death Penalty: Essays on a Cruel and Unusual Punishment,* ed. M. L. Radelet (Philadelphia: Temple University Press, 1989), 171.

60. In the entire New York State penal system, which today houses approximately forty thousand felons, only one long-termer is so unmanageable as to require special isolation. See F. Butterfield, "A Boy Who Killed Coldly Is Now a 'Prison Monster,' " *New York Times,* 22 March 1989, A1 and B5.

61. T. Flanagan, "Time Served and Institutional Misconduct: Patterns of Involvement in Disciplinary Infractions among Long-Term and Short-Term Inmates," *Journal of Criminal Justice* 8(6):364, 365 (1980). [Italics in original.]

62. G. Wardlaw, "Are Long-Term Prisoners a Management Problem in Australian

Prisons?" *Australian and New Zealand Journal of Criminology* 13(1):9 (1980).

63. Flanagan (n. 61), 365, 357, 363.
64. See CONtact, "Lifers," *Corrections Compendium* 5(10):1–5 (1981).
65. H. E. Williamson and J. K. Thomas, "Prison Misconduct among Life-without-Parole Inmates" (Paper presented at the American Academy of Criminal Justice Sciences, Spring 1984).
66. For a review of the pertinent literature, see R. Johnson, *Hard Time: Understanding and Reforming the Prison* (Pacific Grove, Calif.: Brooks/Cole, 1987), esp. Chap. 4.
67. S. Cohen and L. Taylor, *Psychological Survival: The Experience of Long Term Imprisonment* (New York: Pantheon, 1972).
68. John Stuart Mill, quoted in L. S. Sheleff, *Ultimate Penalties: Capital Punishment, Life Imprisonment, Physical Torture* (Columbus: Ohio State University Press, 1987), 60.
69. J. Barzun, "In Favor of Capital Punishment," *American Scholar* 31(2):189 (Spring 1962).
70. Ibid., 189.
71. J. E. Hopkins, "My Life above Virginia's Electric Chair," *Washington Post,* 30 June 1985, G2.
72. William Tallack, quoted in Sheleff (n. 68), 62.
73. A critical review of this literature is provided in T. Flanagan, "Lifers and Long-Termers: Doing Big Time," in *The Pains of Imprisonment,* ed. R. Johnson and H. Toch (Prospect Heights, Ill.: Waveland Press, 1988).
74. See J. S. Wormith, "The Controversy over the Effects of Long-Term Incarceration," *Canadian Journal of Criminology* 26(4):423–437 (October 1984). Research with geriatric American prisoners, the vast majority of them lifers, revealed that

> many of the experiences associated with aging in open society including retirement, loss of spouse, and financial insecurity were not present and that traditional physical and emotional deterioration resulting from work and stress was absent. Inmates appeared and reported feeling younger than their chronological age. (431)

Lifers also tend to have better mental health than regular prisoners and to be generally better adjusted to confinement than other prisoners (431–432).

75. Warden Lewis Lawes, quoted in Sheleff (n. 68), 71.
76. J. P. Conrad, "Research and Development in Corrections," *Federal Probation* 48(2):59–62 (June 1984).
77. See Sheleff (n. 68).
78. For a thorough and thoughtful discussion of the legal and penological ramifications of true life sentences, see J. Wright, Note: "Life without Parole," 43 *Vanderbilt Law Review* 1990 (forthcoming).
79. H. A. Bedau and M. L. Radelet, "Miscarriages of Justice in Potentially Capital Cases," *Stanford Law Review* 40 (1): 21–179 (November 1987).

INDEX